The Spirit
of Celibacy

An Examination of the *Denkschrift für die Aufhebung des den katholischen Geistlichen vorgeschriebenen Zölibates (Memorandum on the Abolition of the Celibacy Requirement for Catholic Priests)*

Johann Adam Möhler

Edited, annotated, and with an Afterword
by Dieter Hattrup

English Language Edition edited by Rev. Emery de Gaál
Translated from the German by Cyprian Blamires

HillenbrandBooks

Chicago / Mundelein, Illinois

Litany of Our Lord, Jesus Christ, Priest and Victim" on p. xxiii–xxv is reprinted from *Gift and Mystery* by Pope John Paul II, copyright © 1996 by Liberia Editrice Vaticana. Used by Permission of Doubleday, a division of Random House, Inc.

Nihil Obstat
Reverend John G. Lodge, SSL, STD
Censor Deputatus
July 13, 2007

Imprimatur
Reverend John F. Canary, STL, DMIN
Vicar General
Archdiocese of Chicago
July 16, 2007

VOM GEIST DES ZÖLIBATES © 1992 Bonifatius GmbH Druck-Buch-Verlag Paderborn. The English edition published by agreement with Bonifatius GmbH Druck-Buch-Verlag, Karl-Schurz-Str. 26, 33100 Paderborn, Germany.

THE SPIRIT OF CELIBACY © 2007 Archdiocese of Chicago: Liturgy Training Publications, 1800 North Hermitage Avenue, Chicago IL 60622; 1-800-933-1800, fax 1-800-933-7094, e-mail orders@ltp.org. All rights reserved. See our Web site at www.LTP.org.

Hillenbrand Books is an imprint of Liturgy Training Publications (LTP) and the Liturgical Institute at the University of Saint Mary of the Lake (USML). The imprint is focused on contemporary and classical theological thought concerning the liturgy of the Catholic Church. Available at bookstores everywhere, through LTP by calling 1-800-933-1800, or visiting www.ltp.org. Further information about the **Hillenbrand Books** publishing program is available from the University of Saint Mary of the Lake/Mundelein Seminary, 1000 East Maple Avenue, Mundelein, IL 60060 (847-837-4542), on the web at www.usml. edu/liturgicalinstitute, or e-mail litinst@usml.edu.

Cover photo from Photos.com.

Printed in the United States of America.

ISBN: 978-1-59525-023-0

HSPCEL

To Johannes Joachim,
Archbishop of Paderborn, with gratitude!

Contents

Preface to the English Language Edition

The world is in need of nothing more than good and credible priests. From priesthood goes forth a fascination that transforms the world into its true self. Its greatness lies in the translation of one single word into human existence and a life-long commitment: the *"adsum"* (I am present) the priest utters on the day of his ordination. The worldwide sympathy and fascination the late John Paul II's long ministry as priest and as pope can be explained exclusively by his loyalty to the *"adsum"* he spoke when being ordained priest on November 1, 1946 in the obscurity of a chapel in Krakow, Poland.

Celibacy is the outward visible sign of a charism lived by countless priests, deacons, and religious alike. On the occasion of the silver anniversary of his papacy in 2003 John Paul II (1978–2005) wrote: "In the reality of the Church and the world today, the witness of chaste love is, on the one hand a form of spiritual therapy for humanity and, on the other, a form of protest against the idolatry of instinct."

The renowned German priest and theologian Johann Adam Möhler's (1796–1838) thoughts on priestly celibacy occasioned in his day a rediscovery of the meaning of priesthood and a rise in vocations. Perhaps this translation of his reflections on this central issue of Christianity will prove helpful after some serious disappointments in recent times.

Please bear with the text's at times polemical tenor. This is due to the acrimonious atmosphere of Möhler's age. In addition, in the then novel medium of theological discourse, the scholarly periodical, authors attempted to gain attention. Such style was often used to convey better a theological position. His contemporaries agree unequivocally: there was certainly no theologian as gentleman-like in composure and irenic in intentions as Johann Adam Möhler. For good reason he was called by friend and adversary alike "the noble Mohler." His text has been edited slightly for contemporary understanding.

I should not fail recording words of heartfelt gratitude for all who made this book become a reality: Dieter Hattrup for permitting the use of his commentary, the publisher Bonifatius, in Paderborn,

Germany, for granting rights for the English language edition, Father Aidan Nichols, OP and Stratford Caldicott for suggesting the translator, Cyprian Blamires, DPHIL (Oxford) for his evenly superb rendering of Möhler's literary German and Hattrup's demanding style into elegant English, and last but not least Kevin Thornton, editor of Hillenbrand Books, for arranging the translation and publication. Fathers Dennis Spies and Burke Masters, priests in the Joliet Diocese and graduate students at Mundelein, were the first to suggest this translation.

May this small book remind seminarians, priests, and indeed all Christians of the priesthood's charisma. May it contribute to a rekindling in priests of singular priestly magnanimity, steadfast commitment to making Christ present in the world, and their unique call to relate the spiritual and material realms to each other. In short, may priests once again set the world on fire.

Rev. Emery de Gaál
Mundelein Seminary

Editor's Introduction to the English Language Edition

JOHANN ADAM MÖHLER: LIBERALITY AND ORIGINALITY

Every theologian is called upon to interpret anew the gospel for his or her age. As a priest and scholar, Johann Adam Möhler did this in the first half of the nineteenth century. He did justice to this challenge by being both "liberal" (that is, free to interpret the gospel) and "original" (that is, faithful to the origins in Christ) in the truest sense of these two words.

The turmoil following the French Revolution (1789) profoundly and irrevocably changed all of Europe. The old German "Reichskirche" (Imperial Church) dating back to the ninth century had collapsed. As a consequence of the Congress of Vienna (1814–21), the assembly that reorganized Europe politically and socially after the Napoleonic Wars, there existed now the kairotic opportunity to start ecclesial life radically—in the literal sense of the word (*radix* = root). This new beginning could not be restricted merely to organizational and institutional aspects of the Church. By then a large number of the clergy had been influenced by the spirit of Enlightenment. In this historically unparalleled situation, the clergy doubted its mission. Were priests impersonal officials of a magical cult, men merely popularizing the newest philosophical trends or simply Enlightenment's liberating messengers? It comes therefore as no surprise that they often tended to advocate a national church along episcopal lines, convening frequently democratic and firmly institutionalized synods, and abolishing celibacy altogether. These and other calls invited a rediscovery of the meaning of central theological terms such as "Scripture," "theological hermeneutics," "Church," "Holy Spirit," "liturgy," "revelation," "dogma," "priesthood," and last but not least "celibacy." By and large the German clergy perceived itself as being the civil servants to a state's bureaucracy. An appreciation for the spiritual or theological dimensions of the Church and of the specific charisma of priestly vocation had been lost. Vocations to the priesthood were on a decline and its morale was certainly not inspiring.[1]

Moreover, theology was provoked to respond to state institutions gradually asserting their control over Church life, the German phenomenon of "Staatskirchentum." Courageously the Tübingen School of Theology confronted this challenge head on in the first half of the nineteenth century. The responses this school, and others, formulated proved of long-term relevance, influencing even the Second Vatican Council (1962–65). As one of the Tübingen School's most significant members, Möhler discovered afresh for his generation the nature of the Church, and taught that she is not a human association but first and foremost a living divine-human mystery. Without tending to extremes, he apprehends the Church, in the vein of the Christological definition of the Council of Chalcedon (451), as possessing both divine and human components. The Church mirrors the divine-human constitution of Jesus Christ (hypostatic union). This is the case in such an intimate way that, in fact, according to Möhler, Christ lives on and works in and through the Church, in space-time as a human being. Indeed, the Church is nothing short of the elongation of the incarnation.

At the beginning of the twenty-first century, our own age is fascinated by scientific-technical progress and the economic integration of the globe. Both the humanities in general and theology in particular suffer from this imbalance. Also in our day, it is sometimes difficult to grasp the true spiritual nature of the Church, the ennobling and transforming essence of the sacraments and the beauty of the spiritual life. All too often we are beholden to a superficial knowledge. As the understanding of the Church's essence suffers, invariably also that of religious life in general suffers and unfailingly also the specific sacerdotal charisma and lifestyle must be either ignored or held in low regard.

It was not Möhler's concern to accommodate the Church to the fashions of his time, but to renew the Church from her own origins and living wellsprings, so that all the faithful might praise the creator and redeemer. Only then are human beings not heteronomously

---

1. For a helpful survey of nineteenth-century intellectual history cf. Ninian Smart, et al. eds., *Nineteenth Century Religious Thought in the West*, 3 vols., Cambridge: Cambridge University, 1985. For a brief discussion of Möhler, see vol. II, pp. 125–39.

determined—by alien, outside factors—but able to relate to both their existence's true origin and goal as they live sacramental lives. In the process he discovered this reality: the Church as the genuinely liberating agent, as the temple of the Holy Spirit and the Mystical Body of Christ. This did not deceive him into facilely embracing a romantic understanding of restoration—his was the age of Romanticism—but to spell out prophetically the Church's authentic nature in fullness. Ensouled by the Holy Spirit, tradition is no longer something rigid and lifeless but takes on the features of a profoundly dynamic reality: a living organism. He would inveigh equally against fundamentalism's fixation and modernism's arbitrariness. The Church is "living faith and holy tradition." As with everything alive, the unity of the Church occurs in tension. When tensions cease to exist, death enters. Upon the background of Pentecost, according to Möhler's memorable words "neither one nor everyone can desire to be all; only all can be all, and only when all are united can they be complete."[2] There can be no unity without diversity and diversity can only exist where there is unity. This is Möhler's definition of the Catholic Church.

His understanding of the Church as Spirit-centered communion eminently influenced the Second Vatican Council. The Church thus becomes protector of a humane society and enabler of human freedom.

Möhler's Life

Johann Adam Möhler was born on May 6, 1796 in Igersheim, near Mergentheim in Württemberg, Germany, as the son of a reasonably well-off baker and innkeeper. In 1815 he began studying Catholic theology in Ellwangen.[3] After this school's merger with the University of Tübingen in 1817, he continued in that picturesque town. He completed his studies in 1818. After spending a year in the seminary,

2. As quoted by Walter Kasper: "weder, einer noch jeder alles sein wollen; alles können nur alle sein, und die Einheit aller nur ein Ganzes." in Harald Wagner, ed., *Johann Adam Möhler (1796–1838), Kirchenvater der Moderne*, Paderborn: Bonifatius, 1996, p. 9. Cf. Johann Adam Möhler, *Unity in the Church or The Principle of Catholicism*, ed. and trans. by Peter C. Erb, Washington, DC: Catholic University of America, 1996, pp. 166–205.

3. For this section cf. Harald Wagner, "Johann Adam Möhler, Die Kirche als Organ der Inkarnation," in: Peter Neuner and Gunther Wenz, eds., *Theologen des 19. Jahrhunderts, Eine Einführung*, Darmstadt: Wissenschaftliche Buchgesellschaft, 2002, pp. 59–74.

he was ordained priest in 1819 and served subsequently as parochial vicar in Weil der Stadt and Riedlingen. In 1821 he returned to the famous Wilhelmsstift in Tübingen and taught there as tutor ("Präparand und Repetent"). At that time many considered him "liberal." In 1822 he was appointed "Privatdozent" (junior professor) for Church history. To expand his horizon and in keeping with the customs of the day he undertook "a literary journey." This brought him to the major cities of academic life in Germany: Würzburg, Bamberg, Jena, Halle, Leipzig, Göttingen, and finally Berlin. He thereby also made the acquaintances of prominent Protestant theologians such as Gottlieb Planck, Johann August Wilhelm Neander, Philipp Marheinecke (Protestant founder of comparative credal theological studies), and Friedrich D. Schleiermacher, the then pre-eminent Protestant theologian. From 1823 until 1826 he taught as "Privatdozent" in Tübingen. In 1826 he was appointed extraordinary professor and in 1828 full professor with chair, teaching first church history, then canon law, and finally apologetics.

He became famous by writing *Unity in the Church or The Principle of Catholicism, Presented in the Spirit of the Church Fathers of the First Three Centuries.*[4] This book's "warmth and fervor"—the then young theology student Ignaz v. Döllinger[5] observed—immediately exerted a fascination upon students of theology. In this book he discusses the Enlightenment's juridical view of the Church as a human society and critically demarcates the Church from this view and sees her as "life" and "liveliness." She is constituted by God's own revelation. By the power of the Holy Spirit she is life-giving and possesses a body. As this Spirit is always Christ's Spirit, the incarnation becomes the point of departure for the "enfleshment" of the Holy Spirit, the Church. Connecting with Romanticism's understanding of symbol (cf. Friedrich Schlegel and Friedrich Creuzer), the Church is apprehended as the symbol of the infinite Spirit of God and as God's revelation manifest in history. Revelation is handed down via scripture, liturgy, creeds, etc. Here one might detect both Marheinecke and the Berlin philosopher Georg Hegel influencing Möhler's understanding

---

4. For a presentation of Möhler's ecclesiology see Michael J. Himes, *Ongoing Incarnation, Johann Adam Möhler and the Beginnings of Modern Ecclesiology,* New York: Crossroad, 1997.

5. J. Friedrich, I. v. Döllinger, *Johann Adam Möhler, Gesammelte Schriften und Aufsätze,* Regensburg: G. Joseph Manz, 1839–40, (vol. I, München, 1899), p. 150.

of the normative features for the Church. The "religious idea" divests and transforms itself into the faithful, thereby obtaining a subjective life and finally becoming objectified in a creed ("symbolon" in Greek). The creed unites spiritual and material realms, the infinite and the finite, and is both representation and presence of the divine in the world. This will be the central concept in his later book *Symbolism, Exposition of the Doctrinal Differences between Catholics and Protestants as evidenced by their Symbolic Writings,* Möhler's most significant contribution. In 1827 he authored important articles on Anselm of Canterbury[6] and a book on Athanasius. Both anticipate *Symbolik,* published in 1832. Probably the Protestant theologian Marheinecke's book *Christliche Symbolik* (1810–13) and the Tübingen Protestant theologian Christian Friedrich Baur's lectures on "symbolism" in Tübingen awakened confessionalism in the jubilee years 1817 and 1830 and induced Möhler to write his book. In it Möhler focused on questions of Christian anthropology, delineating the differences between Catholicism and the main currents of Protestantism and presenting their creeds and books in *Symbolism.* This book remains a classic of nineteenth century Catholic theology and is a pioneering accomplishment, establishing the basis for ecumenical dialogue one century later. In 1835 the liberal-minded Bavarian King Ludwig I appointed Möhler professor in Munich, where he died on April 12, 1838.

It was fitting to name the renowned German Catholic institute for ecumenical studies located in Paderborn the "Johann-Adam-Möhler-Institut" (founded in 1959).

Church Unity

His understanding of revelation is significant and influenced the Second Vatican Council's perception of revelation as contextual in the conciliar document "Dei Verbum." Revelation does not approach a person "extrinsically" in the fashion of a divine decree

---

6. Johann Adam Möhler, *The Life of St. Anselm, Archbishop of Canterbury; A Contribution to the Knowledge of the Moral, Ecclesiastical, and Literary Life of the Eleventh and Twelfth Centuries,* trans. by Henry Rymer, London: T. Jones, 1842. This translation is a compilation of articles Möhler had written in 1827 and 1828 in the *Theologische Quartalschrift* vols. 9 and 10 on Anselm and which had been reprinted in Döllinger's Collected Works of Möhler 1:32–176 (cf. above).

as some neo-Scholastic manualists assumed, nor is it a fairly common natural phenomenon as some Protestant circles presumed. Rather, it occurs at a concrete place and at a specific time. Going back to the etymological meaning of the Greek word "symbol" (a contraction of the words *syn* [together] and *ballein* [to throw]), he discovers revelation as symbolic, as the encounter of the infinite and finite. The mystery of God becoming incarnate in Jesus Christ plays a pivotal role. Christ is the real symbol of God in the world, having the Church become the definable and tangible place of Christ's spirit in the world. In this sense the symbol, Church not only indicates God's reconciliation with the world but occasions it. In *Unity in the Church* Möhler writes "The Church itself is the real, realized reconciliation of human beings with God through Christ. Because of this, individuals are reconciled with one another through Christ and through love in him as a unity with him."[7] Thus the Church is understood as manifestation, as a real symbol, of God's salvific will. One is only able to appreciate the historic event of the incarnation, God's entering history, when seeing this epochal event conjoined with the in history perduring phenomenon of the Church. "Thus, the visible Church, from the point of view here taken, is the Son of God himself, everlasting manifesting himself among men in a human form, perpetually renovated, and eternally young—the permanent incarnation of the same, as in Holy Writ, even the faithful are called 'the body of Christ.'"[8] The Church is the concrete locale in which the Holy Spirit continually keeps Christ alive. Thus Pneumatology and Christology belong inseparably together.

In his book on Athanasius,[9] Möhler sees in this fourth century patriarch of Alexandria the anticipation of the Catholic position found also in the nineteenth century. A leitmotif for him is going back to the sources and thereby uncovering "in the beginning the fullness." He perceives clear parallels between Arianism and Protestantism. Both arrive at untenable positions as regards justification because they err

---

7. Möhler, *Unity in the Church*, p. 247.

8. Johann Adam Möhler, *Symbolism, Exposition of the Doctrinal Differences between Catholics and Protestants as evidenced by their Symbolic Writings*, with an introduction by Michael J. Himes, New York, NY: Crossroad, 1997, p. 259.

9. Johann Adam Möhler, *Athanasius der Grosse und die Kirche seiner Zeit, besonders im Kampfe mit dem Arianismus. In sechs Büchern, 2 Theile*, Mainz: Florian Kupferberg, 1827.

in the foundational area, namely in Christology, i.e. in the divinity of Christ.

THE CONSTITUENTS OF FAITH

A Protestant crypto-Catholic, Johann August von Starck may also have inspired Möhler to a thorough comparative study on Protestant and Catholic doctrinal differences. In their day, frequently the demand was made to gather together ecumenically for the declared purpose of celebrating a Christian cult, while ignoring dogmas. Both Starck and Möhler reject this notion. For both men, liturgy is the *expression* of faith. Starck had rejected the concept of absorption, meaning that a confession surrenders its particularities to enter communion with another denomination. Both Starck and Möhler perceive reunification as necessary to reestablish Christianity's universal credibility. However, they insist such reunification in one faith must be equally God's deed and a human deed. God must will reunification, human beings must achieve it. This comes about by practicing openness, charity, and tolerance. Arguing against trite naturalism, Möhler divines in Catholic faith a force humanizing and educating people.

Symbolism is a scientific presentation of the doctrinal differences that arose from the the Reformation. The first volume of this, the first serious Catholic study of doctrinal differences, discusses the controversial doctrinal issues of Catholics, Lutherans, and Reformed. Its six chapters discuss the original state of man, origin of evil, justification, sacraments, church, and eschatology. In the second book he turns to "smaller Protestant sects" (Mennonites, Quakers, Herrnhutters, Methodists, Swedenborgians, Socinians, and Arminians). Central for a comparative study of doctrinal differences for this scholar is that one have a clear unequivocal confessional position. Significantly, such a comparison may never be apologetical or polemical. Probably influenced in this point by Hegel, he argues such a study must present the "objective" opposites. Möhler's ecumenical achievement cannot be appraised too highly. Until then all discussion had been clad in bellicosity in relation to the opposing side. While in general praising him for his speculative powers and sagacity, in this regard Möhler criticizes even Robert Bellarmine for his subjective approach, his stressing controversial points, and unnecessary digressions. From Veronius'

Regula fidei[10] and Bossuet's *Exposition de la doctrine catholique*[11] he borrows the sober style and clear differentiation between official Church teaching and the positions of scholars. Thereby he wishes to uncover the driving forces underlying each denomination's creeds, its specific features, presuppositions, and symptoms and thus, by analyzing parts, arrive at the whole of its respective faith. His scholarly curiosity is urged onward not by the motivation of a qualifying comparison but by the quest for truth. In all probability Hegel functioned as *"spiritus rector"* in this case. Yet he significantly modified Hegelian dialectics. Ecclesial unity is the statement; heresy is opposition to or contradiction of unity. Therefore heresy is not a true but a failed and missed opposition to ecclesial unity. Heresy makes unity impossible. The resolution of this contradiction he calls reunification and synthesis. Thus heresy cannot suspend or eliminate the Church, as it is not a genuine contradiction. Contradictions and oppositions can be dissolved only within the Church. Insofar he is in direct conflict with his Tübingen colleague Baur, for whom Hegelian dialectics is the interpretation par excellence of history and the preferred instrument for achieving ecumenical unity.

ANTHROPOLOGY AS KEY TO FAITH AND PRIESTHOOD

In the introduction to *Symbolism,* Möhler communicates his firm conviction that the Occident rotates around the concept of a Christian anthropology. All of modernity is but a direct and necessary logical result of questions the Reformation had raised.[12] Upon this background Möhler develops such controversial theological areas as the original state and sin, original sin, concupiscence, etc. These were focal and foundational areas for disputations in the sixteenth century. However, the ramifications of these issues go far beyond theological controversies. Möhler observes in *Symbolism:* "We again repeat it:

---

10. François Véron, *De regula fidei catholica, seu de fide catholica,* Paris: J. P. Migne, 1853.

11. Jacques Bénigne Bossuet, *Exposition of the Catholic Church in Matters of Controversy, with copious Notes by J. Fletcher,* New York: Christian Press Association, 1895.

12. Thus Johann Adam Möhler, *Symbolik oder Darstellung der dogmatischen Gegensätze der Katholiken und Protestanten nach ihren öffentlichen Bekenntnisschriften,* ed. and intro. by Josef Rupert Geiselmann, Köln: Jakob Hegner, 1960, p. 18.

the meaning of the doctrine, the Word is become flesh, the Word
is become man, was never clear to Luther's mind."[13] For someone who
is as familiar with the texts of the Church Fathers as he is and even
more with Scripture the matter in question is unambiguous: *"Caro est
cardo"* (flesh is the crucial issue). Salvation history intends humankind.
His central concern is the harmony of all people who are dispersed
over the whole planet and yet feel empowered to enter a large fellowship
to support one another in living more meaningful lives. By receiving
reconciliation from God, they are now able to grant one another
reconciliation and live in unity.[14] Shortly thereafter, he writes on the
Church and revelation as being closely connected to the purpose
of ennobling people ethically and religiously. By the very fact of the
incarnation, ideals and human fulfillment are no longer hollow ideas.
Indeed the transforming impulse of Christianity unleashes new
energies and permits novel, unheard of things to become reality.
Christianity alone is able to produce the freest and therefore the most
disinterested of people. No doubt Möhler shows here clearly a debt
to the influences of the Enlightenment and Romanticism. However,
his thought is not arrested in or limited to these historic epochs.
The Church is in time, but a foretaste of eternity. There exists something in the Church that is not conditioned by time. He shifts theology
anthropocentrically on an incarnational basis. In the second half of
the twentieth century this will become commonplace, worked out in
detail by Karl Rahner and Henri de Lubac.

  Influences of Romanticism manifest themselves also in
another area: Möhler sees connections to community. The individual
human being is in need of community. Such a need for society would
remain completely incomprehensible if everyone could be his or
her own God. Human beings are acutely aware of their limits and con-
tingency. Pure individualism in his judgment is unable to countenance
the contingent state of the human condition. Social linkages are
prerequisites for humanity. On the other hand community may not
threaten the individual. A healthy society positively forms its individual members. This becomes truly a reality in the Church as a social
phenomenon. Christ has members, who constitute his Mystical Body.

---

13. Möhler, *Symbolism*, § 48, p. 333.
14. Cf. ibid, §37.

Human society finds its perfection in the thus constituted Church. Surprisingly, it will take well over a century for his thoughts to find common expression in the texts of the Second Vatican Council. The Möhlerian communio-ecclesiology is enabled time and again by the Eucharist and therefore by the celebrating priest. Communion with God enables genuine intra-human community. The selfless pro-existence—i.e. living for others—of the priest enables true human communion by illustrating the consequences of someone who lives existentially from a spiritual relationship, namely one with God. The God-man Jesus Christ belongs in the center of an authentic human community. The Church as unity preserves God's revelation and bears witness to Christ. A therein fashioned free human being can become a parable of God's covenantal loyalty.

Almost echoing Möhler, Henri de Lubac's *Catholicism* (1938) speaks of the consequences of Catholic dogma for human society in general. Following the trajectory Möhler to de Lubac, "Lumen Gentium" states: "The Church, in Christ, is in the nature of a sacrament . . . of communion with God and innermost unity among all of humanity" (LG 1).

INFLUENCES ON ENGLISH THEOLOGY

One can never assess Möhler's influence too highly. In the nineteenth century alone, *Symbolism* appeared in no less than twenty five editions and had been translated into all major European languages. In a time when Catholic faith was contested during the *Kulturkampf* (1872–87),[15] his writings were cause for self-assurance. At the same time he opened the Catholic intelligentsia to ecumenism both in Germany and abroad. While not founding a theological school of his own, he became a spiritual father of countless. He sensitized people for liberality, the quest for originality, and history as an organic phenomenon. Readers now once again appreciate Church history as a vehicle for religious truth. History mediates truth by allowing every age to raise issues and each generation allows history in turn to speak to it afresh. Ecclesial tradition is the mode of the Holy Spirit's abiding presence.

---

15. *Kulturkampf* was the conflict between the German imperial government and the Roman Catholic Church, chiefly over control of education and ecclesial appointments.

A *Wirkungsgeschichte* (intellectual history) of Möhler still awaits being written. It is difficult to determine how and where he impacted the history of theology and Church life. Once the French theologian and influential peritus at the Second Vatican Council, Yves Congar, OP, wrote the insightful words: "Möhler genuit Passaglia; Passaglia genuit Schrader; Passaglia et Schrader genuerunt Scheeben et Franzelin."[16] This quotation illustrates the sustained influence he had on the Roman school of theology that dominated in the century and played a decisive role during the very short First Vatican Council (1869–70). Schrader and Franzelin had authored a schema that should have presented an ecclesiology. Giovanni Perrone's published university lectures reflect a non-Scholastic approach, arguing in the vein of Möhler. It is a well-established fact that Perrone had repeatedly and quite intensively read *Symbolism* since 1837. In the unfinished ecclesiological papers of Passaglia some passages seem taken verbatim from *Unity*. Passaglia as well as the whole of the Roman School, acquired the notion of the Church as "the Mystical Body of Christ" from Möhler.

Möhler's ecclesiology influenced the high Christology that was to dominate theology until the 1960s. Cases in point are Karl Adam's (1876–1966) numerous and popular books and the encyclical "Corpus Christi Mystici" of 1943.

For the English-language reader Möhler's influence on British Catholicism will be of particular interest. Himes relates "[t]he English translator of *Symbolik*, James Burton Robinson (1800–1877), managed in the course of his life to touch directly or indirectly many of the most influential Catholic figures of his century."[17] Having traveled extensively, and translated *Symbolism* already in 1843, he thus made Möhler's thoughts available to the English-speaking world at a relatively early stage. Robertson had known Nicholas Wiseman, Daniel O'Connell, and John Henry Newman well. In fact, in 1855 Newman appointed him professor of modern history and geography

---

16. "Möhler gave rise to Passaglia, Passaglia to Schrader and both to Scheeben and Franzelin." Yves-Marie Congar, "L'Écclesiologie de la révolution français au Concile du Vatican," in: Maurice Nédoncelle et al. (ed.), *L'Écclesiologie au XIXe siècle*, Paris: Cerf, 1960, pp. 77–144, at p. 109.

17. Michael Himes in the introduction to J. A. Möhler, *Symbolism*, p. xvii.

at the nascent Catholic University of Dublin, of which Newman was rector at that time.

Robertson had been a regular contributor to *The Dublin Review*, which had extensively discussed Möhler's theology. Early on Nicholas Wiseman makes frequent references to Möhler in "Sermon: 'The Development in the Christian Church'" (1839), which may be considered a precursor of Newman's *Essay on the Development of the Christian Church*. The ecumenically inclined Anglican William G. Ward often discussed both Newman and Möhler.

Newman had made the acquaintance of Wiseman in 1833. At that time Wiseman had already been familiar with Möhler's books *Symbolism* and *Athanasius*. It is certain that by 1834 Newman was familiar with Möhler as a significant Catholic continental theologian. Although he did not understand German, Newman mentioned Möhler at the occasion of a discussion of his *Lectures on the Prophetical Office of the Church*. It is also a fact that he suggested to Wiseman in 1845 a translation of Möhler's *Unity*. In correspondence between Newman and Perrone in 1847, Möhler was mentioned approvingly. It is certainly no exaggeration to state that Newman had been intimately familiar with Möhler's theology and that via Newman and Wiseman the Tübingen theologian influenced English theology.[18]

DIETER HATTRUP: RECONCILING THE SPIRITUAL AND MATERIAL REALMS

As Dieter Hattrup edited, commented, and initiated the reprint of Möhler's present book in 1992 and penned its epilogue, a brief introduction to the person and concerns of Rev. Dr. Hattrup for the English-speaking reader is in order.

Dieter Hattrup must be counted among one of the better known Catholic systematic theologians in Germany. Since 1991 he has held the chair of dogmatics and the history of dogma at the

---

18. Günter Biemer, "Leben als das Kennzeichen der wahren Kirche Jesu Christi: Zur Ekklesiologie von Johann Adam Möhler und John Henry Newman," in: Harald Wagner, ed., *Johann Adam Möhler (1796–1838), Kirchenvater der Moderne*, Paderborn: Bonifatius, 1996, pp. 71–97.

Catholic theological college located in the city of Paderborn. Occasionally he appears on German television.[19]

It is one of his central concerns to delineate the borders between the natural sciences and theology and to overcome the supposedly unbridgeable gap between these two realms. The sciences on their own accord conclude a naïvely subscribed to naturalism, i.e. the claim that nature totally and exhaustively defines reality. It is a serious fallacy with fateful consequences. There exists a real "something" that nature on its own is incapable of explaining. This accounts also for Hattrup's interest in celibacy in general and in Möhler's here presented short study in particular. Priestly celibacy powerfully reminds every age anew that "not all of reality is nature." The priest prevents humankind from "amputating" the spiritual and religious aspects from life.

Hattrup was born in 1948 in Herne and studied mathematics, physics, and Catholic theology at the universities of Münster, Regensburg, and Bonn. In 1978 he earned a doctoral degree in the area of mathematics with a thesis on "The D-Operator on Products of Strictly Pseudo-Convex Areas." In 1980 he was ordained diocesan priest. Subsequently he served for seven years in parish ministry. In 1986, he earned a doctoral degree from the renowned University of Tübingen with a dissertation on categories in the natural sciences and the Christological mediation of being and history. He crowned his theological studies with a study on the Christological epistemology of Bonaventure in 1990, earning him a "Habilitation" from the same university. Since then he has published numerous books and articles. Among these publications (in German) *Einstein and the God Casting Dice* (2001), *The Drama of the Search for Truth in the Natural Sciences and Philosophy* (2003), and *The Dream of a World Formula* (2006) figure prominently. Along with Norbert Fischer he wrote *Freedom and Grace in Augustine's Confessions* (2003).

---

19. Compiled from hrz.uni-paderborn.de/~rhatt1/bibliohatt.htm and de.wikipedia.org/wiki/Dieter_Hattrup as accessed on 11/01/2006.

Selected Bibliography

Primary Sources[20]

Johann Adam Möhler, *The Life of St. Anselm, Archbishop of Canterbury; A Contribution to the Knowledge of the Moral, Ecclesiastical and Literary Life of the Eleventh and Twelfth Centuries,* trans. by Henry Rymer, London: T. Jones, 1842.

___, *On the Relation of Islam to the Gospel,* trans. by J. P. Menge, Calcutta: Ostell and Lepage, British Library, 1847.

___, *Symbolism: Exposition of the Doctrinal Differences between Catholics and Protestants as evidenced by their Symbolic Writings,* trans. by James Burton Robertson (in 1843), introduction by Michael Himes, New York: Crossroad, 1997.

___, *Unity in the Church or the Principle of Catholicism: presented in the Spirit of the Fathers of the First Three Centuries,* edited and translated by Peter C. Erb, Washington, D.C.: Catholic University of America, 1996.

Secondary Sources

Serge Bolschakoff, *The Doctrine of the Unity of the Church in the Works of Khomyakov and Moehler,* London: SPCK, 1964.

Charles Chaillet, ed., *L'Église est Une: hommage à Moehler,* Paris: Bloud & Gay, 1939.

Christina Maria Crose, *Johann Adam Moehler: The Method of Historical Theology,* Dissertation: Portland State University, 1972.

Yves Congar, "Sur l'évolution et l'interprétation de la pensée de Möhler", in: *Revue des Sciences Philosophiques et Théologiques,* vol. 27 (1938), pp. 205-12.

Joseph Fitzer, *Moehler and Baur in Controversy, 1832–38: Romantic-Idealist Assessment of the Reformation and Counter-Reformation,* Tallahassee, Fla.: American Academy of Religion, 1974.

Rudolph E. Gawlik, *The Concept of Tradition in Johann Adam Moehler's Die Einheit der Kirche,* Dissertation: Catholic University of America, 1969.

Josef Rupert Geiselmann, *Lebendiger Glaube aus geheiligter Überlieferung. Der Grundgedanke der Theologie Johann Adam Möhlers und der katholischen Tübinger Schule,* Freiburg i. Br.: Herder, 1966.

___, *Theologische Anthropologie Johann Adam Möhlers; ihr geschichtlicher Wandel,* Freiburg i. Br.: Herder, 1955.

Hans Geiser, *Glaubenseinheit und Lehrentwicklung bei Johann Adam Möhler,* Vandenhoeck & Ruprecht: Göttingen, 1971.

George B. Gilmore, "J. A. Möhler on Doctrinal Development", in: *Heythrop Journal,* vol. 19 (1978), pp. 383–404.

Michael J. Himes, "'A Great Theologian of Our Time': Möhler on Schleiermacher", in: *Heythrop Journal,* vol. 37 (1996), pp. 24–46.

___, *Ongoing Incarnation: Johann Adam Möhler and the Beginnings of Modern Ecclesiology,* New York: Crossroad, 1997.

---

20. An effort has been made to list all English language editions of Möhler's writings as well as all English titles dealing with his theology.

Henry Raphael Nienaltowski, *Johann Adam Möhler's Theory of Doctrinal Development; its Genesis and Formulation,* Washington, D.C.: Catholic University of America, 1959.

Philip Rosato, SJ, "Between Christocentrism and Pneumatocentrism: An Interpretation of Johann Adam Möhler's Ecclesiology", in: *Heythrop Journal,* vol. 19 (1978), pp. 46–70.

Hervé Savon, *Johann Adam Möhler, the Father of Modern Theology,* trans. by Charles McGrath, Glen Rock, N.J.: Paulist, 1966.

Gustav Voss, "Johann Adam Möhler and the Development of Dogma", in: *Theological Studies,* vol. 4 (1943), pp. 420–44.

Litany of Our Lord, Jesus Christ, Priest and Victim

Lord, have mercy. *Lord, have mercy.*

Christ, have mercy. *Christ, have mercy.*

Lord, have mercy. *Lord, have mercy.*

Christ, heed our prayer. Christ, *heed our prayer.*

Father in Heaven, GOD, *Have mercy on us.*

Son, Redeemer of the world, GOD, *Have mercy on us.*

Holy Spirit, GOD, *Have mercy on us.*

Holy Trinity, one GOD, *Have mercy on us.*

JESUS, Priest and Victim, *Have mercy on us.*

JESUS, Priest forever, according to the order of Melchisedech, *Have mercy on us.*

JESUS, Priest sent by GOD to preach the Gospel to the poor, *Have mercy on us.*

JESUS, Priest who at the Last Supper instituted the form of the Eternal Sacrifice, *Have mercy on us.*

JESUS, Priest living forever to make intercession for us, *Have mercy on us.*

JESUS, High Priest whom the Father anointed with the Holy Spirit and virtue, *Have mercy on us.*

JESUS, High Priest taken up from among men, *Have mercy on us.*

JESUS, made High Priest for men, *Have mercy on us.*

JESUS, High Priest of our Confession of Faith, *Have mercy on us.*

JESUS, High Priest of greater glory than Moses, *Have mercy on us.*

JESUS, High Priest of the true Tabernacle, *Have mercy on us.*

JESUS, High Priest of good things to come, *Have mercy on us.*

JESUS, holy High Priest, innocent and undefiled, *Have mercy on us.*

JESUS, faithful and merciful High Priest, *Have mercy on us.*

JESUS, High Priest of GOD, on fire with zeal for souls, *Have mercy on us.*

JESUS, perfect High Priest forever, *Have mercy on us.*

JESUS, High Priest who pierced Heaven with Your own Blood, *Have mercy on us.*

JESUS, High Priest who initiated us into a new life, *Have mercy on us.*

JESUS, High Priest Who loved us and washed us clean of our sins in Your Blood, *Have mercy on us.*

JESUS, High Priest, who gave Yourself up to GOD as offering and
        victim, *Have mercy on us.*

JESUS, sacrificial victim of GOD and man, *Have mercy on us.*

JESUS, holy and spotless sacrificial victim, *Have mercy on us.*

JESUS, mild and gentle sacrificial victim, *Have mercy on us.*

JESUS, peace-making sacrificial victim, *Have mercy on us.*

JESUS, sacrificial victim of propitiation and praise, *Have mercy on us.*

JESUS, sacrificial victim of reconciliation and peace, *Have mercy on us.*

JESUS, sacrificial victim in whom we have confidence and access
        to GOD, *Have mercy on us.*

JESUS, sacrificial victim living for ever and ever, *Have mercy on us.*

Be gracious! *Spare us, JESUS.*

Be gracious! *Hear us, JESUS.*

From rashly entering the clergy. *Free us, JESUS.*

From the sin of sacrilege, *Free us, JESUS.*

From the spirit of incontinence, *Free us, JESUS.*

From sordid self-interest, *Free us, JESUS.*

From every lapse into simony, *Free us, JESUS.*

From the unworthy administration of the Church's treasures,
        Free us, JESUS.

From the love of the world and its vanities, *Free us, JESUS.*

From the unworthy celebration of Your Mysteries, *Free us, JESUS.*

Through Your eternal priesthood, *Free us, JESUS.*

Through the holy anointing by which GOD the Father made You a
        priest, *Free us, JESUS.*

Through Your priestly spirit, *Free us, JESUS.*

Through the ministry by which You glorified Your Father on this earth,
        Free us, JESUS.

Through the bloody immolation of Yourself made once and for all on
        the Cross, *Free us, JESUS.*

Through that same sacrifice daily renewed on the altar, *Free us, JESUS.*

Through the divine power that You exercise invisibly in Your priests,
        Free us, JESUS.

That You may kindly maintain the whole priestly order in holy
        religion, *Hear us, we beseech You.*

That You may kindly provide Your people with pastors after Your own
        Heart, *Hear us, we beseech You.*

That You may kindly fill them with the spirit of Your priesthood,
    Hear us, we beseech You.
That the lips of Your priests may be repositories of knowledge,
    Hear us, we beseech You.
That You may kindly send faithful workers into Your harvest,
    Hear us, we beseech You.
That You may kindly increase the faithful dispensers of Your
    mysteries, *Hear us, we beseech You.*
That You may, kindly grant them persevering obedience to Your will,
    Hear us, we beseech You.
That You may kindly give them gentleness in their ministry, skill in
    their actions, and constancy in their prayer,
    Hear us, we beseech You.
That through them. You may kindly promote the veneration of the
    Blessed Sacrament all over the world, *Hear us, we beseech You.*
That You may kindly receive into Your joy those who have served
    You well, *Hear us, we beseech You.*
Lamb of GOD, Who takest away the sins of the world, *Spare us, O Lord.*
Lamb of GOD, Who takest away the sins of the world,
    Graciously hear us, O Lord.
Lamb of GOD, Who takest away the sins of the world,
    Have mercy on us, O Lord.
JESUS, our Priest, *Hear us.*
JESUS, our Priest, *Heed our prayers.*
Let us pray. *O GOD, sanctifier and guardian of Your Church, stir up in her, through Your Spirit, suitable and faithful dispensers of the holy Mysteries, so that by their ministry and example, the Christian people may be guided in the path of salvation with Your protection. Through Christ, our Lord. Amen.*
GOD, Who, when the disciples ministered to the Lord and fasted, ordered that Saul and Barnabas be set aside for the work to which You called them, be with Your Church as she prays now, and You, who know the hearts of all of us, show those whom You have chosen for Your ministry. Through Christ, Our Lord. Amen.

Abbreviations

CSEL   *Corpus Scriptorum Ecclesiasticorum Latinorum,* Vienna 1866ff.

DH   *The Sources of Catholic Dogma,* translated by Roy J. Deferrari from the thirtieth edition of Henry Denzinger's *Enchiridion Symbolorum,* 653 pp, Fitzwilliam, NH: Loreto Publications, 1955. *See also,* Denzinger-Hünermann, Heinrich Denzinger, *Kompendium des Glaubensbekenntnisse und kirchlichen Lehrentscheidungen,* impr., exp. Original German edition, edited by Peter Hünermann, Freiburg-Basle-Vienna, 40th edition, 2005.

HThK   *Herders Theologischer Kommentar zum Neuen Testament,* Freiburg, 1953 ff.

LG   *Dogmatic Constitution of Vatican II on the Church 'Lumen Gentium'*

LThK   *Lexikon für Theologie und Kirche,* 2nd ed., ed. J Höfer/K Rahner, 10 vols., Freiburg-Basle-Vienna, 1957–1965

MBTh   Münsterische Beiträge zur Theologie, ed. Bernhard Kötting and Bruno Schüller, Münster, 1921ff.

PG   *Patrologia Graeca,* Migne, Paris, 1857–1866.

PL   *Patrologia Latina,* Migne, Paris, 1844–1864.

PO   Decree of Vatican II 'Presbyterorum Ordinis' over the service and life of the priest.

RGG   *Die Religion in Geschichte und Gegenwart,* ed. Kurt Galling, 6 vols., Tübingen, 3rd ed., 1957ff; study edition 1986

SL   *Corpus Christianorum, Series Latina,* Turnhout, 1953ff.

STh   Thomas Aquinas, *Summa Theologiae.*

ThGl   *Theologie und Glaube,* Paderborn, 1909 ff.

ThQ   *Theologische Quartalschrift,* Tübingen, 1819ff.

Translator's Notes

1. All quotations from the bible are given in the New Jerusalem Bible version (Darton Longman & Todd, 1985).
2. All the footnotes to the Möhler text consisting of Latin or Greek quotations are original notes by Möhler himself. Where other footnotes are original to him they are prefaced with the words [Möhler's notes].
3. All quotations from the *Denkschrift für die Aufhebung des den katholischen Geistlichen vorgeschriebenen Zölibates* (the work on which the present Möhler text is a commentary) have been translated from the German original by C. P. Blamires.
4. Fr. Hattrup's German edition of the Möhler text has modernized the author's German in certain places and includes footnotes to indicate any such changes; these have been omitted from the present English translation, but all other footnotes have been included.

About the Editor and Translator

Rev. Emery A. de Gaál, PHD is an Associate Professor, Department of Systematic Theology and Pre-Theology, University of St. Mary of the Lake and author of *The Art of Equanimity: A Study on the Theological Hermeneutics of Saint Anselm of Canterbury.*

Cyprian Blamires has degrees in languages and theology and a doctorate from Oxford University in history. Formerly an ordained minister of the Church of England in London, he was received into the Catholic Church in 1979. He has translated numerous books and articles and has published widely in the history of ideas.

Chapter 1

Celibacy in the Year 1828[1]

MARRIAGE AS A SPIRITUAL REMEDY?

It is clearly a most welcome development when members of the laity decide to speak out on Church issues. If the priests are really slumbering, nothing could be better than for laypeople to proclaim the laws and works of God in the full flood of divine inspiration like the Old Testament prophets to the sons of men. Fine examples of this have been seen in recent times both in the Catholic and in the Protestant Churches. But those who wish the Church well will not be happy with the way that the Freiburg Professors have gone about their task. It has undoubtedly been a great relief to see the Catholic Church in Baden put on a secure footing after a long period of waiting, and there has been a perfectly justifiable expectation that any movements springing from this crucial development—a development that promises to open up a new and momentous source of deep inspiration for believers—would emerge from the very heart of Christian life and come to embrace everyone and everything, triggering a surge of new vitality and nurturing a whole mass of fruits everywhere. In short, people had been longing for what would unmistakably appear as a fresh outpouring of the Holy Spirit, penetrating everything creatively and raising everything to a higher level of existence.

---

1. Möhler inserts the following preliminary observation: "The work I am commenting on here has filled me with infinite melancholy. It has brought to my attention the petitions of Duttlinger and Rottek among others to the Archduke of Baden, the parliament of Baden, and the Archbishop of Freiburg for the abolition of celibacy (for these three petitions are the supporting documents *(Aktenstücken)* of which the title speaks) and the more precise reasons for their demand, the real content of the *Denkschrift.*" The work studied by Möhler was: *"Denkschrift für die Aufhebung des den katholischen Geistlichen vorgeschriebenen Zölibates. Mit drei Aktenstücken,"* Druck und Verlag Friedrich Wagner, Freiburg 1828 *(Memorandum for the Abolition of the Celibacy Requirement for Catholic priests: With three Supporting Documents).*

What a dreadful disappointment then when we find that so many professors from Freiburg, the *Metropolis*, think that the circumstance of *such a time as this* are precisely the ones to justify the abolition of celibacy; that they *only* begin to think of such a measure in such a time as this; and they think *only* of such a measure at such a time as this! Not to mention that from the purely practical viewpoint their idea is quite pointless anyway, given that there is simply no purpose in taking as your starting-point something that, even supposing it were indeed highly desirable, could never actually happen unless a whole series of other things happened as a preliminary to it.

It is said that the Baden clergy are in general (though we trust that there are many exceptions) neither very bright nor very spiritual. They are reckoned to have a rather materialistic and worldly attitude. Apparently they do not show much sign of a noble enthusiasm for the gospel nor of a deep or lively feel for it. They are not necessarily thought to be especially ignorant, the problem is more that they are almost completely devoid of any real spiritual life, and there is no sign of real spiritual fruit among them—only a stiff and lifeless formalism. Personally I cannot vouch for the truth of this proposition, but what I do know is this. When I myself was in Freiburg, there had been nothing in the teaching but negative interpretation and one-sided criticism for nearly half a century. I will mention just two theological subjects—dogmatics and Church history. I am not acquainted with the current teachers of those subjects, but in my day dogmatics was covered from a purely historical viewpoint and with external proofs, and there was neither any deeper grounding nor any real speculative spirit. Instead of it demonstrating the guidance of Christ or the workings of the Holy Spirit in the Church to the students, instead of it presenting the inner progression of events in a higher connection without prejudice to the normal historical sense, Church history was studied as a *histoire scandaleuse,* with a preference for reviling popes, bishops, Councils, monks, and Church institutions. A program of reform was in fact promoted from above for quite some time, but for all its unquestionable merits, this was concerned almost exclusively with a great variety of pure forms and externals. Whenever there was any reason for the clergy to deliver addresses, they dissipated their literary skills in endless arguments over purely liturgical, pastoral, and moral matters, and received not the slightest encouragement to dig down to the deepest roots of Christianity as a whole or to analyze the roots and foundations of Christian faith and life. Indeed they had neither the capacity nor the drive to get a real living feel for the deepest and the highest. If truth be told, whenever there was the least sign of anything of that kind, all the stops were pulled out to suppress it as "mystical" and "scholastical." In the light of all this, the idea that the Baden clergy of today are rather worldly seems more than a little plausible.

Where then can we hope to see intellectual and (even more importantly) spiritual revival coming from? As things stand today, what is needed if we are to witness the blossoming and ripening of a profound and inward religion, a true joyfulness in believing and a noble inspiration? The Catholic clergy in Baden will find it difficult to identify even just a handful of men of philosophical and speculative talent who have come from their ranks and who *have had any encouragement from them.* For talent prospers only where thinking is not merely on a negative superficial level, where attention is not focused exclusively on pure forms and externals, and where faith is not merely not attacked but not clung on to defensively either, where faith is not something out there that is detached from our lives or floating above our heads, but rather something that we embrace in living fashion so that all our higher powers blossom under this heavenly light.

More than one passage in the *Denkschrift* [public memorandum] suggests that the Freiburg non-theological professors are fully aware of this spiritual emptiness and hardness, this unspiritual character of a greater or lesser number of the Catholic priests of their region (and things seem, if possible, to be even worse with the Baden Protestant clergy), and the remedy they are proposing for it is the abolition of celibacy. So inwardly and spiritually impoverished are the Baden priests described above, they are such shadows of intelligent spiritual men, that they are reduced to living the shallowest of lives and looking for joy outside themselves; so the cry has gone up from them: "Who will give us wives?" No doubt with the best of intentions, the authors of the petitions[2] state their complete agreement with them,

---

2. The three petitions from the year 1828 were each worded similarly and were addressed to the Baden Parliament, to the Archduke of Baden, and to the Archbishop of Freiburg. The supporting arguments adduced were rather insubstantial, unlike those put forward in the rather more solid *Denkschrift* of the same year by Professors Zell and Amann, which Möhler is here

joining in the chorus: "Give them wives." But do they really believe
that wives can give priests what they lack? It is of course true that
some parents are all too happy if they can find a wife for a son who is
leading a dissolute life, in hopes that marriage with a girl from a good
family will help to settle him down. But there the point is to get
someone settled into enjoyment of this life—without the least thought
of the next. I must confess that I personally have never previously
come across the suggestion anywhere that the provision of *wives* is an
appropriate means of giving new life to ossified members of the body
of Christ or of guaranteeing a supply of sound and stimulating theologians and inspired preachers; nor has it occurred to anyone before
to propose that possession of a wife be made an important benchmark
for assessing the quality of theologians and preachers.

When Holy Scripture wants to represent Barnabas as one of
the finest of St. Paul's helpers, it says that he was a man "full of the
Holy Spirit and of faith."[3] *This* then was what the author of the Acts
of the Apostles thought was most important, and I must say I am
astonished that there has been no call for the encouragement of *such
qualities as these* as a means to the much-needed reinvigoration of
the Baden clergy. It would have been so much better and so much more
in accord with the thinking of the gospel, if the professors in question
had come together and sung prayerfully and wholeheartedly as the
Church does in such situations:

> Come, Holy Spirit, Creator blest,
> and in our souls take up Thy rest;
> come with Thy grace and heavenly aid
> to fill the hearts which Thou has made.[4]

How very appropriate too the Whitsun sequence would have been
for them:

> Without your divine will,
> there is nothing in man,
> nothing is harmless.

---

answering. See Winfried Leinweber, *Der Streit um den Zölibat im 19. Jh.*, pp. 591 ff. (MBTh 44),
Münster, 1978; here: pp. 58ff.

3. [Möhler note] "πλήρης ἁγίου πνεύματος καὶ πίστεως , Acts 11:24."

4. "Veni, Creator Spiritus, Mentes tuorum visita, Imple superna gratia Quae tu creasti
pectora . . . ."

Wash that which is unclean,
Water that which is dry,
Heal that which is wounded.
Bend that which is inflexible,
Warm that which is chilled,
Make right that which is wrong.[5]

What is actually needed today is for the people of Baden to pray earnestly for the provision of men with such a bond to the higher powers that their blessing would draw down streams of divine grace, men who would hover with creative power over the chaos[6], men who would combine the profundity of an Augustine, the erudition of a Jerome, the rhetorical talent of a Chrysostom, and the gentleness of a Hilary with the sharpness of the implacable Ratherius of Verona. · Unquestionably, the first thing such a group of men would do would be to encourage the clergy to pay close attention to a small passage in a Preface which they sing or pray each year during Lent—without apparently having got any particular inspiration from it thus far: "everlasting God; Who by this bodily fast, does curb our vices, dost lift up our minds and bestow on us strength and rewards . . . ."[7] The term "fast"[8] is here to be understood in a broad sense, it does not refer simply to abstention from eating and drinking, but to the general desire for earthly pleasure and material distraction. What other means such a group of men would employ to get a campaign of renewal started, I leave of course entirely up to them.

I can only congratulate the authors of the Petition for their call for a more capable clergy, for better things will be achieved only when voices are raised publicly against unworthy, ignorant, and superficial pastors; indeed if such voices come from within the heart of the community, they will themselves be proof of the fact that a much nobler element is present in its ranks. *Their complaint will also represent a powerful testimony against many principles hitherto prevailing*

---

5. "Sine tuo numine nihil est in homine, nihil est innoxium. Lava quod est sordidum, riga quod est aridum, sana quod est saucium. Flecte quod est rigidum, fove quod est frigidum, rege quod est devium."

6. Genesis 1:1.

7. "(Deus) qui corporali ieiunio vitia comprimis, mentem elevas, virtutem largiris et praemia . . . ."

8. "corporale ieiunium."

*in Baden, in the University of Freiburg, in the Seminary at Meersburg,
and in the episcopal administration: it will confirm that nothing profitable
has ever been done by these principles nor ever can be done by them.*
One of those principles is the notion that celibacy should be abolished.
Who does not remember that the strongest attack on celibacy was
made in the *Freimütigen*, published in Freiburg? That the institution
of celibacy was particularly attacked by men who came out of this
university or who are attached to it—Werkmeister, Huber, Weinmann?
But the truth is that this hostility to celibacy is very much a part of the
whole worldview that was originally to blame for the current wretched
state of a greater or lesser part of the Baden clergy—so painful and
so much to be lamented. It is no accident that attacks on the celibacy
requirement for Catholic priests have come at a time when the
Baden clergy are in a decadent state, and it is my contention that the
thinking of the *Denkschrift* itself flows from those same dark waters
which its own authors find tasteless, from that very plant whose
fruit nauseates them: in a nutshell, the *Denkschrift* stands in contradiction with itself. The mindset which has produced the *Denkschrift* is
itself the very one that has been responsible for destroying the Baden
clergy, even while its authors admit that they are deeply dissatisfied
with the same clergy. On the other hand there is a positive side to all
this, for the *Denkschrift* writers have pushed matters to the point where
their position has become unsustainable because of its internal contradictions: the cause is at odds with its effects and the reasons with
what they are supposed to justify.

UNCATHOLIC THEOLOGY

With respect to this connection between hostility to celibacy and
other principles which, I have argued, had a morally poisonous influence on the Baden clergy, I will say only the following. The outward
coincidence that a hostile attitude towards the institution of celibacy
developed at the same time as these harmful maxims suggests an inner
connection. The 1780s saw the onset in the Protestant Church of
Germany of assaults on the basic teaching[9] of Christendom, and these
became more and more commonplace with the general spread of

9. Möhler's antipathy is aroused here by a weak Enlightenment theology known as Neology.
Neology equated the content of the credal confessions (the foundation teaching!) with the

shallow thinking. Although a deep reverence for dogma was almost a second nature for Catholics, and this prevented them from simply making common cause with the Protestants, there was all too much visible evidence of spiritual apathy and raw indifference to the basic teachings of Christianity and the Catholic Church. There was also plenty of evidence of hostility to all the Church institutions established in the earlier ages of faith, which were now frequently made the object of frivolous and trivializing commentary. Nobody will dispute this—not even the authors of the *Denkschrift*. The loss of the depth and liveliness of the old faith was necessarily accompanied by a loss of sensitivity toward it and of the capacity to understand and value what had come from it.

Examples are not always welcome, however much they clarify facts, but since the subject seems important to me, I will offer one. Werkmeister[10] started out as one of the staunchest opponents of the disciplines of the Church, but toward the end of his life moved right away from the Church (though rumour has it that he returned to the fold at the last). I know that there are exceptions and noteworthy exceptions—but I also know that they are *only* exceptions. Those like Thomas Freikirch who deny the inerrancy of the Church[11] (and hence her origin from Christ as well as her eternal life), those who do not share with her the belief that the salvation of souls can be found only in her (and that where there is nonetheless redemption outside her, it is owed only to her existence)—how can such persons understand and love an institution like the priesthood which requires such total devotion to the Church, such total sacrifice of oneself, which requires that a person live only for her and work only for her in the furtherance of her welfare? Of course they cannot! Nobody in his right mind gives everything up for the sake of nothing—or for the sake of something he can find absolutely anywhere.

At this point I want to discuss just one doctrine, for the weakening or the passive acceptance of this doctrine have become

---

religion of reason: God, freedom, morality, immortality. See Karl Barth, *Protestant Theology in the Nineteenth Century. Its Background and History*, 666 pp, London, SCM, 1972; here 163–173.

10. Benedikt Maria Werkmeister (1745–1823), first a Benedictine, later a radical Enlightenment figure; cf. Article "Werkmeister" by H. Tüchle, in: LThK (2nd ed) 10, 1054 ff.

11. I.e. the infallibility of the Church, which gives testimony in her life and in her teaching to the fact that God has revealed Himself in Christ. Infallibility is a consequence of the real entry of God into history.

crucially relevant in the present case. Even reason can see very clearly that every individual good is only a good insofar as it flows from the source of all good, and that every being can only remain good through a permanent living connection with that which is good in itself, i.e. the sole source of moral power and true life. Hence the teaching about the gift of grace through Christ Jesus—which means that this union with God has been won again for us through His merit and *that we can only do anything through Him who strengthens us*— is a key teaching of the Gospel and the Church. Wherever naturalistic and materialistic ideas have spread, this teaching has been abused and mocked. The teaching about a *prevenient and concomitant grace*[12] etc. has been rejected as scholastic foolishness, as if all good will were not the work of the Holy Spirit in us, as if His grace did not go with us to help us translate good will into deed. Instead, people argue that man is separated from God and left to himself, so that he has knowledge only of nature and not of grace. This ignores the fact that although nature is able to overcome itself, it cannot do so by itself; or that nature is able to destroy itself and is not really master of itself. Naturalistic ideas have been spreading for a long time within the Catholic Church too, so there was necessarily going to be an assault on celibacy from that quarter. Was there any way this could be avoided, once we saw men trying to embark on the great work of the priesthood alone and without God's grace—an approach which could only end up making the whole enterprise look like foolishness and madness?

If we now turn from a consideration of general principles to a study of the actual arguments put forward in polemical writings against the celibacy requirement, we find our conclusions confirmed. A careful perusal of such texts gives rise to a sense of astonishment at the complete absence of anything that might be evidence of a faith in the ongoing working of the Holy Spirit through all our best and holiest instincts. In his polemic against celibacy, Trefurt[13] even falls into materialism, asserting that it is impossible not to satisfy the sex drive!

I have no desire to be unjust to anyone, and I am anxious not to give the impression that any person who attacks celibacy is bound

---

12. "gratia praeveniens, concomitans."

13. Christoph Trefurt, *Der Cölibat aus dem Gesichtspunkte der Moral, des Rechts und der Politik betrachtet*, Heidelberg-Leipzig 1826; Trefurt was a Baden jurist and high-ranking civil servant.

to be irremediably hostile to fundamental Christian truths. Many have
been taught to despise celibacy by others and may well have rejected
celibacy without having any idea of the reasons for the rejection as
originally adduced by those who taught them. So many people contradict themselves, they believe very firmly in certain conclusions while
at the very same time hotly denying the very principles on which those
conclusions must be based; such people are as little accustomed to
reflecting on the connections between phenomena in the inner realm
as they are on those of the external world. Even those in whom the
hatred of celibacy first began to fester can seldom have been in a
position to explain where their hatred came from. So I would like to
challenge celibacy's opponents generally not to hide from themselves
what it was that initially gave rise to their inner and really *general*
antipathy to the gospel and Church teaching, but to face up to the real
implications of their attitude.

    The end result of all this is to show that current attacks on
celibacy are in reality part and parcel of the whole recent wave of
hostility to the gospel and the Church, and that they cannot be considered in abstraction from it. But there is a further implication in what
I have said that needs to be more closely examined: namely, that
wherever they have had any impact, the attacks on the celibacy requirement of the Church—allegedly motivated by a desire to improve
clergy morale—have in reality had a negative effect on the clergy. This
can be proved very easily. I shall not discuss here the inner connection
between efforts to eliminate the celibacy rule and contemporaneous
unchristian tendencies of other kinds and their influence on the weakening of moral fibre. I am going to focus purely on the direct impact of
anti-celibacy polemic on priests.

    The effect of forty years of attacks on celibacy has been to rob
many clerics of their previous cheerful naturalness, something they
badly need if they are to be strong in themselves and have an effective
ministry. Hearts that had before been settled and peaceful about their
condition were now troubled and their spiritual power was undermined. Hearing people assert that it was immensely difficult or even
downright impossible to observe the celibacy rule induced them to feel
uncertain about their own powers. This doubt [Ger. *Zweifel*]—a word

which, as Marheineke[14] observed in another connection, rhymes with only one other German word, the word for devil *[Teufel]*—carries within itself the virus of impotence. Even the best of men harbours a residual attraction to the pleasures of the flesh, and this will of course greedily awaken and feed any sense of doubt. The alleged injustice of the celibacy requirement will nag away at him, and guilt for sin will be transferred to those who have laid down what is depicted as a harsh and horrible law and who continue to uphold it—so that in the end there will be nothing to prevent a person from sinking into a state of profound moral wretchedness. Although there is fairly reliable evidence that even then priests usually stop short of sexual indulgence, the truth is that where one passion is denied, people are all too quick to believe that they indulge others instead or at least make excuses for them. But the most likely scenario in such cases is that the man who was spiritually strong before will be reduced to a poisonous inner dividedness, to nothing more than a withered flower or a broken reed, and all his joyfulness in life, all his spiritually productive power will vanish forever. Furthermore it needs to be borne in mind that many of those entering the priesthood at the present time will be infected by the negative attitudes to celibacy prevalent in so many minds and so many writings; consequently they will be beginning their priestly lives not with joyful naturalness, noble self-confidence, and trustful devotion, but in a state of uncertainty and ambivalence. What else is to be expected?

　　The one conclusion I want to draw from the argument so far is this: if it is certain that recent attacks on celibacy stem from an era which was to the highest degree hostile to the Church and the Gospel, if it is clear that hostility to celibacy has *the same* origins as modern, shallow, unspiritual, and basically vacuous ways of thinking about Christianity and the Church in general, this circumstance must surely make every opponent of the discipline in question pause for thought. If at the same time it is also demonstrable how very damaging these attacks are and must be, I would have thought that we ought to consider it our holiest duty to impose an eternal silence upon ourselves in regard to the topic, a silence to be broken only if and when—and I speak here from the viewpoint of the opponent—it becomes crystal

---

14. Philipp Konrad Marheineke (1780–1846), Berlin Protestant theologian of a speculative Hegelian tendency.

clear that directly after the appearance of a writing or a speech against
the celibacy rule, this rule would be abrogated. I have long been
fully aware that no book can ever bring the rule of celibacy to an end,
any more than an essay could ensure the continuance of an institution
in the Church or indeed introduce a new one into it, and I would not
have entrusted a word on the subject to paper, if I had not had in mind
the extremely advantageous moral consequences of refuting objections
to the celibacy of the priesthood.

   Thus much is clear. But one vital consequence of the fact that
these anti-celibacy views are basically rooted in the hostility to Church
and Gospel, which became current at the same time as they did, is
that they betray a mindset that is not really able to grasp the true
meaning of Holy Scripture. I will now show in greater detail how they
evacuate Scripture of its real power, how they touch on it only at its
most superficial level and indeed how they positively misrepresent it.
I shall also show that these ideologues completely misunderstand
Church history and present a totally distorted picture of it. In fact,
failure to comprehend the Gospel and failure to understand the
Church and her history always go hand in hand.

   In order to familiarize the reader with the general approach of
the *Denkschrift*, let me begin by explaining that it is composed of three
parts. The first promises a history of the celibacy requirement, and
it is followed by a comparative study in the second of the supposed
advantages and disadvantages of the requirement for celibacy in
priests. Finally the third part considers how and on the basis of what
canon and civil law principles abandonment of this requirement is to
be undertaken. The first section then is devoted to proving that Christ
and the Apostles did not impose the celibacy requirement and also
that they no more despised marriage than did the Early Church!
But all this is nothing less than a huge waste of time. No German theologian would dispute the first proposition, while contempt for marriage
would be regarded as blasphemous by absolutely everyone. Any
Catholic attacking marriage would incur anathema[15,] as has always
been the case in the Church. No really serious polemic of any integrity
against the continuance of the rule regarding priestly celibacy could

---

15. Anathema means exclusion from the community of the Church on the ground of a grave
offense against the Spirit of Christ. It is biblically based, and anathema was first threatened by
St. Paul (Galatians 1:9).

ever have dreamed of insinuating that its defenders are reduced to underestimating or even entirely forgetting the dignity and sacramental status of marriage. The author of the *Denkschrift* was clearly guilty of contempt for his masters in not making this same assumption (page five shows us that this man wrote at the service of the petitioners).[16]

16. "These pages . . . . will provide precise grounds for, and a broader development of, the petition that has been presented and for the views set out there only in outline" (*Denkschrift* [see above note 1], p. 5ff.).

Chapter 2

The Biblical Counsel

JESUS ON MARRIAGE AND CELIBACY (MATTHEW 19)

It will be no surprise whatever to the reader who has followed us thus far that the opponents of celibacy are forever trying to muddy the waters in relation to all the Bible passages in which virginity is praised. They sense that everything rests on this. I will first of all therefore take issue with our champion of a married priesthood on his determination to discourage people from reverencing virginity on the basis of Scripture.

To begin with then, our author[1] comments on Matthew 19:12. In this key passage he finds nothing more than the principle that virginity *"is not impossible."*[2] Yet when Christ says "There are eunuchs born from their mother's womb, there are eunuchs made so by human agency *and there are eunuchs who have made themselves so for the sake of the Kingdom of Heaven,"* he is evidently talking about a positive *reality* that takes the possibility of celibacy for granted and completely discounts any supposed impossibility! And still our author puts it only negatively, claiming that this Scripture shows only that celibacy is not impossible! Instead of rejoicing from the bottom of his heart that the Christian faith has given men the power to live wholly for the Kingdom of God, to apply themselves wholly—heart, will, and mind—to the eternal and to the divine, instead of agreeing with the general jubilation of the Church over the descent of the Holy Spirit in whom we have been made participators of this divine Life, and instead

---

1. Confusingly, Möhler sometimes attributes the anonymous *Denkschrift* to one author, at other times to several, see note 2 in Chapter 1. But he suspects that there were at least two authors, and he shows greater respect towards the writer of the second part than toward the person who wrote the first; cf. Chapter 4, p. 48 below.

2. Cf. *Denkschrift*, p. 8.

of singing with her "[Christ] who ascending above all in the heavens . . . poured out the Holy Spirit upon the children of adoption. Wherefore the whole world doeth rejoice with overflowing joy . . . ,"[3] he observes frostily "it is not *impossible!*" Then he goes on to say: "so that people do not see this abstinence as something everyday, something easy, which can be required of *all* [whoever suggested such a thing!] or even just of many [in a village of 100 souls just one person is significant!] the divine teacher adds: *"Let anyone accept this who can."*[4] What the author of the *Denkschrift* really means then is: "Christ supposes that every hundred years at most someone will come along and apply this to himself."

The following consideration will be quite sufficient to demon-strate how far the author is from the mind of Christ when he inter-prets the words "let anyone accept this who can" as if they meant: "There are so many obstacles to the preservation of virginity that we can expect to see it only very rarely." The Pharisees had asked the Savior whether and to what extent divorce was allowed.[5] He explained that it was permitted in the case of a marriage breakdown to the extent that a man could leave his wife, but that in such a case that man was not permitted to marry again, and if he did so he would make himself responsible for the marriage breakdown. Furthermore, anyone who married a divorced partner would thereby become a participant in the marriage breakdown. Finding themselves on the same footing as the Pharisees in their views on marriage, the disciples were so astonished that they exclaimed: "If that is how things are between husband and wife, it is advisable not to marry." The Savior answered: "It is not everyone who can accept what I have said, but only those to whom it is granted." And then, in order to show that celibacy is quite definitely possible, he added: There will certainly be some who *do not marry* for the sake of the Kingdom of God, those who quite simply abstain from marriage. And Jesus Christ concluded this with the saying: "Let anyone accept this who can." This same sentence actually crops up twice, with only one word different (which has no relevance for the meaning). After his teaching about divorce the Savior says: "It is not

---

3. "Qui ascendens super omnes coelos . . . promissum spirituarum mundus exaltat . . ." (Preface for Pentecost).

4. Cf. *Denkschrift*, p. 8.

5. Cf. Matthew 19:3.

everyone who can accept what I have said, but only those to whom it is granted," and after predicting that complete continence will be practiced in times to come, he again states: "Let anyone accept this who can." I ask then, what is the meaning of this sentence about the prohibition on a man remarrying when the first wife he has divorced is still alive? Our author comments like this: "So that people do not regard such a renunciation as something normal or easy, to be expected of all or at least of many, the divine Savior adds: 'It is not everyone who can accept what I have said, but only those to whom it is granted.'"[6] Our author will certainly have the courage to be one of their number, since such an interpretation would open the floodgates to promiscuous divorce and remarriage, and it would in fact correspond precisely to the frivolous view of marriage as put forward in the school of Hillel,[7] a view Jesus was opposing. But if this had really been what Jesus meant, then the disciples would have had no reason whatever to be astonished. We shall have to look then for another interpretation, and it is hardly very difficult to find, indeed it is right there in front of us. To the teaching of Christ about marriage and its indissolubility the Jews opposed the law of Moses, which permitted that a letter of separation be given. The Savior's answer was this: in the old law a temporary exception had been made on account of the hardness of heart of the Jews, but Christianity will bring something entirely new. The words: "It is not everyone who can accept what I have said, but only those to whom it is granted" contain the contradiction between Mosaism and Christianity, and their meaning is this: "from the standpoint of Mosaism my words cannot be understood, they seem impossible. But for the person who is united with me through faith and to whom as a result higher powers are imparted, they make sense." Jesus spoke in similar terms after telling the parable of the sower: "Anyone who has ears should listen!" (Matthew 13:9) and later on to his

---

6. We do no injustice to Möhler and do nothing to discourage admirers of Christian virginity if we accept that his argument is artificial. Verses 11 and 12—wonderful in their intuition—both relate to *singleness*, not at all to the prohibition on divorce or the renunciation of marriage. Cf. Joachim Gnilka, Das *Mattäusevangelium* 2 Teil in: HThK I/2, 552 pp., Freiburg-Basle-Vienna 1988; here, p. 155. Möhler lets himself be seduced by his opponents into a preoccupation with the question of how many persons will be affected by this teaching of Our Lord on marriage. The words of Jesus are free from quantitative anxiety, they express the full gracedness of virginity. But grace also springs from marriage, since Christ alone and not human strength makes it possible to live marriage as renewed from its original nature.

7. In the time of Jesus, the School of Rabbi Hillel defended divorce.

disciples "to you is granted to understand the mysteries of Heaven, but to them it is not granted . . . they look without seeing and listen without hearing or understanding." The expression: "Let anyone accept this who can" has the same meaning after the words "There are eunuchs who have made themselves so for the sake of the Kingdom of Heaven." It all seems totally incomprehensible to the worldly person who stands outside the Gospel, the person to whom the mysteries of the Kingdom of God have not been revealed, the person who does not know the miracles that happen in the inner man through faith and community of life with the Reconciler. He simply cannot understand how high a human being can raise himself above nature for the sake of the Kingdom of God.

Jesus wanted then to explain his teaching about marriage— a teaching which seemed impossible not only to the Jews but also to his disciples, who had the same viewpoint as the Jews on this—by referring to a life that would be real in the future, a life which to them seemed impossible. In the light of all this, how can anyone try to argue that he was wanting to convey how rare the celibate life would be and how difficult it would be to live? These modern exegetes want him to have said: "Not to marry again after divorcing one's wife is perfectly easy. It's just that it will be very rare and almost impossible not to marry for the sake of the Kingdom of God." Unfortunately on this reading the conclusion is totally out of line with the premise!

The interpretation of Matthew 9:12 which we have shown to be fallacious suggests not the least hint of the Savior's infinite greatness, sublimity, and fortifying power, which the passage actually conveys, but turns it into something soft—hardly surprising since it came out of a soft era so often bereft of all higher powers. Instead of raising the spirits of all Christians and especially the clergy, it depresses them; instead of inspiring and blessing hearts with uplifting ideals, it brings them down to the commonest heathen reality and weakness. Its lack of the least feel for exegesis is also very damaging.

St. Paul's Pressing Recommendation

Equally striking is the way that the message of St Paul in 1 Corinthians 7 is interpreted. What the Apostle says there about virginity is explained by the author as opinions (!) elicited by worries about

the circumstances of the day and the dangerous and precarious situation of the first Christians.[8] He consequently translates: "On account
of the present crisis."[9] And when Paul observes that the person
who marries does well, while the person who does not marry does
better, our author explains this by stating that in such times of great
crisis, to remain single was preferable to getting married.[10]

First of all it would actually be very difficult to prove that the
Corinthians were living under particular conditions of crisis at that
time or that they were in fact being persecuted. Neither of the letters
to them contains any hint of this. Indeed, according to the First Letter
to the Corinthians, they were living in such peaceful relations with
the heathens that they were having meals with them in the temple of
the gods.[11] If they had in fact been in the throes of persecution, would
Paul not have offered them some sort of words of consolation? But
there is no word of such consolation in either Letter! Furthermore,
it is related in the Acts of the Apostles that when an accusation against
Paul had been made by the Jews of Corinth to Gallio (Acts 18:12),
the Proconsul acquitted the apostle on the spot, which seems to cast
doubt on the idea that there was a great crisis for the Christians of
Corinth at that time.

Before going on to point to more of the glaringly evident
grounds for my objections to the arguments of the *Denkschrift*, I want
to offer a few preliminary remarks. I initially harbored doubts about
putting such observations to an interpreter who is apparently ignorant
of even the most general hermeneutical rules, and to whose judgement
one cannot submit with much hope of success. But on reflection I
think this will help other readers to see the emptiness of the exegesis
which I am combating all the more clearly.

---

8. Möhler points here to a problem with so-called historical-critical exegesis which has not
been resolved even yet and which indeed cannot by definition be resolved; by its very method
such exegesis has constantly courted the danger of explaining the unpopular statements
of the Bible as conditioned by the worldview of their authors and of reducing them to "the
contemporary situation." In the end the only words credited as being those of the "authentic"
Jesus or Paul are those that suit the spirit of the age.

9. V. 26, " . . . δια την ενεστωσαν αναγκην . . . "

10. "A clearer understanding of these sayings can be found by reference to v. 26, from which
it emerges that the Apostle was supremely aware of the dangerous and threatened situation of the
first Christians" (*Denkschrift*, p. 9).

11. "εν ειδωλειω κατακειμενοι" (I Corinthians 8:10).

1.   In verse one, Paul responds to the doubts referred to
him in writing, which (as becomes clear in the wider context) are the
motivation for his reflections. The Apostle had recommended continence. His enthusiasm for it must have been remarkable, for his
speech had had such an impact that wives were actually withdrawing
from their husbands and husbands from their wives, indeed they
were talking about complete separation, while the widows and virgins
were thinking they *ought* not to marry at all. People were tending
to conclude that all of this was a Christian's *duty*. Obviously Paul had
been misunderstood. The question now occurs as to how his words
could have been formulated to make such a misunderstanding possible. There is no way he could have been misunderstood in this area
if the point at issue was continence and the avoidance of marriage
because of persecution. Had that been the case, how could those *already
married* have had any reason to apply it to themselves? Their continence would have had no power whatsoever to stop or even to miti-
gate persecution and oppression. Furthermore, if continence had been
recommended in the light of persecution, how can we make sense
of the fact that the Corinthians themselves seem not to have been
aware of the reasoning behind Paul's recommendation? When there is
any question of curbing the desires of the flesh, people are generally
very attentive to the existence of any possible escape clause. But apparently here, the Corinthians simply did not notice the very point that
would have allowed them some latitude! They heard only that it was
good not to marry! Why? They didn't even notice the reason! They did
not notice the reason for such a fundamental requirement! The truth
is that I can think of nothing more strange than the position in which
the Corinthians would have found themselves had there been any
basis for the assumption of those who attribute Paul's recommendation
of virginity to the (dangerous) circumstances of the day. On this
reasoning, his recommendation was not followed on moral grounds,
and yet the Corinthians themselves did not even register the argument that appealed to the circumstances of the day. They simply got
the idea that they *should* not allow their daughters to marry, adopting
this rigid attitude without any ground whatever, until at long last it
finally occurred to them to ask Paul for rather more precise guidance!
If we follow the thinking in the *Denkschrift*, nothing less than pure
thoughtlessness on the part of the Corinthians could give any sort of

explanation of the seventh chapter of Paul's First Letter to them!
So how then is the possibility of their misunderstanding and their
need for written teaching on the subject to be explained?

There is just one interpretation that makes perfect sense:
in the last days of his stay at Corinth, the Apostle had spoken with
immense warmth and love of virginity and eulogized its value.
The reason why this teaching only came up at the end of the apostolic
preaching at Corinth was that it belonged not to the fundamentals
but to the superstructure of Christianity, and indeed it could only be
appreciated if a person was already a Christian (" 'Let him who can do
it, do it!' says the Lord"). These Corinthian converts were of necessity
complete newcomers to the whole question, they were hugely inspired
by the whole preaching of the Gospel to a serious view of life, they
were fired up by the apostolic presentation of virginity, and all this to
such an extent that they understandably saw what Paul was depicting
so worthily and rightly to them as a moral necessity. They failed to
consider the question of distinguishing the different gifts which are
given to men (verse seven), they came to the issue in a state of heated
excitement rather than in a mood of cool reflection, and they also
failed to distinguish between counsel and command,[12] concluding
naively and good heartedly that married couples should break up and
widows and virgins be discouraged from marrying. It was only when
St. Paul had gone away on his travels that the difficulties involved
in this drastic policy began to emerge, and it was only then that they
had to address their queries to him in a letter. It is on the assumption
that Paul had recommended virginity to the Corinthians on *moral*
grounds, grounds therefore valid under all circumstances—and *only*
on this assumption—that otherwise insuperable difficulties in this
text can be overcome. According to our way of looking at things, the
answer that Paul gives relative to the married is perfectly appropriate.
If we follow the logic of our opponent, the Apostle must have been
aware that his recommendation of continence had no relevance to the
Corinthians, because their embattled situation would not have been
relieved in any way by it. In fact, however, the Apostle advised that
instead of the lifelong abstention his Corinthian disciples were trying
to practice, they should limit themselves to occasional short periods

---

12. "συγγνωμη and επιταγη," ibid., 6:25.

of abstinence.[13] Why? In order to improve their embattled situation a little? In order to make the pains of persecution bearable? Not at all! Rather the Apostle emphasised the purely moral dimension: "So that you can devote yourselves to fasting and prayer."

2. In verse 25 Paul says: "About people remaining virgins, I have no directions from the Lord, but I give my own opinion." Could the Apostle possibly have expressed himself in this manner if he was talking about a recommendation to virginity on account of the painful circumstances of the day? It goes without saying that an express divine command relating to the behavior of Christians in each of the different situations in which they may find themselves was hardly to be expected. If the Corinthians had understood the issue purely ethically,[14] if Paul was placing the issue in this perspective, if he was actually wanting to inculcate an inspired single-mindedness ready to sacrifice everything, if he wanted to offer consolation in his teaching and calm troubled consciences, it was in order to make clear that absolutely no general Christian-ethical law or command of God was infringed if a person relinquished their state of virginity to get married.

3. The same applies when Paul believed he had to declare expressly *that it was no sin* if a virgin married. Here the purely ethical character of the object in question was if anything brought out even more sharply. It really could not have occurred to the holy teacher to give his disciples the assurance that they did nothing bad in itself if they married, unless he had been made aware of their very high moral valuation of virginity. If the issue was of virginity as a purely prudential means to make troubled circumstances less painful, and if Paul was rejecting this as a strategy, he would surely have spoken comfortingly in these terms: "the truth is that the pressure of persecution will certainly not crush you if you get married." What he could not have said was "getting married is not a sin," since everyone knew this. The statement "If you marry, you do not sin"[15] is only the negative way of

---

13. "προς καιρον" (5).

14. The ethical or moral conception is, according to Möhler the only possible one appropriate to 1 Corinthians 7, which means that singleness is not a duty, but is only recommended by Paul. This contradicts the conception of the *Denkschrift*, according to which the Pauline recommendation was dictated by current persecution.

15. "εαν δε και γημης, ουχ ήμαρτες," v. 28.

putting the statement "the person who marries does well,"[16] so the verse we have been discussing cannot be equivalent to: "the person who marries, does prudently; the person who does not marry, does more prudently."

4.   Verse 36 tells us that according to Corinthian traditions it brought shame on families if a daughter remained *a virgin* all her life, so people were reluctant to leave their daughters unmarried. But it is a highly pertinent question to ask whether the members of the Christian community in Corinth, if they were being harassed and persecuted by the heathen, would ever have been bothered by worries about a matter of pure convention like this one! Or whether they even *could* have been bothered by such worries! Surely the thought of the danger to the whole family would immediately have relegated to insignificance any concern about being respected for something that was really only a matter of vanity! In the midst of the general weight of contempt and shame which would have tormented them if it was a time of persecution, could the Corinthian Christians possibly have had a moment to trouble themselves about shame on that level? Would those who were enduring insult and contempt *for the sake of the name of Christ* not have considered the matter of such social conventions as far too trivial and demeaning to raise with Paul? Anyone who knows the heart of man will be asking questions like this with us. And indeed there is yet another question. Is there the least degree of plausibility that those who for some reason did not respect advice that was given to them only under pressure of certain outward circumstances, advice that had no moral significance, would wonder whether they should let themselves weaken purely out of respect for the prejudice of others? Is there the slightest likelihood moreover that the one who gave the advice would answer, as happens here: "Such a person does not sin?" What we said earlier applies here again: only if higher issues that touch the spiritual life were at stake could someone have asked in this kind of way, and only on the same presupposition could this kind of an answer have been given.

5.   I would also like to point out the construction of verses one and eight. In verse one, St. Paul—the one to whom of course the

---

16. "ὥστε ὁ εκγαμιζων καλως ποιει," v. 38.

Savior Himself appeared on the road to Damascus[17]— says: "It is a good thing for a man[18] not to touch a woman." In the second: "I should still like everyone[19] to be as I am myself," namely unmarried. Note the sweeping nature of Paul's expressed wish, transcending individual circumstances of place and time, embracing all future Christian times and spheres! That of course is precisely the character of purely ethical and spiritual principles. But Paul—whose sensible prudence is wonderfully close to an enthusiasm that transcends all understanding— does not here express a desire that he would seriously expect to see fulfilled in its authentic sense. He is fully aware of the impossibility of that, having already noted in verse seven that there are individual differences between men that derive from the Creator. That is the way of things with humankind in this world. When good-natured men who find their happiness in the pleasures and the well-being which the earth offers have an experience of overflowing feelings of delight, they not only want all the world to witness their joy, but also to share in it, even although they are perfectly aware that this is impossible. Likewise Paul, spiritually joyful on account of the *moral* good which he possesses in his virginity, would like everyone to share in his joy even though he is fully aware and clearly states that there is no prospect of the fulfilment of his desire. The truth of this affirmation is easy to demonstrate. In verse five the apostle recommends to the married occasional periods of abstinence on the basis of mutual agreement stemming from their heartfelt longing for God—"so that you may both devote yourselves to prayer and fasting." But he does not lay down the law on this, he only makes a recommendation in verse six. *For although he would like all men to be like himself,* he nonetheless does not want to make this the object of a law but only to give advice, because each man has his own gift from God, one this way, another that way. On this point the Apostle's thinking was determined purely by factors within the ethical realm.

It is in the context of these observations therefore that we interpret the passage where the question of pressing need is discussed.[20] Here Paul is clearly speaking in the same terms about suffering

---

17. Acts 9.

18. "ἄνθρωπω."

19. "παντας ανθρωπους."

20. "δια την ενεστωσαν αναγκην," v. 26.

in the flesh, which such persons will not avoid.[21] What this means
is explained well enough in the following verses 29 to 31. The suffering of the flesh or for the flesh[22] consists in the fact that those who
have wives are to live as if they had none—as also in verse 31 the world
is to be used as if it were not being used. This means that all earthly
relationships must be influenced by higher relationships and understood with reference to God; the spirit must not be dragged down into
the earthly, rather the earthly must itself be hallowed by the consecration of the spirit. Paul holds this to be difficult in marriage however,
and wanting to convey what a high degree of self-mastery will be
required, he says in verse 28: "They will however have suffering in the
flesh." The phrase referred to above about pressing need can have only
this sense and I translate: "On account of the natural drive that rebels
so easily."[23]

   With verses 32 to 35 he introduces another justification for
his recommendation of virginity: the unmarried person focuses on
Christ's work and seeks to please him, the married person focuses on
earthly relationships[24] and on how to please his wife. Of course this is
only a matter of degree. The Apostle means that the mind of the
married person is directed more towards externals by his family situation, while the mind of the unmarried person is directed more inward,
for he can give himself up wholeheartedly and with undivided attention to higher things. After observing that nonetheless he is not going
to issue any command, St. Paul adds that the person who marries does
well, while the person who does not marry does better. Since in verse
38 directly before this the issue was *only* about purely moral principles,
I have no idea how a thinking person can foist onto these words
the meaning: "In the present oppressed situation of the Corinthian
Christians it is better for them not to marry than to marry." The
Apostle closes the whole chapter with the words: "She would be happier

---

21. "ὔλιψιν δε τη σαρκι ενουσιν ὁι τοιουτοι," v. 28.

22. "ὔλιψις τη σαρκι."

23. [Möhler's note] "That ενιστημι has the meaning given to it here needs no proof;
αναγκη as 'drive, natural drive, sexual drive' is found however for example in Heroph. De venat.
C. VII: 'ἡ γαρ ὡρα προς τας αυξησεις των κυνων κρατιστη αυτη εισι δε τετταρες και
δεκα ἡμεραι εν ἁις ἡ αναγκη αυτη εχει.' On this passage Weiske observes: 'αναγκη αυτη,'
'drive to Venus,' which thus quite necessarily requires the connection; furthermore Arian's
expression is to be compared with it: 'τη αναγκη εχεσθαι.' "

24. "τα του κοσμου" (33).

if she stayed as she is, to my way of thinking—*and I believe that I too have the Spirit of God.*" All I want to say about this is that the authors of the petition to the Archduke of Baden trace the celibacy rule that we defend back to the *Zeitgeist* of earlier centuries, but the *Zeitgeist* always comprehends only the *Zeitgeist:* ultimately it merely succeeds in dragging down even what is of the essence of the Spirit of God to the level of the *Zeitgeist.*

As long as people looked at the question impartially and with their minds truly enlightened and let themselves be led by the Spirit of God rather than by the spirit of the age, what Paul taught in the Letter to the Corinthians was universally accepted by the faithful. But when the spirit of the age obscured and darkened the thoughts of men, people started to say: this will devalue marriage. Of course people still had enough pious reverence not to want to criticize Holy Scripture directly. Instead, they complained about the Church and twisted the words of Scripture—to which they were no longer faithful because they didn't want to understand it any more. This is what always happens when people lose the spiritual power to believe or even to be receptive to a teaching of Scripture.

The *Denkschrift* is obsessed with the idea that the reason the Church chose to place such a great value on virginity was that the physical side of marriage was regarded as bad. This kind of notion can emerge only where there is an inability to be properly clearsighted about the purely spiritual way. The Apostle recommends the life of a virgin for the reason that it offers the opportunity to follow a free[25] and living way to the divine and the eternal with a gaze that is firmly focused on Christ the Lord. He recommends it for the reason that to it everything external seems to be a matter of indifference:[26] no need for a man is felt, for life is bearable, cheerful, and joyful, and it finds support, a purpose, and a meaning above all in union with others. For Christ alone is all of that to the virgin and is so close to her that he very meaningfully called her *bridegroom.* Individuals of this kind are rated as highly from the religious viewpoint as they are poorly rated from the common political viewpoint. How on earth would a wife with the mindset of a Christian—for a wife without that simply cannot

---

25. "ουχ ίνα βροχον ύμιν επιβαλω" (cf. verse 35).

26. An "αδιαφορον."

judge in this matter—feel devalued in conceding the priority to *such* a virgin? She will after all surely be mindful of how Christ taught us that in the future life people neither marry nor are given in marriage, since what we call marriage will no longer exist.[27] Unfortunately the author of the *Denkschrift* has no respect at all for such purely inward and spiritual principles, for he argues crudely that sexual relationships in marriage are in themselves a stumbling-block for the defender of virginity; in themselves they are just as indifferent to him as the virgin's continence is to her when it is considered purely outwardly. Our opponent regards the lifestyle of the virgin as something wholly negative, whereas the Apostle and the Church after him stresses the positive. That is what treasuring the spiritual means!

At this point the *Denkschrift* refers to 1 Corinthians 9, where Paul wants to show by his own example that not all that is allowed ought therefore to be practiced, and so he observes in verse five that he too could if he wanted have as a companion a Christian wife[28] as the other Apostles do. If he has not done this it is for the reason that he does not want to put any obstacle in the way of the Gospel. It is quite amazing how clumsily our esteemed author defends his case. I will pass over the differences of opinion to be found in the commentaries about the meaning of the term translated here as *Christian wife,* of which our author seems to know nothing. I will also pass over the fact that this is nothing to do with a permission to marry, but with the fact that Paul, like the other Apostles, would have been more of a burden on the communities he served had he been asking them to feed not just himself but a companion too; and then of couse there would also have been the fear in his mind of some kind of a scandal.

Surely every noble Catholic priest could say with the Apostle: "Could I not avail myself of my freedom too? To whom was I united when I denied myself marriage? I have made myself independent of all, I have put myself at everyone's service in order to win some." But how does our author dare to use these words of the kind of priests on whom they can only reflect everlasting shame? Was the Apostle timidly complaining, as if regretting his own free choice? Was he so completely shameless and so much in the grip of inner weakness

---

27. See Mark 12:25.

28. "αδελφη γυναικι."

as to lament his own disgrace whingeingly and cursingly in front of
the whole world: "Woe is me, that people should take me at my word!
Woe is me, that people thought I was a man, a Christian! Woe is me,
that people didn't actually dismiss me as a cowardly and pitiable devil
or a godless hypocrite, when I took on obligations before the altar
of the Lord and in the sight of His communities, obligations not laid
on me by any human authority but only at my own behest, nor did
they reject me or see right through me as someone unworthy!"

Our champion, the opponent of celibacy, says that Paul is
referring in the passage discussed just now by us to the *sacrifices* that
he is making to the cause of the Gospel. The fact that our author
can persistently talk about sacrifice as if it meant a joyless, unwilling,
and hesitant gift shows that not even the faintest spark of religious
inspiration can have glowed in his heart, nor can the remotest spiritual
affinity be found between him and the Holy Apostle! On the other
hand, this attitude makes perfect sense in an apology for persons whose
constant complaints contain the clearest indication that they have
fallen as far below being men of apostolic calling as Saul came far
below the level of the prophets.[29] Meanwhile our esteemed author was
prudent enough to overlook the following passage in the same chapter
of the same letter: "Every athlete concentrates completely on training, and this is to win a wreath that will wither, whereas ours will
never wither. So that is how I run, not without a clear goal; *and how
I box, not wasting blows on air. I punish my body and bring it under
control, to avoid any risk that, having acted as a herald for others, I myself
may be disqualified.*"[30]

The *Denkschrift* also refers to the First Letter to Timothy and
the Letter to Titus, where the Apostle requires among other qualifications that a priest be the husband of *one* wife (I Timothy 3:2). One
thing is crystal clear from this, as our apologist for a married priesthood so shrewdly recognizes — the apostle does not turn out to have
been a despiser of marriage! But that is an observation whose truth
actually stares out at us from almost every page of the Bible, from the

---

29. Here Möhler uses an earthy term of mockery used in the bible of people who have
aspired to a position above their station in their choice of the priestly calling. Just like these men
following their apostolic calling complainingly Saul, having once been filled with the Spirit, fell
into despair when the Spirit left him; see 1 Samuel 10:11f.

30. I Corinthians 9:25–27.

first verse of the New Testament: "Roll of the genealogy of Jesus Christ, son of David, son of Abraham" to the last: "May the grace of the Lord Jesus be with you all!" Meanwhile our champion insists on one among the vast number of things that are *not* to be found in any verse of the bible, something that so far nobody in our Church has looked for in there, something that actually has no place there, and yet remains absolutely silent about something that quite certainly is to be found in the Scriptures, even though it has a direct bearing on his claims. I cannot overlook this, for it has its part to play in the resolution of the point at issue.

The Apostle says then: the priest is to be the husband of *one*[31] wife. Everyone knows that this sentence does not mean that the priest is obliged to have a wife. Protestant clergy completely ignore the fact in their popular commentaries, and with good reason. If the Apostle were really asking here for the priest to have a wife, but only *one*, his stipulation could be read in two ways. First, it could be saying that the priest may not have several wives at the same time, which means either not having two actual wives living with him in formal marriage, or as Theodoret[32] took it, having no mistress alongside his wife. We can safely ignore this first reading of Paul. Given the general level of immorality prevalent in his day, some might be tempted to think that it was what Paul had in mind, yet in reality it is just not plausible. For if we were to accept this reading, it would follow that the Apostle could tolerate such a man perfectly well as a lay Christian in the Church, just not as a priest! It would also follow that this kind of relationship must have been very common at the time of the Apostles in the ordained ministry of the Christian Church, since St. Paul considered it necessary to deliver a special broadside against it. Only those who can square this with what we know about the morals of the first Christians—and with the spirit of Paul in particular—are liable to find this interpretation acceptable.

Then we should consider this: men who indulged in this kind of behavior were generally called marriage-breakers[33] in Holy Scripture and in several places this is how St. Paul himself refers to them.

---

31. "μία."

32. Theodoret of Cyrus (393–c.466), a voluminous patristic writer; cf. Alberto Viciano, *Theodoret von Kyros als Interpret des Apostels Paulus*, in: ThGl 80 (1990), 279–315.

33. "μοιχοί."

Had he had in mind such unchaste husbands, he would certainly have opted to say "marriage-breakers are not to be chosen as priests." Moreover there is the crucial point that Paul repeats the same stipulation with regard to those widows who are to be received into the service of the Church. He ordains that they too are to be the wives of only *one* man (I Timothy 5:9). Here it is simply not possible—even abstracting from all the customs and laws of the Roman Empire—that a widow should be told that she may not have two husbands at the same time. For a woman who has even just *one* husband is clearly not a widow. For the same reason Paul surely cannot have meant to refer to "a lover" when using the term "husband" and undoubtedly he would have called such a relationship adulterous.[34]

If the passage we are discussing cannot be interpreted in the manner referred to, there is nothing for it but to read Paul as saying that a man who has taken a second wife after the death of his first is not to be a priest. This interpretation is supported by I Corinthians 7, where Paul expresses a general preference for widowers not to contract second marriages and shows an inclination to prefer widowers who have not married again to others. The practice of the Early Church also fits in with this, for she consistently barred the twice-married from the clerical state. This custom could not be one that arose from a reading of our passages, for Paul will certainly have refined his doctrine in his preaching and teaching and confirmed it himself by the choices he made. The communities will have followed their normal tradition and interpreted these passages in the light of their tradition rather than first forming a tradition on the basis of their interpretations. Continence is emphasized in a special way here, and the truth is that the Protestant clergy offend against a clear biblical precept if they marry again after the death of a first spouse.

I will deal with the further consequences of all this later on, after the distortion of Church history by our champion of marriage-loving priests has been exposed. His reference[35] to I Timothy 4:2, in connection with which he quite unashamedly calls the defenders

---

34. "μοιχαλις."

35. "He, who strives in holy wrath against the coercive rules opposed to true Christianity of all future overheated enthusiasts and Pharisaical hypocrites, 'seduced by the hypocrisy of liars whose consciences are branded as though with a red-hot iron: they forbid marriage and prohibit foods . . . (1 Timothy 4:2)" (quotation from the *Denkschrift*, p. 11).

of the church law of celibacy "Pharisaical hypocrites," betrays such great ignorance or prejudice that it simply does not deserve our respect. In the passage in question, what is under discussion is the case of persons who forbid any and every marriage, but the Catholic Church not only does not reject marriage in general but does not prevent any individual from marrying.

Chapter 3

External Influences

The Heathen Origins of Clerical Celibacy?

The author of the *Denkschrift* reasons that neither Christ nor the Apostles placed much value on virginity. His problem then is to explain the phenomenon that virginity has always been so highly prized in the Church. In his view this respect could not be regarded as a legacy from the founders of our Church, since there was nothing of the kind to be inherited from them, so it must have come into the Church from outside. Drawing on a so-called anthropological principle of explanation—which even the author himself does not think can explain very much—he observes: "This kind of idea was to a large extent just the development of heathen and Jewish notions and tendencies with the addition of certain oriental philosophical teachings which led to the same conclusion."[1]

Let us consider the argument, and first of all the suggestion that celibacy is a legacy from heathendom. There is something very remarkable about this idea today; for ours is an age which is deeply Hellenized in its thought and in its way of doing things; it is an age that has opted very abruptly for the complete abandonment of the real Christian view of God and the world, of history and nature; it is an age which has been inclined to see in Christ Himself nothing more than a Confucius, a Plato, or a Socrates; it is an age which cannot laud and honor Greek and Roman art and science enough and that finds the real foundations for all finer and higher education in them; it is an age that generally dedicates a very considerable part of its noblest powers to the critical and exegetical study of heathen writers and to knowledge of the ancient world in general and

---

1. See *Denkschrift*, p. 12.

which honors the man who is gifted at this with the respected name of philologist. How can it be that such an age can criticize the Catholic Church so harshly because there is something in her *liturgy* and *discipline* that has its analogue in pre-Christian times? Do our author and those in whom he has found inspiration really believe that we need to resurrect the age of St. Jerome, who believed an angel had told him bluntly in a dream not to read any more works by the heathen Cicero and his ilk?[2]

Our author baldly states that celibacy is heathen[3] without troubling to delve any deeper into the question. He seems to think that it must *ipso facto* be reprehensible because traces of it are found in prechristian religions. Does our excellent author think that the whole prechristian era was devilish in all its ways and that all that happened in the world of men in those days was inspired by the evil principle? This is certainly what the Reformers taught, and they were quite logical in doing so, since they denied the moral freedom of man. But the Church has always rejected this principle as dishonoring God and man in equal measure. Not everything heathen is Satan's work. The heathen too believed in God. Is that a reason for us not to believe in God? They too built temples to the deity. Is that a reason for us *not* to build any?

The whole heathen world was shot through with fragments of truth and traces of the divine. In it we encounter deep intimations, dimmer or clearer ideas of a higher world order, a feeling and indeed

---

2. "Suddenly I was caught up in the spirit and dragged before the judgement seat of the Judge; and here the light was so bright, and those who stood around were so radiant, that I cast myself upon the ground and did not dare to look up. Asked who and what I was I replied: 'I am a Christian.' But He who presided said: 'Thou liest, thou art a follower of Cicero and not of Christ.' For 'where thy treasure is, there will thy heart be also.' Instantly I became dumb . . . ." ("Cum subito raptus in spiritu ad tribunal iudicis pertrahor, ubi tantum luminis et tantum erat ex circumstantium claritate fulgoris, ut proiectus in terram sursum aspicere non auderem. Interrogatus condicionem christianum me esse respondi. Et ille, qui residebat: 'Mentiris,' ait, 'ciceronianus es, non christianus; ubi thesaurus tuus, ibi et cor tuum.' Ilico obmutui . . . ." St. Jerome, Letter XXII, CSEL 54, 190.

3. Möhler's observation remains relevant today, for it reaches far beyond the limited circle of the classical Hellenism of a Winckelmann, a Goethe, or a Hölderlin. There is no point struggling to strip away the layers of "Greek" influence from the Bible or from dogma, that would be a totally anachronistic enterprise, for our modern world is itself "Greek" in its sciences and culture. The truth is that the only result of attempting to rid the Bible of "heathen" or "Greek" elements is to reduce revelation to a matter of mere talk. This quest has led only to historicization; and instead of the Spirit of Christ coming into our time, he has fled from so much pure science and returned to his own.

a desire (however weak) for something better, a widespread yearning for union with the divine. Everything that was believed in its fullness and divinely in Christianity we find foreshadowed in heathendom in outline, as a nucleus and a seed. Where priestly celibacy is concerned, hearts full of yearning inevitably strove to go beyond earthly relationships and rise above them to divine and eternal ones, happily praising those persons who managed to achieve this. As one would have anticipated, they formed the notion of a noble priestly ideal and could only think of the person who embodied the living representation of that ideal as one devoted in mind and spirit completely to God, indeed they thought of him as living *only* for God. Yet what souls longed for and what minds recognized as noble was not to be attained in the prechristian era, for the needful living divine power was absent, and it only began to flow again to poor men in their subjection to death in Christ Jesus, who was poor so that we might become rich.

The essence of heathendom—the eternal yearning of the human heart and its simultaneous powerlessness when it wants to aim high by its own strength alone—is truly and beautifully expressed in Indian myth. According to legend Birmah created the Brahma, the priest, and out of him the three Patriarchs of the three other castes: each was assigned a wife except Brahma. "But Brahma complained that he alone among his brothers was without a spouse, and Birmah gave him the answer: *he should not dissipate his energies, but should focus only on teaching, prayer, and divine worship.*"[4] When Brahma kept on pestering him for a wife, Birmah gave him a Daintany, a demonic woman, and the Brahmin were the direct fruit of their union.

Let us study this myth rather more closely. It shows us that Indian Antiquity quite clearly accepted celibacy as part of its priestly ideal. And how beautifully the myth expresses the reason why the priest was not to marry! Brahma begs impetuously for a spouse, and one is with reluctance eventually conceded to him. What can this part of the myth possibly mean other than the melancholy awareness of an unavoidable disparity between knowing and perceiving on the one hand and powerful willing and doing on the other? Awareness of that human weakness which can actually see what should happen, while yet it remains unwilling to put the thought into practice! We cannot

---

4. [Möhler's note] "As Creuzer relates (*Mythologie und Symbolik*, 2nd ed., Th. 1. p. 600)."

however assume that this disparity will last forever, or that it is a contradiction fixed in the eternal being of man. For the myth points to a future resolution of the contradiction that it finds: this intuition of the Indians was fulfilled in Christ Jesus, in whom, since he was at once God and man, the human was again taken up into the divine.[5]

There is even more to be found in this myth however. In order to make it absolutely clear that a married priesthood is unnatural, a Daintany, a demonic woman, is given to the Brahma. So little thought had been given in creation to the provision of a wife for the priest that when he insisted on having one, she had to be taken from quite another species of creature. According to the myth they had not been created at the same time and for one another, as though it wanted to make the point that Brahma's marriage subsists only for a time and is nothing more than a provisional arrangement.

Now let us turn from the profundity of the Indian sages to the Greeks. The prophet,[6] the high priest of the Eleusinians, did not marry, or if he did have a wife, he avoided marital relations with her. Such requirements are all the more remarkable given that he could not be High Priest at all if he had more than one wife,[7] a condition which throws a great deal of light on the Pauline passage discussed above.[8] That only virgins maintained the holy fire of Vesta is a fact too well known for us to have to linger any longer with these Roman priestesses. Even in the deepest Germanic North, traces of a celibate priesthood are to be found. I am referring to the researches conducted by Mone[9] and also to the German maiden seers Veleda and Aurinia as depicted by Tacitus,[10] who tells of sacred pimps in the second book of his History of the German people. What Creuzer[11] observes when he

---

5. Möhler points to redemption through Christ: if divinity and humanity had not been united in Him, there would have been no way to God. Man would have remained unredeemed forever or would have had to achieve redemption by his own efforts. Modernity tells the story of the outcome of this freely chosen destiny.

6. "προφητης μυσταγωγος."

7. [Möhler's note] "(See Creuzer, loc cit. Th. IV p. 482, where reference is made to the evidence which Meursius, Saintecroix and Sylvester de Sacy provided)"

8. See above. Chapter 2.

9. [Möhler's note] "(Geschichte des Heidentums im nördlichen Europa, Th. 1. p. 237)."

10. Tacitus speaks about this in his Germania: "In the reign of the deified Vespasian, we have seen Veleda for a long time, and by many nations, esteemed and adored as a divinity. In times past they likewise worshipped Aurinia and several more . . ." (Chapter 8).

11. [Möhler's note] "(loc. Cit. Th. II. p. 47)."

relates the myth of the virgin priestess Cybele and the chaste Marsyas is very true, that generally there is a great deal of evidence for the celibacy of the priests in the primitive nature religions.

At this point we should also note that neither among the Indians nor in the Eleusinian Mysteries nor in Phrygia with the cult of the good Mother of the mountains, Cybele, nor in the Roman and Nordic myths are the kind of dualistic conceptions[12] found, which might lead us to suspect that people disapproved of a celibate priesthood because they thought matter was evil. The truth is that the association of celibacy with the priesthood represented the naïve and as yet unclouded expression of a purely human way of looking at the matter. People reckoned it to be in the highest interest of a fully human life to devote themselves with stern and undivided attention to the divinity and with their *whole* soul. Virginity was thus taken into the ideal of the priest, who was dedicated to the service of the divinity in a particular way. Indian myth contains a clear expression of this.

Incidentally, if the author of the *Denkschrift* thinks he has to condemn something because it is found in heathendom, I am really not clear why he does not transfer his animus to the idea of a married priesthood. For this is found everywhere in heathen religions, it was absolutely necessary for the reason that priests typically had their own power base and this could be developed only by marriage. It is the married priesthood that is truly heathenish, we cannot fairly claim that celibacy goes with heathendom. The seeds of a celibate priesthood clearly go back to pre-heathen days and belong to a time when, as was noted above, feelings were purer, views clearer, and generally the heart was more open to the acceptance of the divine. Heathendom did not however root this seed properly, it lay dormant and hidden as the faintest of memories, making its appearance only in very occasional and only half-implemented institutions. We shall see very clearly how strongly real heathendom was opposed to virginity when we explain below[13] how highly the life of the Christian ascetic was lauded by the early apologists over against the heathen, in hopes of making them

---

12. Critics often deduce celibacy from some kind of dualistic conception, tracing it back to a hostility to the idea that the body was created good, etc. Möhler shows that there can be affirmation without negation, despite the fact that in naturalistic thought generally the praise of one good is always accompanied at the same time by the devaluing of another.

13. See Chapter 4, p. 48.

aware of the power of the Christian faith; those apologists simply could not have followed this line of thinking if celibacy had really been at home in heathendom. No one is surprised to come across ordinary native plants. Before leaving this topic, I need to provide a more adequate foundation for an observation I made earlier when I drew attention to a crucial dual connection: the external historical and also inner interconnection to be found in the deepest root of religious life and thought between modern attacks on virginity in general and the celibacy of the priests in particular and the whole anti-Christian and uncatholic orientation of recent times.[14] This connection comes in here again. Anyone familiar with the history of the opinions and errors of the last fifty years knows how scholars have been hunting for the foundations of Christendom in heathendom. When a melancholy dullness of the higher sense gave rise to such a far-reaching mental weakness that a gulf opened up between the receiving spiritual power and the object to be received—an object which, being of sensory vastness and grandeur, requires an infinite power for its conception; in a word, when the powerful Christian faith no longer fitted the human mind even though the human mind still did not want to completely deny a faith for which it retained real respect, the human mind resorted to manufacturing a new kind of Christian faith that was more to its taste, consigning whatever elements of the Christian faith it had grown too weak to cope with to heathendom.

So it came about that the origins of the teaching about the Incarnation of the Eternal Word and the Trinity were "discovered" in Egypt, India, and the Mithras myth; the origins of the Resurrection of the flesh in Parseeism; the origins of the teaching about original sin in the Talmud, etc. The foundations of the Gospel were thus transplanted to heathendom, as morally corrupt men make virtues out of their vices and allege that the true virtues they do not possess are actually vices.

The same fate was reserved for the biblical teaching about virginity. But in reality, surely, it makes sense to suppose that if Christianity has the capacity to satisfy the needs of the human heart and spirit truly and comprehensively, then dim intuitions, premonitions, and prophecies of its content would have been found everywhere

---

14. See Chapter 1 above.

in primitive times—which would of course provide another deeply—
rooted argument for believing it to be true. On the same basis it
can only be a recommendation for virginity as such in the first place
and then also for priestly celibacy, if witnesses for them are to be
found even in deepest Antiquity. However, we now need to move on
with our research.

The Jewish Origins of Clerical Celibacy?

The continence practiced by the Early Church is also alleged to have
represented a continuation of Jewish morals, and that is somehow
regarded as a damaging slight on Christian virginity and priestly
celibacy! It is perfectly true that the Law enjoined on the Jewish priests
abstinence from intercourse with their wives over the period of Temple
service,[15] and we would in no way wish to deny our reverence for
this ordinance as given or approved by God; if Christians are respect-
ful of it, then their respect certainly cannot be dismissed as if it were
wasted on something taken from a poisoned source. Abstracting from
its divinely revealed aspect, we are left with the observation that the
Jewish law here abandoned its custom of setting its face against the
morals of the oldest nature cults and was actually in full harmony with
them. This gives us an indication of the great antiquity of the custom
under discussion, it must have arisen at a time when the Abrahamites
had still not separated from the polytheists—since the two opposing
sides took with them as a legacy of their original unity that same
requirement for the priesthood. Even if it is argued that both types
of religion happened on this idea of a celibate priesthood quite independently of one another, or else that one of them took it from
the other, it still gives us a secure basis; for that would point to the idea
of a celibate priesthood being something universal and purely human,
given that both of these starkly contradictory traditions found room
for it within themselves and that both of them could accept it or freely
give rise to it.

On the other hand there is also a powerful challenge to us
here to reflect on the emergence of these customs. When the Jewish

15. Cf. Exodus 19:14ff.; 29:44; 2 Chronicles 5:11. In the New Testament the regulation
mentioned by Möhler is seen most clearly in the example of Zachariah, who only returned home
when his service in the Temple was over (Luke 1:23); cf. also Luke 10:31ff.

priest had the Temple service, he was charged with the presentation of sin offerings or thanks- and prayer-offerings. His heart was full of the thought that the sins of his people were so heavy that he merited death like the animals of sacrifice; at the same time he was warmed by the thought that God's infinite mercy graciously pardoned those who were humbled into meekness by these symbolical acts, offering the sacrifice of their heart to the all merciful One. The priest's heart was also replete with the idea of Yahweh choosing the sons of Abraham and planning for them to be his particularly beloved people; the idea of how this people alone had been wonderfully kept from the acceptance of false gods; and the idea of how its whole history was a long unbroken series of highly visible divine promptings, a glorious chain of wonders. The tabernacle held the Table of the Laws which Moses had received from Yahweh on Sinai, and the hearts of the assembly shivered in fear and trembling at the thought of this great frightful-sublime lawgiving.[16] So it was that the priest would bring the thanks offering for all these blessings and for those daily accruing to the people of God.

How on earth then could it ever have been possible for a priest to think of a wife at this point? In the daytime, his pious soul was moved by so many powerful thoughts like these while at night he was overwhelmed by holy and powerful dreams. Inevitably this sublime intercourse with God would have driven right away any thought of intercourse with a wife—who in any case would have remained at a distance while the priest was devoting himself to the Temple service; so the law merely required what was self-evident anyway. But our excellent author must have imagined to himself a priest carrying out the ritual slaughter as mechanically as a butcher and preparing the ritual cakes as if he were just a baker. If our author was not thinking this way, how could he possibly have resorted to such shabby tactics as denouncing the morals of Christian virginity and priestly celibacy on the ground of their origins? What other foundation for this provision of the Mosaic Law could be found than the one I have proposed? That marriage and marital intercourse were held to be something essentially impure? It would then have to be explained how Mosaism teaches us

---

16. Cf. Exodus 19.

to know that all creatures are good and that God Himself is the founder of marriage.

Our gentleman author has unfortunately been hamstrung by the fixed idea that something that is not of itself bad may or must be practiced in all circumstances and in all situations. He cannot understand that there are many things which, though allowable of themselves, are nonetheless excluded from certain spiritual states. This is why such phenomena as those that arose from the deep and tender sensitivities of Antiquity are completely beyond his comprehension.

I will make this clearer with an example. Dancing is not evil in itself, and yet it is out of bounds for priests, and it actually makes good people angry to see a priest dancing. Why should that be? Why condemn this innocent rhythmical movement? My answer runs like this. The inner being of the lover of dancing is dominated by shifting images of gaiety and feelings of flirtatiousness, the tone of his thoughts is one of trivial and careless playfulness. As soon as the cheerful sounds of all those merry instruments impacts on a person in this state of mind, it triggers a powerful impulse in him that sets his limbs going in such a way that his physical actions betray his inner state. It is the kind of inner state that is evidenced by the bodily movements involved in dancing that is not looked for in a priest; here is what elicits the unconscious annoyance of the people. For where we justifiably look for high earnestness, deep feeling, and profound thinking, we find a spiritual emptiness instead, and that is what causes such discomfort in the people and upsets them. *Dancing is not therefore the activity of the true priest.* His fullness of spirit, his gravity, and the force of his thoughts make it impossible *per se* for him to throw his body about light-heartedly.

Just as dancing is alien to the spiritual character expected in a priest even though it does not mean that dancing must be considered a bad thing of itself, since when young people dance everyone considers that normal: likewise Yahweh declares that intercourse with women is alien to the priest because he is specially devoted to service in the Temple. This is the expression of Yahweh's ideal for his priest, even though initially the Law is only negative and observed outwardly. The inner is given, hidden in the outer, and the spiritual is to be built only on states that are remote from all sensual movements. Antiquity did not make the clear distinctions we do: they held that since the outer is the revelation of an inner, the inner is always to be understood together with the outer.[17] If therefore the Mosaic lawgiving had indeed exercised some influence on Christian morals in this area, only an idiot would regard that as a cause for reproach and contempt. But in actual fact the truth is that for Mosaism to have exercised such an influence is in the highest degree improbable, for the early days of the Christian Church were spent in constant struggle with the Jews and any Judaizing was regarded with the utmost suspicion. That which is purely human emerges in all eras and circumstances without there being any need to look for special connections or demonstrable ancestries.

Before I pass on to evaluate a third attempt to trace the ideals of virginity and priestly celibacy back to an impure source (and in the process embark on some real church historical research), I have to say that I really would have preferred it if the gentlemen professors of Freiburg had managed to find for themselves some apologist who did not give such open proof of a superficial and careless approach to Church history, someone who could have succeeded at least occasionally in assembling some solid pieces of evidence. Thus for example our author gives it for an undoubted fact—to show how early false concepts of virginity were spread through misattributed writings—that an Asiatic priest and foolish admirer of the Apostle Paul made up the legend of Saint Thekla; he then alleges that John—who was still alive—discovered and punished the deception![18] He appears to be sublimely ignorant of the fact that besides the seven genuine extant letters written by St. Ignatius, we also have seven spurious ones, for he gives a long quotation from one of the fakes![19] If he goes looking for his supposedly Ignatian passage (dredged up heaven knows where) in the authentic letters, he certainly won't find them there. But if he trawls through the fake letters and reads the letter to the Philadelphians up to the fourth chapter, he will find every word of his quotation in

17. Möhler here alludes to the strongly individualistic and subjectivistic tendency of modern times which results from the separation of subject and object in scientific thought. Such thinking continues to be very much in vogue today.

18. Cf. *Denkschrift* p. 14.

19. "In a letter to the Philadelphians he writes: 'If someone calls marital intercourse with a woman and the generation of children a sin or merely an imperfection, or if he believes that certain foods are to be avoided, the hellish dragon of apostasy dwells in him.' (*Denkschrift*, p. 15). Compare this with the following: 'The seven letters of Ignatius were revised around AD 380 and expanded by additions; a further six letters were also added to them.'" (B. Altaner/A. Stuiber, *Patrologie. Leben, Schriften und Lehre der Kirchenväter*, 672 pp., Freiburg-Basle-Vienna 1978, p. 48).

it.[20] Our author also makes the mistake of including Eusebius and Epiphanius among the Christian authors of the third century![21] Furthermore, he states that Gregory VII (date of death: 1085) managed to send a Legate, John of Cremona, to England to preside over a Synod there in the year 1125![22]

The Gnostic Origins of Clerical Celibacy?

We now need to see if there is anything to be said for the idea that Christian reverence for virginity derives from Gnostic roots. For the sake of the uninitiated I will note that both in terms of their name and in terms of their principles the Gnostics actually had a great deal in common with our modern-day rationalists: they specifically called themselves "those who know" (Gnostics), just as many of our contemporaries call themselves "the reasonable ones" (rationalists), encouraging reason to adopt the same approach to revelation as the Gnostics did.

The Gnostics concluded (among other things) that this world had not been created by the true God. Instead, it had been formed out of eternally present and wholly or half evil matter by a lower spirit. The human spirit, an emanation of God, did not derive from this lower creation but had come down into it mysteriously. They held the human body to be as bad as all other matter, and this impacted on their attitude to marriage as well as to things like wine. They therefore quite simply forbade more or less all marriage, taking precisely the opposite position to our rationalists, who are led by the same reasoning to treat celibacy with contempt. Our author believes that the idea of reverencing virginity and celibacy must have been derived from these rationalists of old as well as from the Jews and the heathen. Incidentally he is certainly not the first to have come up with the idea of such a derivation!

The historian often finds himself in the situation that when he wants to present events in their causal relationship, he can only judge according to the way things usually work and usually happen in the world of men. Let us assume for the present that we do not have any particular data relevant to this issue such as would enable us

---

20. [Möhler's footnote] "(Patres apost. ed. Cotel. Antw. 1698. Tom II. Fol. 80)."

21. Epiphanius of Salamis (c.315–403).

22. Cf. *Denkschrift*, pp. 16, 43,

to figure out causal connections, and let us ask this question: is it really normal that when the most stubborn and bitterest of enemies are squaring up to each other, one side should proceed to adopt the preferred views and opinions of his opponent?[23] Even the most superficial observation of human behavior demonstrates that precisely the opposite is the case: in such cases people glory in adopting whatever is the most contradictory position to that of their enemy. What is really astonishing about the issue under discussion is the phenomenon that the Catholic Church's reverence for celibacy was not derived in any way from a desire on her part to set her face against her contradictors. But in any case no healthy human understanding could possibly imagine that Catholics took the ideal of celibacy into their system from such opponents in such a battle. The Catholic Church's reverence for celibacy must have come to them *before* the battle with the Gnostics, *before* the existence of the Gnostic opponents, and from quite another source. The Church allowed herself as little to be persuaded to oppose virginity unjustly, as she will allow herself in our day to be induced to accord it excessive respect at the cost of the holiness of marriage. In actual fact, in her struggle with the Gnostics the Church scrupulously followed the most middle of middle roads, acting with a prudence and serenity that was truly astonishing. Against the heathen, the Catholics appeal to the infinitely elevating power of the Gospel: "And many, both men and women, who have been Christ's disciples from childhood, remain pure at the age of sixty or seventy years; and I boast that I could produce such from any race of men. For what shall I say, too, of the countless multitude of those who have reformed intemperate habits, and learned these things?" [24] Athenagoras exults as much as Justin does to belong to a religion which communicates divine life in such a measure: "Nay, you would find many among us, both men and women, growing old unmarried, in hope of living in closer communion with God . . . . For we bestow our attention, not on the study

---

23. Möhler holds it to be *a priori* foolish to think that the early Christians would have taken over from their bitterest enemies, the Gnostics, their most treasured opinion. But the study of Church History also shows *a posteriori* that the celibacy of Christians does not spring in any case from contempt for the body but from a deeper affirmation of creation, which far surpasses all rationalism.

24. [Möhler's note] "*Apolog.* 1, section. 15." Justin the philosopher was martyred around AD 160.

of words, but on the exhibition and teaching of actions." [25] Irrespective
of this, the Church acted quite ruthlessly to expel those who dis-
turbed the clarity and purity of her faith, and the Early Christians
were quite unapologetic about the fact that their goal was to live closer
to God, as Athenagoras said. The *Apostolic Constitutions* laid down
rulings relevant to the Gnostics at the time when the latter were at
their most influential; in this text those who forbade marriage along
with certain particular foods were branded instruments of the Devil
and children of wrath.[26] In the next chapter (vi,10) they observe:
"We also say that every creature of God is good and nothing abomi-
nable; that everything for the support of life, where it is partaken
of righteously, is very good . . . we believe that lawful marriage and
the begetting of children, is honorable and undefiled."[27] The forty-
third Apostolic Canon[28] threatened with excommunication any clergy
or laypersons who avoided meat, wine, and marriage not for the sake
of godly discipline, but on the grounds that these things were impure.

I am going to appeal here to the instincts and the healthy
judgement of every student of human history and human life.
Consider the confidence with which this position is affirmed, the
firmness and clarity of vision, the appeal urged on the heathen to the
sublime convictions of the Christians and the preservation of careful
boundaries in the battle with the Gnostics. Consider too the confident
and successful adoption by the Church of a middle way between
two opposites. On the one hand we have the dreariness and weakness
of heathendom, which could not comprehend the worth of a wholly
undivided existence lived for God, could not find the power for it, and
so allowed the spirit to degenerate into matter: and on the other hand
Gnosticism, whose excessive and fanatical enthusiasm drove it to set
up an absolute contradiction between the ideal and the real which
failed to honor God as creator and regarded nature as the work of the
devil. In this thinking of the Catholic Church about virginity, is there
any evidence at all of a second-hand attitude borrowed from outside,

25. [Möhler's note] "*Legat. Pro Christ.*, section. 33."

26. [Möhler's note] "(I. VI. c. 10)." Cf. *The Apostolic Constitutions*: Altaner/Stuiber (see note
71 above), pp. 255 ff.; an edition of the text: *Apostolische Konstitutionen und Kanones*, ed. and tr.
Ferdinand Boxler, 350 pp., Kempten 1874.

27. Cf. Boxler (see note 77 above), p. 189.

28. The *85 Apostolic Canons* are a part of the *Apostolic Constitutions*, cf. Altaner/Stuiber (see
note 71 above), p. 50; Boxler (see note 77 above), p. 326.

and is it not rather her own philosophy that we should credit with being original and primordial?

To anyone who cannot accept the argument I would say this: look at men or at groupings of men who have adopted particular moral attitudes from outside, and observe how insecure, halting, and uncertain they are as to how to live them out. At one moment they are over-indulgent with themselves, at another, they push these ideas to extremes: there is no consistency in their behavior! Notice how quick they are to abandon such principles if the principles lead them into difficulties! They follow them very selectively, behaving one way in the privacy of their own homes, and another way in the world outside! This consideration should throw light on the question whether we may dare to assert that the Church received her understanding of virginity from outside!

Another question our author would do well to reflect on is this: do caricature, distortion, and exaggeration precede the simple and the natural? Is it superstition that gives rise to faith? Does desire for knowledge come out of excessive curiosity? Does prudent research come out of scepticism? Surely that would be to put the cart before the horse? For in reality what we see is superstition attaching itself to a pre-existing faith, and so on. So we have to ask this: are simplicity and naturalness characteristic of the Catholic Church or are they characteristic of Gnosticism? Which of the two, the Catholic Church or Gnosticism, looks more like a caricature? The truth is that it is clearly gnostic rationalism that is a caricature of the simple Catholic view of virginity.

Had our author given due consideration to all this, he would have found it very advisable to adopt the opposite position to the one he has chosen to espouse. For the truth is that under every great error of the human race is a great truth, a deep need of the human heart, a dark mysterious longing and intuition. How else could millions of men, perhaps whole generations, centuries, and indeed millennia have been beguiled and imprisoned by error? What happens is that a fundamental deeply-rooted truth, a sense of some reality is distorted by one-sided conceptions and exaggeration. There really was true intuition concealed in the old nature religions. Not one Christian sect has ever been built other than on the basis of one of the many truths or aspects that Christianity presents to the observer. Likewise this error of the Gnostics we have been looking at here also contained its truth. The simple element, which it distorted to excess, was of course nothing other than the Catholic way of looking at virginity. Our author is however trying to present his vacuous and weak conception of 1 Corinthians 7 as the outline, the distortion of which had given rise to the Gnostic view of marriage and virginity, and in doing so he will turn himself into a *total laughing-stock*. For nothing can only give rise to nothing.[29] Something without any deep root in humanity could never have been abused to such an extent, could never have unsettled the Church for more than two centuries.

So too there is a truth underlying our opponents' view. But over against the Gnostics we set the holiness of nature, and Mr. Trefurt,[30] with whose approach the author unwittingly finds himself at one, emphasises the immateriality and freedom of the human spirit and its elevation by Christianity. Directly denying the one-sided spiritualism of the Gnostics of old as well as the increasingly materialistic views of the moderns, we acknowledge the spirit in union with the body, while anticipating that one day a transfigured body will be given to a transfigured spirit in a union not involving marriage.[31] At one and the same time we applaud those who marry because they desire to do so and we also praise those who—with a view to the future splendour of the children of God—pass over what the present form of the body could give, as being something not belonging to the eternal being of man but subjected to transience.

A purer and finer view of marriage is simply not possible than the one represented by the Church Fathers. St. Clement of Alexandria said: "To be chaste means to have a holy mind," and he remarked about the people, many of whom do not live on the land: misunderstanding the essence of chastity, the people attribute more value to what pertains to the body, to outward behavior, than to spiritual orientation, for without the spirit the body is dust and ashes.[32] Against those who found evil and wickedness in marriage, St. John Chrysostom

---

29. Möhler thinks that the "absence" of a recommendation of virginity in 1 Corinthians— "absence" according to the interpretation in the *Denkschrift* (see above Chapter 2, p. 13.)—would have left Early Christianity entirely bereft of anything substantial for the Gnostics to distort.

30. See above Chapter 1, p. 1.

31. Cf. Mark 12:25.

32. [Möhler's note] "αγνειη δ'εστι, φρονειν όσια. *Strom.* L. V. c. 1.); '(όι πολλοι.)' '(L. c. I. III. c. 6)."

remarks that the Holy Spirit worked in the prophets without reference to their married state[33] and in another place makes the crucial point: "For the greatest thing is charity, and moderation, and almsgiving, which hits a higher mark even than virginity."[34] And yet Clement defends virginity and admires it,[35] while St. John Chrysostom is the eloquent and spiritual author of two apologies for those who live celibate lives. But precisely because to them the life of the spirit represented the only measure for the evaluation of man, they were clear-thinking enough to recognize that those persons in whom such a powerful force and inner acceptance of divine powers was found that they could forego and forget the earth and all that it offered, merited the highest respect in the sphere of religion. St. John Chrysostom praised virginity, which forgets everything else for the love of God, precisely because he set the highest value on love for God in the shape of moderation, gentleness, and mercifulness towards God's creation.

Here I must bring the historical debates to an end insofar as they concern virginity in general, and I simply want to share with our esteemed author the advice that he try comparing many of the quotations I have given from the Apostolic Canons and the Church Fathers with 1 Corinthians 7. For example what Athenagoras says: "The reason for the continence of the ascetics lies in their hope for a closer communion with God" is to be compared with what Paul says in 1 Corinthians 7:35: "so that you are able to give undivided attention to the Lord;" the words of the Apostolic Canons "one can abstain from marriage for the sake of the exercise" should be compared with 1 Corinthians 7:5: "to leave yourselves free for prayer"; likewise, the Apostolic Canons call those who forbid marriage and particular foods "impure instruments of the devil" while Paul (1 Timothy 4:2) designates as "liars whose consciences are branded as though with red-hot iron" those who forbid believers to marry or to enjoy foods made by God. Our author then needs to consult his conscience as to whether the most precise agreement is not evident between the views widespread in the Catholic Church of the first centuries and the

---

33. [Möhler's note] "(*Hom.* IV. In Oz)."

34. [Möhler's note] "το μεγιστον αγαπη και επιεικια, η και παρθενιας ὑπερεκοντισε. *Hom.* XLVI. *in Matth.*)"

35. [Möhler's note] "*Strom.* I. II. c. 1."

teaching of Paul. When he is through with this assessment, then let him pass judgement on himself.

The author clearly knows the Apostolic Canons, which are directed against the view of marriage as something evil, since he refers to them.[36] At the same time he admits that the honoring of virginity in the Catholic Church is also to be found in them. But what then do these Apostolic Canons contain if not the general convictions of Catholics of the first, second, and third centuries? Produced from within the Catholic Church and generally valid in the Church, they are clearly an expression of her beliefs. The only assumption that can explain how our author's theories about the origins of the high valuation of virginity could possibly have arisen is that his mental processes and the powers of his soul have fallen under the influence of his passions. It is as if someone were to claim that Hegel teaches that we do not know the *An sich* of things because he opposes the Kantian principle according to which we can only know the appearance of the *An sich* of things.[37] Of course it is possible and indeed very probable that in the thick of all the Early Church's struggles, the healthy judgment and right feeling of many Catholics succumbed to the influence of the rationalists of the day, just as our own splendid author has himself been ruined by the rationalists of modern times. But that the *whole Church*—with all her hatred for the Gnostics and their errors, a hatred that was so strong, so forceful, and so often (indeed tirelessly) repeated—should have honored virginity so highly out of hatred for marriage (and remember that our author speaks of the tendency of the whole era, not just of certain particular individuals)? Such a suggestion is just too monstrous for the human understanding.

It is perfectly true that our opponent declares himself solely "opposed to a *fantastic* reverence for virginity."[38] The non-fantastic adulators are much preferable to him—those who honored it because

---

36. Cf. *Denkschrift*, pp. 16ff.

37. Möhler's comparison is expressed rather too concisely. He wants to say that among many other things Hegel opposed the Kantian principle of the unknowable *An sich* of things, but of course Hegel was much too original to have based his ideas purely on a dependence on or opposition to another thinker, even when that thinker was of the stature of Kant.

38. "Through the agency of the monks fantastic ideas of holiness, of perfect continence, and of virginal chastity became rooted and widespread both among the people and among the teachers and the legislators in the Church" (*Denkschrift*, p. 22).

of their *"threatened situation"*—just as an officer on half pay for example would have treasured celibacy on account of his "threatened situation": in this case Paul himself would certainly have recommended the bachelor state! There is certainly nothing fantastic in that—at most it all comes down to dreams in the night!

Chapter 4

Celibacy in the Early Church

FROM THE SECOND TO THE FOURTH CENTURY

So then we have defended the Church's beliefs about virginity against their distortion and against mistaken theories about their origins. We have shown those beliefs to be biblical and we have seen that they flowed from the purest sources in the Church. At the same time we have shown that the author of this part of the *Denkschrift* is as little familiar with the history of the Church as he is able to explain the Holy Scripture and its meaning. Even though we have done all this however, the celibacy of the priesthood has still not been historically explained nor its origins and essence clarified. So far we have merely given a justification for its foundation—though this was of course essential if the institution was not to be dismissed right away as a nonsense. I would never have bothered myself so much with its foundation had it not been that my opponent, seeing how much depended on that, had made such a huge effort to destroy it. We must now turn to the history and origins of the ideal of a celibate priesthood, and this will again lead us to pass judgement on the work we are opposing.

Apostolic Canon XXVI runs like this: "Of those who have been admitted to the clergy unmarried, we ordain, that the readers and singers only may, if they will, marry." It is known that the Apostolic Constitutions contain the Church discipline of the second and third centuries. Consequently we can be certain that at the end of the first century it was a custom and more than a custom that priests should not marry. This also emerges very clearly from a Montanist oracle.[1] Between 150 AD and 160 AD the prophetess Priscilla said:

---

1. [Möhler's note] "(in Tert. exhort. cast.)."

"the holy minister knows how to minister sanctity. 'For purity,' she says, 'is harmonious, and they see visions; and turning their faces downward, they even hear manifest voices, as salutary as they are withal secret.'"[2] In this context "holy minister" means a priest living a celibate life. Had our author been aware of this oracle, he would surely have brandished it before us with delight and assurance of victory. He would have shouted "look at the Montanist origin of priestly celibacy!" The reality is very different. Any specialist in Church History knows how the Montanist sect differed from the Catholic Church: in the convictions they were taught by their founder, in matters of Church discipline, and in the way they grounded their basic principles. If someone in the Church fasted once, the Montanists said we should fast ten times. If in the Catholic Church abstention from a second marriage was held to be commendable according to Paul, they affirmed that such an abstention must be turned into an absolute imperative. In a word: they simply exaggerated everything Catholic.

Thus they also simply took the custom of priestly celibacy to such extremes that it was transformed into something ridiculous. Priscilla claimed, in the passage referred to, that the celibate priest has visions, that divine voices are very clearly audible to him which are the all the more holy, the more they remain inaudible to others. Of course the Catholic Church too taught that only the holy person could administer holy things *worthily*,[3] that only the pure is fitting for the pure,[4] and here she was in agreement with the Montanists as long as they did not have in mind some purely external purity. The rest however is attributable to the Montanist sectarian view, and this is easily explicable from the circumstance that they preferred to demonstrate the truth of their principles by appealing to messages given through Maximilla and Priscilla, the ecstatic women, the evidently great and *God-inspired prophetesses*. What we find with the Gnostics in relation to virginity in general is that they mixed very simple and truly Christian elements in with impure additions dreamed up by human

2. "quod sanctus minister sanctimoniam noverit ministrare, purificantia enim concordat, ait, et visiones vident, et ponentes faciem deorsum, etiam voces audiunt manifestas, tam salutares quam et occultas." (Cf. Tertullian, *De exhortatione castitatis*, SL 2, pp.1015–1035; here, chapter 10. This writing comes from Tertullian's late uncatholic and Montanist period.)

3. "quod sanctus sanctimoniam noverit administrare."

4. "purificantia enim concordat."

foolishness, corrupting long-established Catholic fundamentals with sectarian nonsense. This is the only way we can explain how the first and strongest opponent of Montanism that we hear about from Eusebius[5] uttered no word of complaint against the sect for having introduced priestly celibacy. Opponents who were so ardently opposed to Montanus that they condemned him and his female companions with all their charms, ecstasies, and prophecies as nothing less than demonic and wanted to exorcise them by force, were definitely not going to be in the kind of spiritual mood in which they might borrow an institution from those same Montanists. Yet these Montanist sermons contain clear and unimpeachable testimony that priestly celibacy had become *established* right from the middle of the second century, offering powerful support to what is said in the Apostolic Constitutions.

It is equally clear from another passage in the same Tertullian text that towards the end of the second century, men who were not already married when they became priests did not marry at all. Wanting to discourage a man from marrying a second time, Tertullian proposes that he ponder how he can bring intercessions to God for both his wives, the dead one and the living one, through a priest who has either been only married once prior to ordination or who has made his life a eulogy of virginity by virtue of his ordination commitment to celibacy.[6]

In Antioch around the middle of the third century we find only unmarried priests. Admittedly we are given this information in the context of a report that presents these celibate Antiochene clergy in a rather doubtful light, but it does make it very much simpler to answer the purely historical question whether and when the clergy in the Early Church first began to live as celibates. This report informs us that under Bishop *Paul of Antioch*, who denied the divinity of Christ, the priests—who had to go along with him so as not to displease him—had been living in very impure intercourse with their wives, with whom they were cohabiting. This assumes a norm of celibacy on their part. Incidentally, it provides a further illustration of the impossibility of combining belief in a genuinely maintained virginity with a

5. Cf. Eusebius of Caesaraea, *Church History*, Bk. V, ch. 18–19.

6. "Commendabis illas duas per sacerdotem de monogamia ordinatum aut etiam de virginitate sancitum?" (cf. ch. 11; see note 91)

rejection of the essential teachings of Christianity.[7] The celibacy which those early clerics evidently railed against was a celibacy *which custom imposed on them.*

People who rejected the teaching of the divinity of Christ consequently could not believe that divine power and divine life have truly been given to us through him, and so they could not be the first to introduce a way of life that rests simply and plainly on that faith.

As early as the Council of Elvira in the year 305 or 306 and the Council of Ancyra in 314, specific prohibitions begin to be mentioned on priests and bishops who were married when they were appointed continuing to enjoy sexual relations with their wives.[8] Likewise the Synod of NeoCaesarea in the year 314 decided on the exclusion of those who had got married as priests.[9] The Synod of Nicaea, however, to which the regulations introduced by Elvira and Ancyra were recommended as meriting *general* imitation, rejected this at the request of Bishop Paphnutius, who remarked that the requirement of continence could give rise to burdensome wounds of conscience in this case, and stated: *"It would be sufficient . . . that such as had previously entered on their sacred calling should abjure matrimony."* And he called this custom *"the ancient tradition of the Church."*[10]

THE PROPHECY OF JESUS FULFILLED

The material we have been discussing so far offers indisputable proof to any intelligent observer that the custom *not to marry after becoming a priest* took its rise in the earliest Christian Antiquity and was definitely known in Apostolic times. The knowledge that we have of Church

7. Möhler's incidental remark here is an embodiment of the leading character of this writing: only what someone lives can one believe, and only what one believes can one live. Möhler was passionately convinced of the organic unity of the spirit with the life. God manifests himself in the spirit and in the life, in both at the same time or not at all. There is the living spirit of this writing on celibacy. The stages of Church history serve him as examples of this unity of spirit and life. Cf. above in chapter 1 Möhler's main thesis.

8. The decision of Elvira runs: "Bishops, presbyters, and deacons, and all other clerics having a position in the ministry are ordered to abstain completely from their wives and not have children. Whoever, in fact, does this shall be expelled from the dignity of the clerical state . . . ." (cf. DH 119, Can. 33c).

9. Möhler refers to the three Synods corresponding to Apostolic Canons C. XXX; C. X; C. 1.

10. "Κατα την της εκκλεσιας αρχαιαν παραδοσιν," Socrates, *Church History*, 1. B. Ch. XI. (see *Denkschrift* pp. 19ff.).

history from the time of the Apostles onward supports the assumption that this custom was in existence then. Though we cannot trace it back to actual words of institution spoken by the Apostles themselves, we certainly can trace it back to their spirit. Having provided the external proof of this, we now need to see through to the inner essence of the historically accredited facts, to get down to their real roots. The Savior Himself had pointed to the extraordinary phenomenon that there would be some who possessed sufficient spiritual power to make themselves eunuchs for the sake of the Kingdom of God, which means living celibate lives; and the Apostle Paul discusses the form of a spiritual life like this one which devotes itself in its whole undivided essence to Christ. Where in God's name *could* this kind of life be found, where *should* it be found but in the one who feeds the flock of God? It is only what we would expect that such a person should stand on the highest level of the religious life, and that his life should manifest the beauty of God-filled inwardness. That all the great power of the Gospel is revealed in him will not come as a surprise to anybody.

But as I demonstrated earlier,[11] for the Redeemer and his Apostles, virginity is precisely the blossoming and the most beautiful flower of this purest and highest development of gospel power in life.[12] The priests appointed in the Church by the Apostles found in those words of Jesus Christ and his disciple a sign for themselves, and something even more profound than that, for these words came to them as a commanding sign. They were possessed by a spiritual fullness of power, a heavenly yearning to live exclusively for Christ and his institution. So spirit-filled were their hearts, so pure and vibrant their enthusiasm, so deeply and hiddenly rooted in Christ was their thinking, coming to the surface and expressing itself exclusively in the service of his Church, that they never had a thought of marriage: women just weren't on their minds at all. Their hearts were full of other things, *they saw every person without distinction only as redeemed in Christ or as needing redemption.* Not a single one of the biographies of any bishop or priest of early times contains any reference to an engagement party or wedding feast, and we leave it to our learned

---

11. See above Chapter 2, "The Biblical Counsel."

12. [Möhler's note] "I ask here those of my readers who are inclined to dismiss this expression as 'a revamping of monkish foolishness'—as wisdom is styled in the world—not just to revile, not to condemn thoughtlessly, but *to show* that what I am claiming is not biblical."

opponent to find one. Now at last the old ideal of the priest was finally realized, the ideal whose faint echoes had resounded persistently throughout the era of dull heathendom, the ideal of which even in Mosaism only fragments could appear in reality. Our opponent is mired in a trivial way of looking at the things of the Church of the Son of God, as thoughtless as it is blasphemous, for he sees the Church as nothing more than a sewer into which flowed all the garbage from the four corners of the world. But he really should see himself as a Christian and instead climb up to the heights from which he can honor an infinitely rich and characteristic drive to education in the Church and give a better explanation of the deeper ground for the origin of priestly celibacy as it arose in the Apostolic age.

The second thing we notice when we reflect on the historical material we have referred to is that in both the western and in the eastern Churches up to the time of the Council of Nicea, men already married could be accepted into the higher clergy—though it did not happen very often. In this connection however there are two points to be made. First, most of them felt an inward compulsion to abstain from intercourse with their wives; second, the number of such persons gradually decreased. The evidence for this is not hard to find. Everything at the time that was made into a law of the Church or that had been made into a law of the Church had already been current previously as a custom. It would have been quite impossible to proclaim as a law at a few Provincial Synods or to propose for a law at Nicaea that married clerics chosen for higher consecration should no longer touch their wives, if this was not in fact already the existing custom. Moreover, given this prevalent state of mind, celibates were naturally preferred and they grew increasingly numerous with the expansion of the Church. All this is confirmed by witnesses more or less contemporaneous with the Synod of Nicaea. Thus St. Jerome says in his well-known comment against Vigilantius: "What do the Churches of the East do, the Egyptian Churches, the Apostolic See? they accept for the ministry only men who are virgins, or those who practice continency, or who, if married, abandon their conjugal rights?"[13]

---

13. "Quid faciunt Orientis ecclesiae, quid Egypti, et sedis apostolicae? Quae aut virgines clericos accipiunt, aut continentes, aut si uxores habuerint, mariti esse desistunt." (Cf. Jerome, *Contra Vigilantium*, PL 23, par. 2. Elsewhere in *Expos. Fid. cath. c. 21* it says: "Sacerdotium ex *virginum ordine potissimum* constat; aut si minus ex virginibus, certe ex monachis, aut nisi ex

The Transition to the Middle Ages

This was how things stood when the Roman Empire began to sink into chaos, when it succumbed to the invasions of the uncouth Nordic tribes, who spread their barbarity everywhere they went. No part of the empire escaped their influence, whether direct or indirect. From now on, as was only to be expected, a significant number of priests were no longer spiritual enough either to live the ideal of a priest themselves or even merely to tolerate it in others. Uneducated minds did not comprehend—nor did the low moral state allow—the ideal to be reproduced in life. An all-embracing knowledge that penetrates the heart of Christianity, a receptivity to ideals, a spiritual inwardness, an integrity and moral purity are all required if virginity is to be honored in itself and in the priest. Popes and Synods fought both the general barbarism and the particular uncouthness of many priests. But what had in the beginning been born out of the inspired spiritual fullness of heart and the depth of the first beautiful Christian times now had to be accepted as an austere and rigid law imposed from outside. Among so many wild and barbarous men, this was at best able to achieve an outward Jewish kind of righteousness (for no law can ever do anything more than that) which was often circumvented. Not until the end of the eleventh century—when science rose again and the moral anarchy gradually subsided—was the capacity restored to value priestly virginity. First of all it reappeared as an ideal, and then the ethical power to achieve it revived; in short, the era of Gregory VII. In the Reformation there was an issue about the contradiction between faith and works. The Reformers preached that only the former was to make people happy, the latter had no part in it, so celibacy began to arouse opposition again. In recent times for quite other reasons—which I have already referred to at the beginning of this book[14]—opposition to celibacy has revived along with the barbarousness of earlier centuries.

---

monachorum ordine idonei coaptari possunt, *ex his sacerdotes creari solent, qui a suis uxoribus continent*, aut secundum unas nuptias in viduitate versantur." St. Epiphanius confirms this (*Haer.* 59. n. 4) strikingly: "Qui adhuc in matrimonio degit, ac liberis dat operam, tametsi unius uxoris vir, eum nequaquam ad diaconi, presbyteri aut hypodiaconi ordinem admittit, sed eum duntaxat, qui ab uxoris consuetudine se continuerit, aut ea sit orbatus."

14. Möhler is referring here to his main thesis about the morally poisonous influence of uncatholic Enlightenment theology. See above Chapter 1.

After this short survey of the history of celibacy, let us now return to our author. What I find most reprehensible in his argument is the lack of any sense of the contingent historical factors that influence practices.[15] He manages to derive celibacy from here, there, and everywhere, giving a superficial imitation of a shallow Protestant, more or less like someone who thinks he can account for Napoleon's strategic genius as deriving from the military talents of his apprentice cooks, boot polishers, and valets; or like someone who tries to claim that the bold and beautiful dance of a skillful acrobat is an imitation of the crazy leaps of the clown who moves around under the rope making people laugh by mimicking him. Our author has no interest whatever in figuring out the causal connections between phenomena. The only observation he makes of this kind—borrowed from Planck as it happens—states that priestly celibacy spread in countries the same way that monks got a foothold in them.[16] Planck has never provided any evidence for this assertion, and there is in fact a great deal of evidence against it. For example it is well known that the monkish way of life made its first appearance in the East, and specifically in Egypt, and that the ascetic life was first planted in the West with Athanasius and actual monkish life still later (through Martin of Tours, Ambrose, etc.). And yet our bright fellow makes out that celibacy was strongly commended from Rome *by Siricius,* even though we know that the severely ascetic Jerome was not even allowed to remain in Rome under Siricius, but was forced to flee to the East on account of the distaste for monkish ways prevalent in Rome at that period! At a time when the East was full of monks and there were a mere handful of monasteries in the West, our author claims that Siricius established celibacy all on his own,[17] assuring us *"that in the eastern churches the marriage of priests was customary everywhere."* And yet priestly celibacy supposedly developed the same way as monasticism! I am not going to pause here to examine our author's general ignorance of history or his unfamiliarity with the contemporary testimonies I have presented from Jerome and Epiphanius; I am simply pointing out his inconsistency. Or perhaps this is not so much a case of a lack of consistency as a lack

---

15. [Möhler's note] "From p. 56 to p. 62 we can however detect evidence of another hand with a more perceptive approach."

16. Cf. *Denkschrift*, p. 22; the reference is to J. G. Planck (1751–1833), cf. RGG.

17. [Möhler's note] "P. 26."

of historical knowledge, more specifically a knowledge of the way that the monkish ideal spread. He not only seems to think that monasticism arose first in the North, he seems to imagine that the sketic deserts lay in Scythia![18]

Our author gives absolutely no explanation how it came about that from the fifth century up to the eleventh so many priests started marrying again or why the Greeks for the first time in 690 AD at the Trullian Synod[19] deviated from the earlier custom to which Jerome and Epiphanius and Socrates[20] had testified, that the preferred candidates for ordination were to be first of all virgins, then widowers, and then married men who abstained from intercourse. It does not take much in the way of sophistication to sense a connection between this phenomenon and the general character of the age. It is true that the level of historical knowledge around today is pitifully low in comparison with earlier days, but even our modern superficiality cannot fail to see that the fate of celibacy in those times must be regarded as either a cause or a consequence, the cause or the effect of the era of decadence. If neither were the case, nothing could be known of it from the historical point of view, it simply could not be an object of history; either the many priests who married several times brought in the barbarousness, or their behavior was a product of it. Unfortunately our masterly writer on the history of celibacy has no conception whatever of its relation to its historical context and presents the changes that took place with regard to it as mere accidents. But for the historian everything that appears apart from any chain of causal connections is merely accidental. Then he encourages us to treat this chatter as *history* and to rejoice with him that the counsels of popes, synods, and the better men of the age were generally in vain and that celibacy was more a matter of theory than of practice. Our dear author seems above all to be curiously pleased by the unculturedness and barbarousness of those times and by their consequence, the violation of priestly celibacy.

---

18. The sketic deserts were in Egypt; Scythia is an area to the north of the Black Sea.

19. The Trullus was a vaulted assembly hall in the Imperial Palace in Constantinople. The Trullian Synod of 690 (691/2?) was never recognised in Rome. The Eastern Emperor was seeking to establish his state church system against the Pope; in accord with Möhler's thesis he exploited the spiritual weakness of the clergy: a married clergy has always been much better suited to serve the state.

20. [Möhler's note] "*Church History,* V. 6. Ch. 22."

He also remarks that the Arians in Spain were particularly opposed to celibacy.[21] It is true! But what are we to make of this isolated fact? We must get to the root of it, if any *reasonable* reader is to be satisfied. The truth is of course that the Arians, who acknowledged in the Savior only a finite being, were *necessarily* hostile to celibacy. How could they have been supporters of a practice that assumes a belief in a participation in infinite and truly divine power, when they could not possibly know themselves to be in possession of such a power, since a finite being cannot convey and communicate an infinite power?[22] The honoring of virginity could never have developed out of Arianism. Only the Catholic Church could have produced it, or rather could have accepted and promoted the inspiration given by the Redeemer and his great apostle. The Arian sect had of necessity to move on an increasingly divergent path from that of monasticism, a path that was destructive of it, for the honoring of virginity lay at the root of monasticism. It is instructive to remember on the one hand the relationship between the Arian Emperor Valens and the monks, and on the other how the teaching of the divinity of Christ found its most important defenders in the ascetics and monks of the day (Athanasius, Basil, Gregory of Nazianzen, Chrysostom) and in the defenders of monasticism (those just mentioned plus Ambrose, Augustine, and others).

The first 55 pages of the *Denkschrift* are disfigured not just by an ignorance of basic facts in the treatment of the history of celibacy, but by a truly astounding mass of errors—some of them major, some minor. There is no real point for my purposes in identifying every single one of these errors to demonstrate how uninstructed our defender of priestly marriage is, so I will content myself with pointing out just a few of them. On page 21 the Synod of Gangra[23] is introduced as

---

21. "In Spain the decree of Pope Siricius encountered some opposition, and priestly celibacy in particular found no acceptance among the Arians there; but the Spanish Councils held all the more strictly to this prohibition" (*Denkschrift*, p. 31). Beginning with the conversion of King Recared in 587, Spain in time gradually became Catholic. Arian theology was rigid and backward, so the Spanish Synods and Councils strove to become connected to the theology of the universal Church.

22. The Arians denied the divinity of Christ. For them Christ was a model man, indeed the most excellent of the creatures made by God, but still a creature, not God from eternity and himself Creator.

23. "The views on the freedom of priests to marry heard in the first general Council found further recognition and affirmation soon afterwards in a Provincial Synod at Gangra in

recognizing and confirming the views of the Fathers of Nicaea, and our author tells us that this Synod was held "soon after" (the Council of Nicaea) while at the same time dating it to the year 324! But every schoolboy knows that the Ecumenical Synod of Nicaea took place in the year 325, and so it could hardly have been confirmed by a Synod held a year earlier! Leaving aside the mistaken chronology, what point is our author trying to prove? That married priests could celebrate divine worship! It is true that the Gangra Fathers asserted this in opposition to a certain Eustatius and his disciples, but all this tells us is that those sectarians condemned marriage as something bad of itself— not just the marriage of priests but even the marriage of layfolk—and the enjoyment of wine and meat as well to boot. All this is ignored, and sand will thereby be thrown into the eyes of uninstructed readers. If our author had contented himself with showing that at the time of the Synod of Gangra in Paphlagonia there were married priests around, nobody could have denied this—although in all fairness the form of the canon at least supports Bellarmine's view that the priests in questions were ones *who had been married,* rather than ones still married.[24]

What our author claims to be the consequence of the Decree of Siricius to Himerius of Tarragona in the year 385 is frankly as striking as it is shallow.[25] He alleges that it was this decree that signalled the introduction of the law of celibacy into Spain, Gaul, Africa, and Greece. Before I go on to expose all the vacuousness of this proposition, I want to point to something which many would brand as "thoughtlessness," but which I am inclined merely to report without further comment. Further on I will explain how the popes in fact exercised a law-giving power only over a very short period in the Middle Ages. In the teeth of the evidence for this, the introduction of the above-mentioned decree into the said countries is given by our author as a cause for complaint against the Pope, who is thus alleged to have been laying down laws as early as the fourth century! As it happens,

Paphlagonia around the year 324" (*Denkschrift,* p. 21).

24. [Möhler's note] "The author of the *Denkschrift* opposes Bellarmine on the grounds that in the canon it says γεγαμηκως, which is used only of a person who has got married and remains married, not of a person who was once married. We advise him to compare 1 Timothy 5:9, where he will find the definition of a widow γεγονυια ένος ανδρος γυνη. If the use of the perfect tense means that she is still the wife of a man, how could she then have been a widow?"

25. See DH 181–185.

our author seems to be hostile to the rights of papal primacy, arguing that the bishops have the authority to lift the celibacy restriction on their own initiative, and that in this area the right of law-giving would not be an appropriate one for the Pope.[26] When he speaks of the celibacy ruling, however, he assumes that the Pope did have this legislative role, but only so that he can argue that celibacy came into the Church by force. In other words, our author gives himself very extensive permission to contradict himself.

In reality it is quite certain that the popes of that time in no way claimed the direct and immediate right to introduce new laws. Even in the Middle Ages they did not exercise such a right, nor indeed has the whole Church ever exercised it. What happened was simply that principles which had been proved through long practice were gradually raised to the status of a law, and the Popes held it as their most important right to protect such canons. That this also applied in the present case will become clear immediately.

The first thing to be noted here is that Siricius was informed by Himerius that very many priests were continuing to have sexual relations with their wives even while practicing as priests. That Himerius should have bothered to report this shows that the Spanish bishops took it for granted that this behavior was a violation of an older order of things: otherwise why would it have occurred to him to address himself to the Pope on the subject? So then he chose to appeal to the Pope to have such priests punished, as emerges from the well-known decree of Innocent I dealing with the same subject which contains an appeal to his forebears. What we need to focus on here however are the reasons which the married Spanish priests gave for continuing to have sexual relations with their wives. Some referred to the Old Testament ordinance which permitted such behavior to priests. What they noticeably did not do was to complain *that novelties were being introduced and the old discipline harmed,* which they would have done, had this argument been valid as a defense. They made no attempt to defend their behavior on this ground. Others apologized like children for not having realized *that priests may not touch a woman—* a pointless apology if celibacy had only recently been introduced into

---

26. "There is no doubt, that it lies within the attributes of office of the most reverend Bishop of Freiburg to restore the freedom of priests to marry, or at least . . . not to deny any Catholic priest permission to marry on grounds of his status. . ." (*Denkschrift*, p. 107).

Spain. All this, we must not forget, took place before Siricius prepared his decree. Himerius had already reported to him what was
happening and the Pope answered the excuses. How could the Spanish
Bishop possibly have made the clergy who had not been respecting
the celibacy law responsible for their behavior, if the Roman decree,
which had not yet appeared, had prescribed celibacy for the first time?
Finally the Papal Rescript imposes the punishment of dismissal on
those who appealed to the Mosaic Law, while the others were to remain
in their posts but rendered unfit for promotion. Where in the whole
world is someone punished without having infringed any law already
in force? Siricius could simply have requested that these priests abstain
from sexual relations with their wives in the future and supported this
at most with threats. But a punishment—at least of the harshness
stated—would in no way have been justified.

    According to our profound researcher it was also through
Siricius that the celibacy law came to Africa. *Five years* after the pro-
nouncement of the Sirician Decree the second African Synod observed
in their prohibition of priestly marriage "that we too must uphold
what the Apostles taught and what tradition itself has upheld."[27] The
bishops of the African church therefore had the clearest knowledge
of the high antiquity, indeed of the apostolic origin of the institution
in question. What then did Siricius say that was new? Would five years
have been enough in Africa for them to forget that Siricius had been
the real lawgiver? Could a law that had existed for just five years be
attributed to the Apostles or to tradition? We have already discussed
above how far the apostles can in fact be seen as the founders of
priestly celibacy.[28] Yet our author seems to be referring here to a law
written only on paper which went out from Rome. I do not want to
pursue this point further and might perhaps have said nothing about
it, had it not been for the fact that our author wanted quite unambigu-
ously to deny or minimize the existence of a law written in the heart of
the blessed priests of the earlier period. The truth of the matter is that
if the old priestly piety had not already been implanted in Spain, if
some had not lowered themselves to a comparison of themselves with
the Jewish priests while others felt childishly called to ignorance—by

----

    27. [Möhler's note] "quod apostoli docuerunt et ipsa servavit antiquitas, nos quoque
custodiamus" (Cf. *Concilia Africae* 345–525, *Concilium Carthaginense* a. 390, SL 149, 13).

    28. See above, Chapter 2.

which they meant that they had not heard from others what their own hearts and their own inspiration would certainly have said to them as to all earlier priests—the external law would never have been introduced. But should the Church have to abandon her *Christian* priestly ideal just because a certain number of clerics could not rise above paltriness? It is as if someone were to attack the Church for having issued express laws against simony and the like at a later period simply because there had been no such laws in earlier times!

The problem with our patron of a married priesthood is that he constantly relies purely on externals and is incapable of knowing and discerning spirits; thus he deceives himself and others when he claims that the Greeks remained faithful to apostolic mores on the basis of the decisions of the Trullian Synod[29] in the year 690, which allowed already married priests full enjoyment of their marriage, while the Latin Church moved away from this tolerant approach.[30] This kind of talk is typical of someone who prefers appearance to reality. For it is crystal clear that in the apostolic age, celibates chosen to be priests were motivated by their own living zeal for the Kingdom of Christ to abstain from marrying—a custom that only later became a law; it is equally clear that married persons were invested with priesthood only in case of need, and that even then the fullness of their devotion to Christ and his Church for the most part drove out any thought of enjoying further intercourse with their wives. Who then remained faithful to the spirit of the apostolic ways, the Greek Church—which has suppressed the priestly ideal and which now has only married priests at all levels below the episcopate, or the Latin Church which has preserved the celibacy ideal even in the most difficult of times and which has constantly lived the hope of achieving it in fact?

Only a person whose sense of the spiritual has decayed into the merest formalism could believe that in the apostolic age priests abstained from marriage only *after ordination*. Greek clerics who marry still do so before they are ordained, *even though they already have the intention of becoming priests*. A person who thinks that the vocation to

29. See Chapter 2 above.

30. "While in the West laws on celibacy were being promulgated more and more frequently, the Greeks stuck increasingly firmly to the old apostolic ways, and affirmed these joyfully at the Trullian Synod of 690 attended by more than two hundred Fathers" (*Denkschrift*, pp. 23ff.).

the priesthood begins *only with ordination* must have a very lowly view
of priests. In reality, every true priest is born a priest from the moment
of his conception, for he is eternally predestined to priesthood by
God. In fact then he is already a priest long before he actually becomes
one. He prepares himself to be a priest beforehand, he *knows* he will
become a priest. But the person who marries in the knowledge that he
is to be ordained a priest, knowing himself therefore to be a future
priest, has in reality married as a priest. Whether the marriage takes
place before or after ordination makes no difference. I would challenge
any thinking man to ask himself whether the present Greek custom
really does correspond to Christian Antiquity, in which nobody
married after he was ordained! Given all that I have said, what a great
difference there is between the person who marries before his ordination while knowing that he is to be a priest, and the person who in
the Early Church was chosen to be a priest although already married.
For the latter did not get married with the plan of becoming a
priest—far from it, he knew nothing of his future priesthood when
he got married. But the former does know, and in getting married
he represents only a caricature of the ancient custom.

The Catholic custom is of course that if a person recognizes
himself as a future priest in embryo then he abstains completely from
marriage and tends and nourishes the seed of his vocation; when
he goes on to actual ordination he brings the seed to fruition. Nobody
with the least portion of integrity or intelligence can deny that this
corresponds perfectly to the spirit of the earliest Christian Antiquity.
If he gets married before his ordination while actually anticipating that
he will be ordained, he is only making a mockery of the original law,
as the Greeks do. If he gets married after ordination, he is not even
observing the dead form of the law, which even the Greeks do.
Enough said on this topic however!

Our opponent is convinced that Augustine, the apostle of the
Anglo-Saxons, was not able to reach an understanding about celibacy
with the old Christian Britons,[31] and he alleges that they regarded
celibacy as a novelty. Unfortunately it did not occur to him to tell us
the source of this story! I am not referring to the Protestant "sources"
from which he borrowed the idea, for I am as familiar with these as

---

31. The Benedictine monk St. Augustine of Canterbury, who died in 604, not to be confused
with Augustine of Hippo (d. 430).

our author is. I am talking about what we call a historical source in the strict sense—Bede for example,[32] who reports the conflicts between Augustine and the Welsh.[33] In fact Augustine asked three things of the old Christian Britons: that in celebrating Easter they should follow Roman custom, that they should use the Roman rite in baptism, and that they should join him in the work of the conversion of the Anglo-Saxons.[34] Not a word here about celibacy! We have to assume then that it already existed among the British Christians.

It is a sure indication that a man has a narrow-minded view of the world, that he is half aware of his own weakness, and that he has no great inner resources to develop, when he chases after anecdotes and prefers to employ those as polemical weapons where the foundations are lacking for his argument. Thus the author states[35]that John of Cremona, whom he claims that Gregory VII sent 40 years after his own death (!) as Legate to England,[36] was actually himself caught red-handed in a very unseemly intercourse the very night after he had been catechizing the priests about celibacy. If our learned historical researcher had known that Henry of Huntingdon, to whom he attributes this strange tale, also reported that the Synod celebrated under Anselm in London was the first to deny wives to priests,[37] he would surely have cited this ignorant chronicler again for that reason,

---

32. Bede the Venerable, OSB (672–735), English monk and doctor of the Church.

33. [Möhler's note] "*Hist. Eccles.* 1. II. c. 2."

34. "He said to them, 'You act in many particulars contrary to our custom, or rather the custom of the universal church, and yet, if you will comply with me in these three points, viz. to keep Easter at the true time, to administer baptism, by which we are again born to God, according to the custom of the holy Roman Apostolic Church; and jointly with us to preach the word of God to the English nation, we will readily tolerate all the other things you do . . . .'" *Bede's Ecclesiastical History of England*, ed. J. A. Giles, 515 pp., George Bell & Son, London and New York, 1892; here bk ii, c. 2, p. 70.

35. "But history has followed a path which cannot be overlooked here, it shows how Nemesis as it were mockingly punished him. 'After he (relates an old English chronicler) had fought most strenuously at the Council (of London in 1125) against the wives of priests, saying: it is the blackest crime to get up from the side of such a whore and then to bring the body of Christ out of the bread: the following night he himself was caught in bed with a whore, although he had changed bread into the body of Christ on that very day. The fact was so public that it could neither be denied nor concealed'" (*Denkschrift*, p. 43).

36. See above Chapter 2.

37. [Möhler's note] "in quo prohibuit uxores sacerdotibus Anglorum antea non prohibitas" (edit. Lond. 1596 1. VII. Fol. 219).

even though Flodoard,[38] William of Malmesbury,[39] Osbernus,[40] and Lanfranc,[41] among several others, expressly contradict Henry on this. So uncritical is our historian of celibacy! Wherever there is something that he thinks can be adduced to his apparent advantage, he reaches greedily for it without asking any questions about words and their meanings. Yet even if this tale about the papal legate were true, what follows? Are we to condemn marriage just because there are adulterers around?

Faced with a whole plethora of signs of ignorance and extreme superficiality in our author, I will limit myself to pointing out his mistranslation of a particular Greek passage. In the [legendary (*editor's note*)] the address by Paphnutius[42] in which he advocated that married priests should continue to be allowed sexual relationships with their wives if they were called to the priesthood when already married, the Confessor proposed: . . .[43] Our translator gives the first sentence like this: "For not all could endure *complete unfeelingness*." [44] May we not justifiably ask the question whether the author had any other reason for his translation at this point than his own view that celibacy makes a person "unfeeling?" Sozomen reports this same sentence thus: "for it would be difficult to bear."[45] The sentence must have the same meaning in Socrates. When we look at the actual words of Paphnutius, we cannot but be amazed at the impudence with which the meaning is distorted, for it definitely cannot be a matter of pure ignorance. Apathy (Gk *A-patheia*) means being above the passions, here especially above sexual lust, or what is rendered in ecclesiastical Latin as being continent.[46] It should therefore be translated: "For not all could cope with the practice of continency," which agrees precisely with

---

38. [Möhler's note] "hist. Rhem. C. 5."

39. [Möhler's note] "de regib. Anglorum 1. II. c. 8."

40. [Möhler's note] "*vit. s. Dunstan*, c. 39, ap. Sur. Tom. III."

41. [Möhler's note] "*ep. II ad Alex.* II."

42. At the Council of Nicaea in 325, see above p. 53.

43. Paphnutius was a Confessor Bishop from the time of the persecutions of the Christians, this is why Möhler gives him the title of Confessor. "ου γαρ παντας δυνασθαι φερειν της απαθειας την ασκησιν, ηδε ισως φυλαχθησεσθαι την σωφροσυνην της έκαστε γαμετης" [Paphnutius intervention never occured: cf. Friedhelm Winkelmann, "Paphnutias, der Bekenner und Bischof," Peter agel ed., Probleme der koptischen Litereatur (Halle, 1968) pp. 145–53, editor]

44. See *Denkschrift*, p. 20.

45. [Möhler's note] "(*hist. eccles.* 1. I. C. 23) 'χαλεπον γαρ ειναι το πραγμα φερειν.'"

46. "continentia."

Sozomen's formula. The second sentence clarifies the first. For Paphnutius says of the separated wife of the priest the same thing that applies to the priest himself, namely: "Perhaps the continence of the wife of the priest might not be maintained." The practice of continence is thus prudence.[47] We cannot understand what grounds thus existed other than arbitrariness for our author to suggest that Paphnutius regarded the refusal of intercourse with the wife as a matter of "unfeelingness": Paphnutius would certainly not have considered himself "unfeeling."

    This concludes our historical critique, and I will now turn to the second part of the *Denkschrift,* which seems to me to have been written by a different author from the first part, like the foreword to the pamphlet. I do not want to expand on the reasons that lead me to this conclusion, it is not a matter of huge importance. I must however stress that the writer of the second part is definitely entitled to more respect from us than is the one with whom we have been debating thus far.

---

47. [Möhler's note] "Ασκησις της απαθειας thus equals = σωφροσυνη."

Chapter 5

On the Theology of Celibacy

THE FREEDOM OF THE INDIVIDUAL
AND THE CHURCH

The most universal and the most relentlessly reiterated criticism of the celibacy rule for Catholic priests is that it is a mandatory prohibition which imposes extremely harsh restrictions on personal freedom.
One commonly raised question is generally considered unanswerable: how can the Church believe herself to be justified in forcing so many men—a whole body of them—to abstain from marriage? It flies in the face both of divine and of human laws. But to begin with I deny that the question is correctly stated and I propose to recast it in a different form: Has the Church the right to confer priestly ordination only on those whose hearts are anointed with the highest religious consecration, on those in whom the purest and most beautiful blooms of divinely blessed life are unfolding, on those the Apostle speaks of who live completely and wholly for the Lord, those in fact—to put it in a nutshell along with the same Apostle—who have received the gift of virginity?

Nobody can fail to see the great difference between these two ways of stating the question. While the question in its first form must be answered in the negative, the answer to the second can *only* be positive. For clearly the Church has a perfect right to decide the qualities her shepherds of souls should have. It would be strange indeed if we were to begin by denying the neediness of our own spiritual nature and its inadequacy for the office of spiritual shepherd, and then went on to demand that the Church should therefore mutilate her ideal. It would be equally strange if someone found his way into the priesthood only then to discover that he lacked the higher powers he needed for the task, and then complained that because the Church failed to adapt her requirements to his particular makeup, his personal freedom was being violated. It is as if someone to whom nature has given the talents of a corporal, but to whom those of a field marshal have been denied, were to complain that his personal freedom had been infringed because he was not appointed head of the army. Or imagine that as a result of some mistake he actually did become a field marshal, only to discover his personal incapacity to lead the troops victoriously: would he then be justified in demanding that people should be obliging enough to desire of a field marshal no more than he himself, the one promoted, could perform? Moreover, having failed to come up to scratch—as was to be expected—would he be justified in complaining that his freedom had been infringed because he himself was not up to the demands of the job?

There is perhaps an example closer to home. The Church looks for certain spiritual aptitudes in a future priest that will enable him to absorb a considerable sum of knowledge and apply it to life. In the earliest Christian times the requirements in this area would clearly have been much more modest, and indeed the various branches of our linguistic, philosophical, and theological disciplines did not even exist in those days. Now just imagine if someone were to appeal to the example of the apostolic age and give the ecclesiastical authorities to understand that in spite of his talent being quite inadequate to absorb the knowledge required today, he is perfectly capable of being an excellent priest according to the standards of the Early Church? And suppose he were to go on to claim that his Christian freedom would be infringed if a particular level of learning were to be required of him? Who would argue that such a candidate should be anything other than rejected without regard for his complaint, or that any more attention should be paid to him than to the many sects which have in general attacked our church for having obscured the plain message of the Word, so close to the human heart, under a pile of useless learned junk? If such a man had nonetheless been openly accepted into the service of the Church, his bishop would have found his sermons and his catechesis much too simple and inappropriate, and his much-needed refutations of attacks on the Church and the like quite insignificant, while he would have looked in vain for some sign that this priest could compensate for his lack of knowledge by performing appropriate miracles, as in the Early Church. The bishop would therefore be obliged to exhort him to acquire a reasonable mastery of his teaching office and to sweat away night and day to make up for his lack of talent by his diligence. If he still insisted that the qualifications for ordination should simply be lowered and claimed that the refusal of the episcopal authorities to do this constituted an attack on his Christian freedom, this would certainly be dismissed as sheer foolishness.

There is an infinite variety of particular callings among men. Each person exercises his own special gifts and strengths, and the opinions expressed on this question by the law-giving authorities are simply clarifications and interpretations of nature. The only question where in our case doubt might arise is whether particular gifts and strengths are granted for virginity—but I have already shown that this is undoubtedly the case. Each person has to find the calling suited to him among the numerous ones that are available, or rather he must place himself consciously in the place where Providence has called him. Then he will surely not consider that his freedom is limited, for true freedom means moving in response to the calling which God has inspired in our innermost being, a calling which echoes and reechoes in all the twists and turns of our lives.

Our author claims however that all too many are motivated to choose the priestly state purely as a result of external circumstances. And yet the truth is that it is precisely in our surroundings, our family, our friends, and our teachers that Providence comes to meet us. They listen carefully to the sounds to be heard from time to time from the innermost depths of the hearts of the children, lads, and young men around them; then they sift those various sounds to find the basic one in which God's voice may be heard as it calls out from a person's inmost depths for the corresponding calling to be given him from outside. Of course carelessness, apathy, and the like very often fail to hear the gentle voice which a more attentive ear would easily have picked up. But anyone who denies that in the environment in which we are set Providence comes to meet us from outside, so that the call from the soul of man will be entrusted to the proper artist for development and fulfilment, would be denying the influence of divine Providence in the most crucial moments of our education. We also have to sound our own innermost depths for the inspiration we need from God to acquire a precise knowledge of our inclinations and the things that make us happy, our delights and our loves, and by God's grace to decide on our vocation. Anyone who does not do all this must expect to have a very painful life, while anyone who does do it will very rarely be disappointed.

Of course it is true that the young are not sufficiently attuned to the importance of circumstances, something we only begin to appreciate through longer experience of life, and with every decade of his life a person's inclinations and needs do certainly change. This much is beyond question. In general, however, and in terms of the particular application made of it here, this particular argument against celibacy is very mistaken. If taken literally it destroys all life, it makes all education impossible, it turns all consistent effort and consistent relationships into something wavering and uncertain. Who would cheerfully and joyfully subject himself to training for a particular calling, a training which often takes up a period of years, if the thought torments him that all the work he is doing may turn out to be useless for his future? Wouldn't someone have to become a judge first and only study the Pandects[1] afterward? Who could bear to marry, if we could not afford to rely on our inclination until it was actually put to the test by life? Indeed, shouldn't it be made allowable for the marriage bond to be dissolved after a few years? Would there even be any such thing as a marriage any more? The truth is that the end result of the elimination of the celibacy of the priesthood would actually be the elimination of all human life, and it could only have come up as an issue in an era when life had been shaken to its deepest foundations, an era when all firm principles had evaporated, when even religion and the Church seemed to be drifting rudderless, an era resembling a storm-tossed sea.[2] The conflicting opinions and views of the age would dominate by turns, coming in and out of fashion at a great rate, so that

---

1 Collection of laws, Latin *digests*, a collection of Roman and modern legal judgements.

2 Möhler introduces a picture beloved by the Romantics of the Church in the storm-tossed sea of the age: cf. Joseph von Eichendorff's 1848 poem *Das Schiff der Kirche*: "The old towers had long been seen to shiver,/What our fathers had piously built and achieved,/Throne, city and altar/a wild torrent of unleashed ideas devoured.//It spreads wider and wider without limits./A sea where rising up and lifting high/The dark surge pressed from rock to rock,/And every patch of · land for safety was submerged.//Yet over it arched a bow of peace./To which the furious waves could not reach,/And under it a ship went its way/That knows nothing of the water's wild thirst,/That breaks the whirlpool dance of the storm./O Lord, let us all land happily there."

people would be seduced into accepting a theory one day only to deny it the next. No firm moral character could possibly be formed in this kind of social environment. For where the intelligence twists and turns in a constant whirlwind, the will cannot be firm and definite either. Remaining eternally unchangeable in the midst of all the uncertainty of the times, the Catholic Church would likewise lose that firmness of will and that unbreakable resoluteness of character which holds fast to what it has once grasped honorably and wholeheartedly in the sight of God, inspired and strengthened by him up to the last breath of life; it is that which guarantees the indissolubility of marriage and hence also the eternal faithfulness of the Church to those who have devoted themselves exclusively to her.

One thing I am happy to praise in our author is his emphasis on the joys of the moral bonds which maintain family life and which the unmarried will miss, joys which he would prefer to make available to priests. Yet he is surely making a very big mistake in believing that celibate priests are excluded from the advantages which accrue from our experience of legitimate ties of affection. The profound joy to be derived from being honored and loved as the father of a whole community as you carry them all within your heart, watch over the growth of the scattered divine seed, and see fruits for heaven ripen under your hands—that is something which can only be appreciated by those who see it or experience it for themselves. Likewise the happiness which flows from association with those devout souls who are deeply dependent in their inmost being on the true pastor of souls is something that has to be experienced if ever it is to be understood. The more you feel that you live your office of shepherd to the utmost and that all your longings and joys are taken up with it, the happier you feel. Love is the measure of love. It is in the nature of things that the person who divides his heart between a wife and a community simply cannot expect to receive the same degree of warmth and tenderness of feeling from the community as the one who is exclusively devoted to them. The more excellent the pastor of souls, the more inward his relationship to the community, the more comprehensive and the fuller his delight. Surely we have here the equivalent of all that the life of the family gives. But anyone who wants to enjoy the one in full measure must renounce the other, and the Church wants the pastor of souls to be able to experience the fullness of the joy which is to be found in the spiritual bonds of religion.

Some also expect the priest to provide a model for the raising of children. Every time I have heard this wish expressed, I have found myself very perplexed as to how it is to be achieved. The aspiration is perfectly appropriate of itself, but in actual fact it is already fulfilled in every good pastor of souls anyway. He is the spiritual father of the whole community and its educator for the Kingdom of God. What are his sermons but words flowing from the innermost place in the heart of a father who longs only for the happiness of his children? Surely the best education comes from parents who develop the idea of a holy and blessed way of thinking and living throughout the course of their whole lives, so that their children see the abstract concepts of piety, virtue, industriousness, etc., embodied in front of them in a bright and lively way and can then gradually incorporate these into their own lives. What on earth is the pastor of souls if not an educator, through the medium of his heartfelt, tender, and ever-watchful care for the whole community which is his family, through his mildness and his severity, his gentleness and his love for his enemies, his mercifulness and selflessness—in a nutshell, through all the virtues and good works shining out from him? If the pastor of souls does not embody the picture of a true educator, *as the Church wants him to be,* then I really have no idea what education means. The representation of the true pastor of souls as a model to parents for their work as educators in the home is a task worthy of a true artist. The moment the child is born, the priest takes it up and consecrates it into the Kingdom of God, and in doing so he makes plain the goal and end of all education. As soon as the first intimations of spiritual powers are visible in the child, the pastor begins to exercise them, holding the highest objects before the child, the only ones worthy of it, advancing in stages from the simplest and easiest level to the highest and the most difficult. He is a child to the child and grows up alongside him to perfection. He takes lovingly all the child's secrets, his innermost thoughts and his most hidden activities up into his father's heart. His children keep nothing from him, all hearts open up to him, he shows compassion, rejoices together with them, comforts, exhorts, advises, and punishes—just the same as the best educator does. If one of his children falls ill, he rushes to his side to console him and accompany him until he has to give him up into the hands of the heavenly Father. If this is not education, if no pattern of true education is given here for all parents, where indeed is education to be found? If he had his own physical family, he simply would not be able to enjoy the kind of relationship with his community I have described, a relationship so radical and so far-reaching. It is precisely because he has no physical children that all can be his spiritual children. It is no accident that Protestant clergy do not enjoy anything like the close relationships with their community that the Catholic priests have. On the other hand it must be admitted that the successful education of the children of a clergyman can bring many advantages for a community. Clergy children are of course often damaged by an ill-advised severity, but I do not want to make anything of that, for after all an inadequate celibate priest will also fail to establish the kind of educational relationship with his community I have described above. But no advantages enjoyed by a married clergy can be compared with the benevolent influence of a Catholic priest, which is precisely what it is because he remains celibate. Consider the relationship between a pastor and his wife: he is able to accommodate to her weaknesses, to compromise with her and to bear patiently with her, but in actual fact he cannot be a model for others in this, simply because *in good families* the respective weaknesses and afflictions and the mutual restraint resulting from them remain hidden from view. Once all this becomes public knowledge, the whole marital relationship loses any value as a model. The same is the case with the relationships between parents and children. What by its nature must be visible to the eyes of the individual Protestant church community is the most ordinary behavior, and certainly not something especially different from what is expected of any Christian family. But the finer and deeper qualities are as a rule observed by nobody outside the home—and perhaps not even by the closest friends of the household. In addition, the particular vocation of the children of a pastor, who of course do not go into farming or business, requires a special education which has little or no general relevance to the lives of villagers.

Among the young, those having high career aspirations that require to be pursued in the context of married life and that are not therefore compatible with celibacy, or those reluctant to tolerate the limitations imposed on their freedom by celibacy, are clearly not going to consider the possibility of ordination, and this is often raised as an objection to the institution of a celibate priesthood. There is an important truth here. The distorted attitudes that our age has adopted toward virginity and priestly celibacy from sources outside the Gospel and the Christian Church can indeed lead to young minds being betrayed, robbed of their noblest inspirations, and diverted from a consciously chosen path of true and unshakable adherence to a calling given to them by God. Indeed, the weakness and prevalent negativity of the age, the earthier senses, the attractions of pleasure, etc. quite often obstruct big commitments and the pursuit of ideals even in better natures. But we have to get to the real root of the kind of views which prevent any noble enterprise from coming to fruition, and we shall find that it has nothing whatever to do with any proposal to abolish mandatory celibacy for priests. I will show, indeed I will demonstrate incontrovertibly that it cannot be considered an accident if the Catholic Church, which honors virginity so much, also has the deepest grasp of marriage and hallows it as a sacrament; I will also demonstrate that those religious movements which treat virginity as something indifferent or contemptible also devalue marriage. For in truth the assumption that priestly celibacy and a high view of marriage are contradictory can only be derived from a very superficial consideration of the issues involved.

In the Protestant theological world only the most mediocre types of mind do homage to feeble rationalistic ideas, and in the Catholic Church only the poorest theologians adopt outwardly negative arguments, and so I nourish the liveliest hopes that in the near future faith, the Gospel, and the mind of the Church will win a decisive victory. Then we shall see the most distinguished among the younger generation fired up with the inspiration to feed the flock of God. Then the natural sure touch of their strong character will no longer be betrayed by a superficial environment, and their rich minds nurtured by a many-sided fundamental education and their deep hearts will grasp the whole idea of the Church and accept it into themselves with living power. Such men will not experience celibacy as imposing any of the limitations on their personal freedom we spoke about earlier, indeed they will dismiss the very idea of that as nonsense. Rather, they will call it the highest freedom to follow the tendency of their own nature as purified by the Spirit of God. The real truth is that the age to which God's merciful Providence has brought us is highly suited to celibacy.[3] The Church will no longer have to battle either with the barbarous ways of the Middle Ages or with the unbelief and superficiality of the modern age. True scholarship, the fundamental study of philosophy, history, and theology, to which barbarousness and unbelief are alike unfavorable, will become increasingly common among the clergy, while spiritual concerns will be suffused with the earthly light of faith. Then we shall have just the kind of priests that are required by celibacy and by the Church's ideal of the priesthood.

Meanwhile, what the claim that "individuals who are particularly well suited for the priesthood are discouraged by the celibacy rule from becoming priests" really amounts to is that young persons from the (so-called) upper classes are deterred by this discipline from seeking ordination.[4] Of course it is highly desirable that well-bred families should give their *talented* sons for the service of the Church, and I have not the least desire to deny that the celibacy requirement discourages many such from entering that service. But the truth is that even were the celibacy rule to be abolished, only a small number of such persons would actually devote themselves to the service of the Church. To spend perhaps one's whole life in the same village, to visit the poorest hovels and to provide the comforts of religion in them, to withdraw from a host of pleasures and distractions allowable of themselves but denied on good grounds to the priest, to be content with what is as a rule an extremely modest income, and to have to accept a lowly level of honor, rank, and respect in the world of leisured gentlefolk: what attraction can any of that possibly have for the better sort of family? As long as the German church was still in a position to bestow the possibility of rich outward display, the nobility flocked enthusiastically to claim her offices and dignities. Unfortunately, now that she has been robbed and impoverished and separated from all

---

3 Here Möhler reveals a divinatory far-sightedness whose confirmation he would have witnessed with his own eyes, had he been granted a rather longer life. Soon after he wrote and for the century that followed, many vocations to the priesthood began to appear, and celibacy ceased to be an issue for a long time.

4 "A further oft-lamented disadvantage of the celibacy of the Catholic priest lies in the fact that it appears as a hindrance that keeps so very many individuals who are often particularly well suited to it from the priestly vocation ... Nothing more need be said about the sheer extent of the moral and intellectual power lost to the priestly calling because of it, the huge size of the obstacle put in the way of the effectiveness of the priesthood, and the consequent multiplication of the number of the mercenary-minded who enter the priesthood" (*Denkschrift*, p. 71).

earthly splendor, few members of the aristocracy have any desire to serve her. The conclusion is absolutely clear: it is definitely not the celibacy requirement that keeps the educated classes from rushing to enlist in the ranks of the clergy. The governing elite are in possession of power and might, they stand at the head of the administration and the judicial system, they exercise the greatest influence on those events which are the most important for sensual men, and for that reason they enjoy a reputation and take pleasure in an authority which blinds and binds young minds. By contrast, the work of the priest is discreet and little-noticed, it has to do with what is hidden and inward in man, he does not acquire any kind of brilliant outward reputation by it, and the truth is that there is nothing to be gained by seeking to lure the sons of the ruling elite into the priesthood.

In many countries, most of the families of the ruling classes live lives that are all too unspiritual, lives given over to externals and appearances. Although they are conventionally classed as educated, in reality they are uneducated, unless we understand by education that conventional sheen which adheres only to the surface and masks the crudity of what is on the inside. Real education has nothing to do with having a paltry jumble of knowledge in your mind which enables you to chatter away superficially but not to see beneath the surface of things. Conceitedness is not education. What would the Church really gain by attracting young people like these from such a background? When more inwardness and piety, a deeper seriousness of life, and a true depth of knowledge and learning are found in the majority of families in the ruling elite, then we shall certainly see more devout mothers and fathers committed to the Church awakening and nurturing by word and deed the seed of a priestly vocation in one or another of their sons and bringing it to maturity. Such parents will not have the future glory of their sons in mind but the need and the requirements of the Church. But in any case it is certain that anyone who has a calling to the priestly state that stems not from man but from God will not be repelled in any way by the thought of what this calling denies him, but rather attracted by the sphere of influence that it offers. How often we are deceived in our judgement as to someone's capacity for the priesthood. And when you hear someone say "Mr. X would be just the man for the priesthood if only it didn't involve this or that obligation," it is usually tantamount to saying: "Mr. X would make an excellent soldier if only soldiers didn't have to have this thing about honor." Generally speaking, a person's lack of *one* quality requisite for a particular calling points only too strikingly to the fact that he is completely devoid of an inner calling to it. The coward for example usually turns out also to lack the presence of mind, the staying power, and so forth that are equally important in a military vocation.

THE VICTORY OVER NATURE

I do not recall ever having come across in earlier attacks on celibacy the allegation made in the second part that one by-product of celibacy is unfeelingness. But the way our author chooses to translate a Greek passage that we find in the first part above, along with certain other pointers, leads me to conclude that this assumption is indeed part and parcel of the way of thinking of our new opponent of celibacy.[5] I am therefore obliged to give it due consideration, and all the more so in that it is now beginning to be picked up by others. We should not be surprised at such allegations: it would have been a great deal more surprising if they had not been made here.

It is a fact of history that the celibates of our Church wandered Germany's woods and marshes with the aim of drawing the barbarians out of their damp snow-covered holes into the mild and friendly sun-light, and—what is even more important in the eyes of the Christian—also led them out of their moral darkness into the sun of minds so that they could share in the light and warmth of the immortal soul. It is a fact of history that these celibates taught ignorant hunters horticulture, agriculture, and viticulture, and—what is even dearer to the faithful—sowed the seed of the divine Word in their hearts, eradicated their terrible barbarousness and produced flowers and fruits for heaven. It is a fact of history that when those celibates performed and encouraged both supernatural and natural works—and indeed it could not be otherwise, given the connection between soul and body—and abolished not only the curse that went out in Adam

---

5. "When they were discussing this, Paphnutius stood up in the midst of the assembled bishops and cried with a loud voice . . . they must take care that they do not do great damage to the Church by this excessively demanding requirement: not all would be able to endure complete unfeelingness." (*Denkschrift*, pp. 19ff.). (Cf. footnote 43 in previous section regarding the legendary nature of Paphutios' intervention; American editor.)

over the earth, that it would bear only thistles and thorns for itself, but also the curse bearing on souls, that their works would always be stained with sin and in fact, as Peter predicted, they actually did create a new heaven and a new earth.[6] Yet according to those who think like our author, all this arose not out of their deep religious feelings, from hearts full of compassion for the wretchedness of man, but—*out of a desire for fame.*[7] The celibates of our Church crossed oceans to India, China, Tibet, America, and Africa, confronting a thousand dangers, infinite labors, and the threat of death at any moment, and they did all this for the most part in the service of Christ whose gospel they were proclaiming. But according to the judgement of the wise of today, all these efforts sprang not out of hearts full of love which God had wonderfully remade, but from the Church's lust for power, as we learn from Henke and many others. We go into a hospital run and served by celibate sisters and we are moved to tears to see women in the bloom of youth from prosperous and respected families, good-looking and well-educated, at the service of sick persons who have no earthly connection with them, at the service of the old, the stiff, the paralyzed and the neglected whose shoelaces they cheerfully tie and whose waistcoats they button up, whose neckties they put on, for whom they happily prepare and administer food, treating them as beloved fathers or spouses whose love and faithfulness they are wanting to repay. But according to our opponent's theory we are not to allow the beauty of soul made visible in such behavior to move our hearts to tears, for in the eyes of the wise of our times this is basically all a fantasy, it is an exception to the rule that only heart speaks to heart, for we are being moved by nothing but trickery.

Dear friends! Where on earth does this kind of view of history come from? Surely it comes from the fact that those higher feelings which flow from heaven down to earth and which the Father of love produces in the human breast have become quite alien to us today. Surely it derives from the fact that we ourselves only feel and love in an earthly manner, so that we lack an organ or a receptivity adapted to those higher, more spiritual, and purer feelings by which such persons as these were brought alive and moved in the past and yet still can be

---

6. Cf. 2 Peter 3:13.

7. [Möhler's note] "Henke *christl. K. Gesch.* Th. 1. p. 493. 5th ed."

today? Surely it derives from the fact that we see unfeelingness all around us, simply because we do not meet feelings in the mundane circles in which we ourselves move. What the poet said is true: "Thou art like the spirit thou canst comprehend."[8] It is also true that you will forever misread the mind that is totally unlike yours.

There could actually have been a very plausible foundation for the criticism we are encountering here, and in fact I could have wished it to have been expressed with greater clarity. For the truths we are proclaiming can only be seen in all their glory if the relevant contrasts are set out vividly and with full supporting evidence. I would have been delighted if the *Denkschrift* had generally employed more thoughtfulness, shrewdness, and freedom in deploying its arguments in the full light of day. That would actually have helped me to defend celibacy all the more effectively and successfully. So what I am now going to do is provide the most powerful foundation that the object under discussion can possibly be given from the standpoint of finite thinking, precisely in order to present our holy institution in an even purer light. Here then is a powerful argument for our opponents: it is nature's way that we must go step by step up her stairway, for to try and cut out some of her steps is dangerous. The steps are interconnected and there is no gap between them, as the Ancients so wisely observed.[9]

The power of the self-seeking which is so deeply woven into our whole being is only gradually broken, and it is only gradually that an increasingly purer love take its place. When a man gets married, he gives himself wholly to *another* being. In so doing, he begins to go out of himself and the first fatal wounds are inflicted on his egoism. Nature repeats the same attacks on self-seeking with each successive child with which the marriage is blessed. Without being really aware of it, the man lives less and less for himself and much more—indeed

---

8. Goethe, *Faust* 1, Nacht.

9. The Scholastic principle: "Nature does not make any leaps." *Natura non facit saltus.* Not because of any spiritual kinship, but for the sake of greater understanding, Hegel too makes a point of mentioning the old saying: "'tis said, *natura non facit saltum;* . . . But we have seen that the alterations of being in general are not only the transition of one magnitude into another, but a transition from quality into quantity and *vice versa,* a becoming-other which is an interruption of gradualness and the production of something qualitatively different from the reality which preceded it." *Hegel's Science of Logic,* translated by A V Miller, 844 pp., London, George Allen & Unwin/New York, Humanities Press, 1968, vol. I, section 3, chapter 2, p. 370.

only—for others. In proportion as the family grows, self-seeking weakens its grip and the heart's narrowness gives way to generosity. What anxiety if his wife is ill! What worry, when dangers threaten his child! All this makes his feelings grow purer and stronger. Just as his inheritance is generously shared with many, so his whole inner life is also shared with them. This family life becomes the firm basis on which the life of the individual develops more and more breadth and his love grows greater and more perfect. So many new relationships and associations are acquired either directly through marriage or as an indirect consequence of it. His love for his spouse extends to all her own family. Sons and daughters too form new connections and to that extent the scope of the father's affections broadens out. In the Dark Ages, canon law quite benevolently forbade marriage between relations even when they were only in a very distant degree with the aim of helping to widen this circle of relationships, something that is very difficult for crude uneducated types who just want to withdraw into themselves. Now the ground is prepared and moral powers are strong enough to love the whole Fatherland and beyond it all of humanity. According to this argument, the celibate by contrast, desiring to reach straight for the highest without following the steps prescribed by nature, cannot escape the power of self-seeking. He dares to embark on an Icarian[10] flight which can only fail. If someone wanted to get up to the fiftieth step of a ladder from the first at a *single* leap, he would not even manage to get a foothold on the first rung but would fall powerless to the ground and perhaps never recover the courage to have another go, and this is just what happens with the celibate. Observation thus clearly demonstrates what experience as such might still leave uncertain—that unfeelingness and self-seeking are necessarily part and parcel of the celibate life.

All finite thought operating outside the sphere of Christian ideas is nothing, and that applies to this style of argument too. There is an entirely opposite argument which claims that a husband's love for his wife is nothing more than self-love, and that the best kind of marriage is contracted on the basis of just this kind of feeling, thinking, and wanting. On this theory, the husband loves the wife

---

10. Möhler is referring to Greek Myth. Icarus did not want to listen to the restraining counsels of his father Daedalus. He loved to disobey prohibitions. Hence he failed to grasp the laws of nature, flew too close to the sun with his feather wings, and fell to his death.

precisely because he meets himself in her and loves only himself in her. Far from destroying egoism in the act of marrying, he merely displays the evidence that in the whole wide world he has only himself in view. The case is even worse if the husband, reflecting on his outward circumstances, notices a certain void and sees attachment to a wife as the most appropriate means of filling it. The parents grow young in the children and are born again. They devote love to themselves all over again. As the natural man prefers to cherish himself, understandably his wife and children do the same. The harsh truth is that the real person he has in mind in all these things is himself. That is the reason why he himself suffers when they are ill. Moreover, everyone knows how often it can happen that family relationships are only tools for the attainment of deeply self-seeking goals, so that for example nobody makes his way in the world easily in town or in country life unless he is either related to the leading families or becomes related to them by marriage. The whole world also knows the sad heights often reached by mutual hatred when two similar families get in each other's way in the pursuit of their self-seeking. Typical examples from history are furnished by the Italian cities in the Middle Ages or the Abencerrages[11] in Granada. On this argument then, the married person only reaches out to embrace others in order to return the stronger back to himself, as Cicero says: "The fellowship between men and their common bonding will best be preserved if the closer someone is to you the more kindness you confer upon him."[12] The same can be said of love of the Fatherland; it is in reality composed of the national pride in which each individual glorifies himself and worships his own excellence along with his desire for security for himself and those whom he loves for his own sake. That is certainly the justification that Cicero gives for representing love of the Fatherland as the highest form of love: "Parents are dear, and children, relatives and acquaintances are dear, but our country has on its own embraced all the affections of all of us."[13] Self-seeking thus penetrates all these social relationships—though in ever-new forms—and it is hard to see how such relationships could ever

---

11. Moorish-Islamic dynasty that played a role in the battles with the kings of Spain.

12. "Optime autem societas hominum conjunctioque servabitur, si ut quisque erit conjunctissimus, ita in eum benignitatis plurimum conferetur" Cicero, *De Officiis*, Book 1, (50).

13. "Cari sunt parentes, cari liberi, propinqui, familiares: sed omnes omnium caritates patria una complexa est" Cicero, *De Officiis*, Book 1 (57).

break the power of that same self-seeking. So which of these two arguments corresponds the more closely to experience?

The Christian standpoint is the only one that can offer a solution to our dilemma. If self-seeking is an essential part of our fallen nature, one does not need to be especially intelligent to see that we cannot be set free by natural means through something that is itself not freed by its development from nature. Nature may refine itself, yet however much it may bring us by our experience of its changes to an awareness that we are blemished with it, it cannot disappear and go over into *its opposite*. There is no more a gradual stage-by-stage transition from self-seeking to *Christian love* than there is a possibility that some number could open up the way to the transition from a finite quantity to an infinite one.[14] There is no such number that can take us beyond the natural order. The truth is that if self-seeking is natural to us, then *Christian love* must necessarily be supernatural. It is clear that there are no leaps within the natural order,[15] but it is equally clear that supernaturality could *only* ever be reached by a leap—a leap which must make the married person like the celibate person if he wants to be taken out of the eternal circular movement of nature. When you stand on the thirtieth rung of a ladder, you are no nearer to the boundary of the realm of the senses, of (infinite) space, than when you are standing on the first rung—for the simple reason that the first rung is not even the beginning of space.

If *Christian love* could arise in the way discussed, the Church's teaching would be reduced to nothing more than a simple straightforward supplement to state education. But for this to be the case, the coming of the Son of God would have to happen, for it is his Spirit through whom, as the Apostle Paul says, love is poured out into our hearts.[16] Marriage itself must be hallowed and transfigured by the Christian principle if it is to be pleasing to God and if what is pleasing to God is to develop out of it. The Gospel message is very far from teaching the error that Christian love gradually grows out of marriage and the relationships deriving from it. This higher Christian principle

---

14. The mathematical example hits the nail on the head: no addition or multiplication of a finite number by another finite number can make it infinite. Of course the sum 1+2+3+4 will grow inordinately, but at no time does the addition take us beyond the finite realm.

15. See note 9 above.

16. See Romans 5:5; Galatians 4:6.

may be added to marriage, Christian love may first be added to natural marriage through God's particular grace, but marriage *as such* contributes nothing to the production of Christian love and Christian feeling, both of which can penetrate and enliven hearts quite independently of marriage. Before Christianity marriage was not something to be avoided, for it required the natural virtues—i.e. such as they can be without the Christian principle—and that is the truth in the first argument above. But now in Christianity the highest can be attained without marriage, as Christ and Paul said and as both showed in their lives, so the necessity of celibacy was given along with the possibility. All phenomena that are *possible* through the Christian principle *must* become a reality. All the attacks on celibate priesthood amount to nothing, simply because celibate priesthood is in fact a necessity. This is the most profound reason for the fact that ascetics and then monks made their appearance with the beginnings of the Christian Church. Abstracting from the fact that the priestly state tends of itself to celibacy, celibacy became established only in the priestly order because whereas the monastic orders may disappear—as in the greater part of Germany—there are always priests in the Church. Thus that possibility which is a necessity always becomes a reality in the priesthood.

In addition to having clarified the issue of the supposed "unfeelingness" of those who are celibate for higher motives, we have now also given the answer to the claim in the *Denkschrift* that celibacy ought to be abandoned if its necessity cannot be strictly demonstrated.[17] The Church is indeed driven by a higher necessity, and that higher necessity is in fact the possibility of virginity, a necessity that in the case of most of those who embrace it operates unconsciously to elicit a willing acceptance, while with some it reduces to the need for the achievement of all kinds of church aims whose attainment they consider possible only through celibacy; but these are, to be frank, often fairly modest in their scope.

THE VICTORY OVER THE SPIRIT OF THE AGE

At a later stage in his text, our worthy author observes that the spirit of the age—meaning modern morals and opinions—calls for priestly

---

17. "Only a demonstration of its most absolute necessity can reconcile us with a measure against which natural feeling and the natural understanding rebels" (*Denkschrift*, p. 65).

marriage, and that to want to ignore it or trivialize it is very pernicious.[18] I am far from being ignorant of the power of the spirit of the age. But I believe we can stand above it, assess it truthfully, and accept only what there is of good in it as not absolutely bad: the rest however we must oppose. What a vast amount would have to be thrown away as outdated if we simply bowed to prevailing opinion! There would be no place for anyone to be a Catholic and indeed not even to be a Christian! Such a way of reasoning is far too vague to have any substantial significance.

On the other hand, there is another aspect to all this. Something that does not present as a symptom of any kind of actual unholiness but merely as a vague threat may open the way for the anti-celibacy view to grow in importance against the background of a very widespread lack of Catholic understanding and an almost universal indifference on the part of so many towards the interests of Catholicism, so that it ultimately appears to form a real counter-claim to that of the Catholic Church. My answer to this point is only that since celibacy makes no other claim than to be numbered among the disciplinary laws[19] of our Church, it might perhaps be allowed to fade off the scene along with a hundred other similar ordinances in preference to even just a little damage being done to souls. We could potentially accept a married priesthood somewhere in order to avoid a separation, as we have done with the Greek Uniates, where it was allowed to subsist in order to make reunion easier. On the other hand, the great difference between these two cases is blindingly obvious. The Greek Uniates were drawn to the inner essence of the Catholic Church, and in a case like this a matter of Church discipline should be no hindrance to letting the mutual attraction develop to a full reunion. But if someone wants to separate from the Church on account of a discipline, in that case the inner essence of the Church is either not

---

18. "Most of those who are familiar with the state of things in Germany are of the opinion that in tune with the spirit of the age and under the inspiration of a mysterious impulse, not just bad Catholics but moderate and true ones in Germany nowadays generally prefer a chaste marriage to an unchaste celibacy" (*Denkschrift*, p. 48).

19. Möhler is not quite consistent. He has already said that celibacy is necessary, but here he presents it as a disciplinary law. A discipline can be changed, a necessity cannot. More precise biblical knowledge about the unconditioned eschatological character of the message of the Kingdom of God and a deepened view of the Church as the original sacrament in Christ points towards a real relationship between the office of service in the Church and deepened celibacy, the Evangelical Counsels.

known to him or it is being misjudged, so the opposition could not really be said to be caused by discipline issue. A person who leaves the Church on account of a discipline was never in the Church for the sake of her dogma in the first place. There is no living inner relationship between such individuals and the Church, and indeed they are certainly no members of the Church. How could the Church be pressured for the sake of people like this who do not even belong to her to abandon an institution that has become dear to her? They are in no position to value it or to understand its foundations, nor are they qualified to do so since they stand outside the Church or as long as they do not understand how they are outside the Church.

The application of the rules of higher criticism to the various striking contradictions I have uncovered in the *Denkschrift* has led me to the conclusion that it must have been a joint production of the shallow minds and the lightweight thinking of several authors, so I can perhaps dismiss this part of the text as an unplanned extra which does not uphold the spirit of the whole. For in the introduction to the *Denkschrift* the people involved in the petition are referred to as being deeply committed to the Catholic Church,[20] and they set their faces expressly against those who, though outwardly members of the Church, in reality belong outside her, either because of their immorality or because of their assumptions about the superfluity or downright absurdity of any positive religion. There is a further question that needs to be put to these worthy men. They must certainly be aware that in proportion to those who believe in the preservation of celibacy they are not even one to a thousand. In particular they must surely have noticed that the people are against the abolition of celibacy. Admittedly the authors of the *Denkschrift* disregard this as a trivial matter, claiming that the people follow "custom, tradition, or a father's faith and calling without the need or the capacity to give an account of what they do." This would be fair enough if it were really true, as

---

20. "With respect to their relationship to the Church to which they belong, we can usefully divide the Catholics of our day into three classes. The first and most numerous class is formed by the mass of the people . . . A second class is formed by those who have given up all participation in their Church . . . Between these two extremes stands a third class of those who combine with participation in their Church and the desire to see her as pure and as worthy as possible a measure of education and knowledge which both invites them and enables them to reflect on Church matters and to test them against generally prevailing ideas of morality and religion" (*Denkschrift* p. 3).

our authors claim, that "celibacy normally emerged in times of great unrest and revolutions, and did so only as a tool."[21] But this kind of talk seems almost like something that might have been heard in the inmost depths of the most absolute Asiatic monarchy. If we did not know for sure that in Baden a constitutional regime has quite definitely been introduced which presumes a guardianship of the people, the most sharp-eyed observer would certainly not have gleaned the information from this passage. There is real food for reflection in the fact that one of the petitioners, Herr Duttlinger, himself a people's representative (i.e. one of those *who should be an organ of the people*), is pressing before the People's Chamber of Representatives for the abolition of celibacy, even though he knows that this institution which the people's representatives want to eliminate is actually supported by the people! If the people are to be declared incapable of making an independent judgement, how can a person who has the calling to be nothing but an organ of the people—which means to proclaim the will of the people to the regime—how can he, I ask, hold himself to be *capable*? Surely it must be the case that expressing the will of someone incapable effectively means declaring oneself to be incapable too, insofar as one is representing that incapable person.

I am moreover struck by the fact that in the third part of the *Denkschrift* the earliest church constitution is referred to as showing that alongside the bishop and the presbyterate the people too had a part in the administration of the Church.[22] What does this prove? That today too the people has its vote to cast which—as has been admitted—is in favour of celibacy? Or that today the question should be decided according to the opinion of the earliest Christian people who first introduced celibacy? I am quite unable to find my way out of this labyrinth; I must continue my quest to resolve these difficult cases using the method appropriate to my own limitations, a method to which I have had to resort several times already in the absence of any other options, namely that of reading this text as the joint composition—or indeed the contradictions—of several authors. But now I must break off to emphasize something else very important.

---

21. Cf. *Denkschrift*, p. 4.

22. "The principle of the Catholic Church is built on the firm foundation that all church power is limited, in the sense that the president may not push through his views against the crucial vote of his presbyterate and the other members of the diocese" (*Denkschrift*, p. 101).

One point that is likely to be made here is that married priests are more closely tied to the state through their families. But to this the answer is that a person who is not loyal to his sovereign out of fear of God will not be loyal to that sovereign for the sake of his family. Concern for his family can indeed make someone more likely to be disloyal to his duty in doubtful circumstances than the celibate priest who needs to worry only about himself. And dependence on the Pope is not likely to be excessive where married priests are concerned, fears of some new Gregory VII would soon be overcome! The approach here is reminiscent of that of someone who is just getting hungry but worrying that he might some time be thirsty! Or as if someone in an advanced stage of tuberculosis were to be worrying and fretting about a possible stroke resulting from his being too much fired up with energy in the future!

Celibacy does of course provide unmistakable evidence of the non-unity of Church and State. As no clear-thinking person could fail to recognize, celibacy is an ordinance which could never have sprung from roots which the state had removed. An institution devoted purely to bringing souls to birth for a higher life beyond this one; an institution wholly unconcerned with the multiplication of earthly citizens in this life and focusing purely on enrollment in an invisible world order and taking cognizance of the citizens of earthly kingdoms only insofar as time streams back into eternity from which it has flowed; an institution like that can never grow on the soil of earthly states and for that reason, as long as it flourishes in the Church, it will form a living protest against all attempts to make the Church lose herself in the state.[23] But precisely because celibacy has always maintained the polarity of Church and State and will always prevent the submission of the former to the latter, it will also limit the extent to which the Church falls into worldliness, constantly thwarting the unfortunate tendencies of certain Church office-holders to subject the state to the Church. The mere existence of celibacy as such shows that we have something very different to honor in the Church than that the Church be subjected

---

23. At the age of only 32 Möhler shows powerful prophetic insight! If any one of the three Christian Confessions had anything to set against state totalitarianism from then until now, it was the Catholic Church—on account of her celibate clergy. One need only think of Bismarck and his nationalism or Hitlerism, one need only think of Marxism, so recently defeated in East and West. The Catholic Church has always been the least prepared to compromise.

to the state as if it were something worldly that is part of the realm of
the state—and justifiably regarded as such. At the same time, celibacy
eternally proclaims that the state is something quite different from
her, that it does not belong to her domain, and that her servants cannot
show more strikingly that earthly power is not their affair by any
better means than through celibacy, which places them in a quite separate circle of government and also points us to a higher order of things.
The issue with celibacy is the polar opposite to the issue with the
state as expressed in the bible passage: "My kingdom is not of this
world."[24] But although this saying has been applied often enough in
modern times to show that the Church possesses no power in civil
affairs, it does in fact also spell out very clearly that no authority over
the Church was entrusted by Christ to the civil authorities. The celibacy of the clergy promotes not just the freedom of the Church from
the state, but also the freedom of the state from the Church.

Here however we appeal against our adversaries not to mere
thoughts and empty ideas but to the clear testimony of history. The
reason that Gregory VII imposed the age-old law of celibacy was to
recover the Church's freedom. But equally, when the Church authority
asserted an excessive dominance over the state authority and threatened to become worldly, the strongest opponents of this secularizing
tendency emerged from the ranks of the celibate clergy itself. Celibacy
bred in those who honored it in accordance with its nature a spiritual,
ideal, and noble outlook higher than the purely earthly one, which
for that very reason inevitably found the involvement of the clergy in
the wordly arena very objectionable. Celibacy contained within itself
the antidote to its own exaggeration. "[a]nd yet those who talk like
this will never tell us, as far as I know, in what place, in what circumstance it happened that one of the apostles made himself a judge
over men, to decide on the division of inheritances or the distribution
of land. I certainly find in Scripture that the Apostles appeared before
judges; but nowhere do I read that they took their places on the
tribunal of judgement: that will happen one day, but it has never happened yet . . . why should they not disdain to pronounce on earthly
and perishable interests, when one day in heaven they will pronounce
on the angels themselves? It is over the crimes of men and not over

---

24. Cf. John 18:36.

their material interests that power has been given to you . . . Where
does it seem to you that more dignity and power is to be found: in
remitting sins, or in settling disputed inheritances? There is simply no
comparison here. These vulgar earthly interests have their own special
judges: the kings and princes of the earth. Why then trespass on the
territory of others? Why take your scythe into a harvest that belongs
to another? Not that you would be unworthy to do so; but it is
unworthy that you should become absorbed in such activities . . ."[25]
Examples of this are St. Bernard, the Minorites under Louis of
Bavaria, Petrarch, Gerson, Pierre D'Ailly, and Nicole de Clemange.
In case these names are too remote and the activities of the men who
bore them too little known, I will refer to a fact which should have
some impact on these particular opponents of ours. Who were the
supreme advocates of Gallican liberties? Who defended the independence of the state from the Church most brilliantly? The leading
names are those of Edmund Richer, Archbishop Petrus de Marca,
Launoy, Dupin, Bossuet, Natalis Alexander, and Fleury, among others:
but everyone knows that these men were all celibates (and that they
were guilty of numerous exaggerations to boot). Riegger, Pehem, Sauter,
and Rechberger, married Canonists all and frequently enough cited in
the *Denkschrift*, actually put barely a single thought into their works
that was not borrowed from the aforementioned celibate theologians.

I could say so much more on this subject, but I will content
myself with one observation. While the above celibate theologians
represented both the effects of celibacy I have referred to in untroubled
unity—the one affirming the independence of the Church over
against the state, the other freeing the state from interference by the
Church authorities in its rights—they also had their caricatures alongside them, and these were equally promoted by celibate priests.
The tendency to spiritualism inherent in celibacy was pushed by these
men to extremes. St. Bernard's ideal was distorted in Arnold of Brescia,
Gerson's in Hus, and that of Erasmus in Luther, who in his lonely
celibate cell exaggerated the spirituality of the Church so much that
he made her quite invisible and robbed her of *all* power. This meant

---

25. Möhler inserts the Latin text in a footnote: "For example *de considerat.* I. 1. c. VI. Non
monstrabunt, puto . . . Non quia indigni vos, sed quia indignum vobis talibus insistere." Cf.
Bernard of Clairvaux, *De consideratione ad Eugenium papam*, in *Sämtliche Werke* Latin/German,
vol. 1, ed. Gerhard B. Winkler, 866 pp., Innsbruck: Tyrolia 1990; here, pp. 643ff.

in fact that she could simply no longer exist, so he subjected her totally to the state. The accusation that celibacy necessarily preserves a hostile relationship between Church and State is thus entirely without substance.

There is a point related to this one that I now want to discuss. No social association worthy of the name can subsist without self-awareness or without the clear knowledge of its value and its worth as a whole. Where such an awareness is not present, what is lacking is not so much the capacity to know as the actual worth and value about which one might know. It is an awareness that really only develops in tension with other associations and it then appears as a spirit of solidarity. Unfortunately, for a long time now events have been conspiring to stifle both the Church's self-awareness and her feeling of solidarity, things which are so crucial if she is to enjoy both well-being and the respect of others, whereas she suffocates for lack of them. Many men perfectly honorable in their way have expended great energy to reduce the independence of the Church and her freedom in her own inner administration to being purely nominal, to intrude the hand of state officialdom into all the branches of that administration, and to leave nothing else to her own powers of knowledge, will and action: in a word, to portray the relationship of governments with Church authorities as that of guardian to ward and to translate just such a way of looking at things into practice. Nobody seemed to notice that this was bound to disseminate and settle in people's minds a notion that was dangerous for the life of the Church, the idea that the Church had become so powerless and weak-minded that she had to be put under administration—like some tired and stupid old crone who was no longer competent to care for herself, so incapable had she become of providing for her own well-being and true needs. There is no need to devote any further consideration to showing how far such a view must weaken all self-confidence in the Church and undermine every joyful and cheerful feeling of life and all encouragement to effective activity, crippling the boldness of her intellectual enterprise—for that is something which can emanate only from awareness of an indwelling power. In the end, what prevails is a dull, lame, and stiff apathy.

The situation that obtains in the Catholic Church is very different from that which obtains in Protestantism. In the Catholic

Church as a true community all self-awareness, all power, all drive to activity, all awareness of the value and worth of the individual and of the bloom and beauty of an inner fullness of life, majesty, and splendor depends on the whole, and when the Church as a whole behaves according to the way prescribed, she develops an astounding wealth of ideas. Then the sciences and the arts flourish and the most wonderful manifestations of life and activity are bred out of inner holiness and brought to the light of the day. Such times produced Augustine, Chrysostom, Aquinas, Erwin von Steinbach, Dante, Michelangelo, Raphael, Bossuet, Fénelon, Bourdaloue, Massillon, Descartes, Malebranche, Racine, and a brilliant swarm of other heroes in the front rank. When the whole as such suffers however, then all power dries up in individuals, all the members stiffen, all joy disappears, all vitality and inspiration weaken.

Things are different with Protestantism. As long as Luther's and Calvin's teaching was accepted as true, there was no poetry, no history, and no philosophy in the Protestant movement. There is absolutely no doubt that as long as the Protestant community was still Lutheran, it had no philosophy, and when it got a philosophy, it was Lutheran no longer. Their faith flees philosophy and their philosophy flees faith. Once the faith that binds everything together had been conquered so that nothing common bound all the members together, Kant came to prominence—and he eradicated all positive religion completely from his church—then Fichte, who had to defend himself before a Court of Justice on a charge of rejecting God, then Schelling, who did not reject God but held everything to be God. Then came Goethe, with inimitable beauty painting life as it is without faith, without hope, and without love.[26] Goethe's *Iphigenia in Aulis*, the work of a complete Hellenist, is on a par with Sophocles and Euripides, and at the same time as a Christian he could come out with the confessions of a beautiful soul. Goethe faithfully mirrored the Protestant Church of his day in its many-sided education, in its high culture of externals, in its taste and its striving for the beauty of forms, in its indecisiveness as to whether and what it ought to believe or not believe, in its wavering between Christianity and Hellenism and between

---

26. It is quite unbelievable how the young Möhler senses that the hidden source of Goethean creativity is nihilism. Beyond faith, hope, and love nothing but cold nature awaits us. Goethe's pantheism ultimately proved to be the illusion of life—nihilism.

heaven and earth—with an overwhelmingly predominant tendency to the latter. That was the golden age of Protestant literature, and it had to be seen in its fullest development for the essence of Protestantism to be made known fully. This essence has now emerged openly into the world of appearances and it can no longer remain hidden from anyone.

Protestant literature is a great phenomenon in the history of mankind, but a very dark stain on the history of Christianity. In the Catholic Church, science and art were always Christian, and when they could not make this character prevail, they preferred to remain silent. What is quite undeniable is that the further the principle of individualism was pushed in Protestantism, the more brilliant its productions. Conversely, the more united and living the community in Catholicism, the more the arts and sciences blossom in her bosom. The Protestants are all that they can be when they destroy all common faith and all of church life, while we are all that we can be when the common faith grips us powerfully and works in us. The weaker the ecclesial sense is in Protestants, the more it is in its element; the stronger it is in Catholics, the more it is in its element.

I will now make the appropriate application of this observation. When the Protestant Churches wholly agree with the states in which they have become predominant, this is not only quite appropriate and essential to their human origin, but also an indispensable condition of their existence. For since they are not capable of producing within themselves any principle that holds them together, they must hold it from outside through the state, which applies benevolent ties to their unregulated and thoroughly ex-centric movements. But these bonds limit the individual very little on account of the fact that the whole, the Church, has actually gone over into the state. For as we have observed, the individual is woven into the whole only by very weak threads, and the character of the Protestant loses very little thereby. When for example the state requires of Protestant clerics that they swear an oath to follow the credal books which are supposed to contain the teaching of the Bible, the pastors are able to make such inner reservations that the oath is reduced to a farce. Some say they are in no way obliged to teach in accordance with the credal books *because* they agree with the Holy Scripture but only *insofar as* they agree (not quia *cum sacris scripturis consentiunt,* but rather *quatenus consentiunt*), while others want to think that this oath merely binds them not to teach *against* those books. Others distinguish between their public and private personae; the former teaches what is required, the latter thinks and writes what pleases. Still others point to the gulf between the faith of the man in the street and the findings of scholarship. Very many pastors preach therefore to the free Protestant people about original sin, the divinity of Christ, and the like, while at the same time scoffing at the one and denying the other in the name of the furtherance of scholarship. Meanwhile they mock the Jesuits for having introduced the damnable mental reservation *(reservatio mentalis)* and for teaching a "poisonous" casuistics. So then we can see that the dissolution of the Protestant Churches into the state does not damage the character of the Protestant and that it is quite in order for the pastors to be married and thereby to be tied by yet another bond to the state. They would not have rushed to embrace the Prussian Liturgy in their hundreds[27]— even though it is too Christian for them—had their hearts not been set on their jobs and their career plans which the need to support a family makes so essential. Such ties do not particularly hinder the further evolution of the Protestant character. The pastors are happy to "put on" the Liturgy, as they say, even while they do not believe in its contents, reasoning that when an actor plays the part of King Thoas in Goethe's *Iphigenia*, everyone knows full well that it is just a job and that if so required he would throw himself with equal bravura into the role of Weislingen in *Götz von Berlichingen*. The Protestant retains his particular character absolutely, irrespective of the fact that his church has lost all its independence and lacks any knowledge of values.

Where the Catholic is concerned, the situation is precisely the reverse. Individually and by himself, as we have seen, he is nothing and can be nothing, he must be taken up into the whole, to which he belongs not externally but inwardly, not according to appearance but according to essence, not just fifty per cent but one hundred per cent, and he shares the destiny of the whole in every way. Now it becomes crystal clear how much credence the *Denkschrift* will gain

---

27. Möhler is referring to the Prussian Union of 1817 in which Reformed and Lutheran Christians were to come together into "a newly revived Christian Church." The introduction of the new order in worship, the Liturgy of 1822, started the liturgy battle, which was at its height at the time Möhler was writing. (Cf. K. Kupisch, Art. "Agendenstreit" in: RGG (3rd ed.) 1, 173ff.)

with reasonable readers when it calls for Catholic priests to be married *in order to make the Church more dependent on the state and to diminish the influence of the Pope on it!* If we go but one step further towards the state, we shall be completely lost. The inevitable result of this would be to detach us from the Church and to undermine our strength of purpose, leading necessarily to radical damage to the fiber of all the longings and nerves not just of the body but also of its *individual members*. It cannot escape any well-intentioned, thinking, and educated observer that German Catholics are called carefully to grasp every factor that can heighten and empower the self-awareness of the Church and her community spirit, so how can we possibly accept the abolition of celibacy, whose opponents openly back its elimination in order to achieve goals which we need to put all our efforts into opposing, goals which threaten our Catholic existence and which involve the denial of all hope for a better future? It is in vain that the sciences are freely praised, or that literary institutions are renewed which a melancholy era had robbed the Catholics of in France, Germany and elsewhere, when the moral force and noble inspiration are lacking which can come to us Catholics only out of a Church that is blossoming as a whole. We cannot be what we should be for the state if we do not first of all stand in a right relationship to the Church.

The Pope is to step more into the background! Because we Catholics are still powerful in him? Because he has just won honorable Concordats for us? Just try leaving the bishops to deal with the regimes, to endow cathedral chapters, seminaries, and the like, and see what a fist they make of it! For the states deal with bishops as with subordinates, whereas the Pope is respected as an acknowledged power independent of all states. In him, we are free. Nothing is more essential for us, as we have said, than to nurture and promote the spirit of community, since nothing prospers among us without it. The Pope is the center point of our community, so anyone who tries to push him out of the way will end up eliminating the community at the same time. The community of the faithful does not consist purely in the idea of an association of believing persons, nor indeed purely in feeling. Rather, when the community feeling itself is healthy and the idea of it powerful and active in life, it is expressed in a common constitution and bound up in its perfection with a *person*. Nobody can understand the Christian religion and love it apart from the person of Christ himself.

In modern times some have expressed regret that we have not managed to retain Christian ideas without Christ, but they have misunderstood Christianity and failed to grasp its essence.[28] In loving our princes we love the Fatherland, and love of Fatherland without love, loyalty, and obedience to the ruler is devoid of truth and power, it is a lie of our time, impure in its origins and destructive for the Fatherland itself. It is in focusing on the princes that love of the Fatherland first discovers its sure and firm object and develops a definite and noble tendency. So it is with Catholic community spirit too. It is first perfected and finds expression, truth, and firmness in the persons of the bishops and the Pope. The intimate inner connection between honor for the Pope and Catholic community spirit is clearly manifest in the way that in modern times the decline of the latter has led to the former being weakened. So if the *Denkschrift* argues for the abolition of celibacy in order to make the bonds which tie us to the Pope looser, then we shall defend celibacy precisely in order to maintain and strengthen the connection with him.

Why is it in fact that the enemies of celibacy always seem to be hostile to the Pope while its defenders are on his side? We have seen how celibacy is a living testimony of faith in a constant outpouring of higher powers in this world and of the omnipotent rule of truly infinite forces in the finite, so that it speaks for the origin of the Church in a higher order of things. Inasmuch as he is the visible center point for all Catholics wherever they are located among the earthly empires, the Pope likewise is a living symbol of the existence of a life lifted above all that is finite and earthly. But given that our age is inclined to see everything only as finite and oppose any faith in an influence of the infinite in the finite—indeed is really hostile to any idea that the infinite may exist in the finite, then the middle point of the Church must necessarily be attacked from the same side as the one hostile to celibacy. Both bear witness to the Church having a higher origin and higher goals than anything that could be understood as deriving from the state. The more people sought to make everything

---

28. The separation of the revealer from the content of revelation, to which Möhler is referring, reached its high point with *G. E. Lessing*. Thus, he writes in the year 1780: "Education gives to man nothing which he might not educe out of himself; it gives him that which he might educe out of himself, only quicker and more easily. In the same way too, Revelation gives nothing to the human species, which the human reason left to itself might not attain; only it has given, and still gives to it, the most important of these things earlier" (*The Education of the Human Race*, § 4).

finite by deriving it from the state, the more the papal primacy and celibacy have to be a joint object of hatred. On the other hand, the inner connection we have been discussing motivated defenders of celibacy to be instinctive defenders of the primacy, and friends of the primacy to be advocates of celibacy.

I am certainly not arguing for the complete separation of Church and State or proposing that they be indifferent or even down-right hostile to each other. Nothing could be further from my intention than this unreasonable starting-point. Nor would I want to offer even the slightest support to the idea that the clergy should trespass outside their spiritual and ecclesial sphere of activity. What I do want is for the clergy to concentrate on living wholly within this sphere rather than pushing their way into state power. For in Germany it is not arrogance that is to be feared on the part of the clergy but *coward-ice*. *Courage* is equi-distant from both of these, and should be encouraged or supported in them, not undermined. In respect of our clergy it is not their *overweening power* but their *powerlessness* that should arouse our concern. Midway between these two there is the state of *being strong in oneself,* and the least that can be desired is that the clergy be strong in themselves. The Church has no wealth to enable her to exercise influence herself or even simply to obstruct overweening external influences on her servants. She has little in the way of rank or honors to bestow in the Church Provinces of the Upper Rhine, for everybody knows that in reality these are in the gift of the government. To be able to bestow money and status is the way to maintain the most influence and the greatest power in the circumstances of this world. So the Church is no longer strong in herself, and therefore celibacy is to be abolished! Why? In order to create a tie that will bind the Church more closely to the state and limit the excesses (!) of papal and spiritual power! In order therefore to abolish almost the only means of allowing freedom of spirit to blossom in our clergy, and a means that is purely ethical, purely Christian, purely Catholic to boot! Only a free ethical motivation will put itself at the service of the freedom of the Church, a motivation which derives solely from religious faith in God's almighty power to work in the hearts of men— but it is this power, a power so specific to the Church, that they are desperate to rid us of! It is perfectly appropriate that the Church has been stripped of worldly glamour and wealth on the ground that she

should not make use of such means.[29] But is she now to be robbed of
her purely spiritual powers as well? Her ethical inspiration is feared
more than any power to bestow wealth and status, and this is perfectly
appropriate. But for that very reason the Church will never be
deprived of her real power.[30]

---

29. Möhler is referring to the secularization of 1803, which nationalized almost all of
German monastic property. He accepts a sense of indifference towards external goods, but he
does not want to see the Church robbed of her spiritual possessions.

30. [Möhler's footnote] "We have nothing to say here about the third part of the *Denkschrift*,
we need only express our surprise at the clumsiness and lack of practical tact which seems to be
typical of the professors. First of all they want to transport the present constitution of the Church
through testimonies from Cyprian and others straight back into that of the Third Century, and
then to remove celibacy in the midst of modern times, and all that in a fortnight!" (Cf.
Denkschrift, Part III, pp 86–120).

Afterword

By Dieter Hattrup

THE SITUATION THEN AND NOW

Tübingen and later Munich theologian Johann Adam Möhler (1796–1838) was called "the noble Möhler"even in his lifetime. At a distance of more than one and a half centuries we can still see the force of this opinion. It is not only his portrait from that time, his outward appearance, that tells us what was meant by that word "noble"— though this does give us a sense of the inspired driving force of his character. A friend from his student days described his appearance twenty years later: "The soulful look, the noble countenance, the earnest and yet friendly-looking eyes, the whole dignified posture of the man had something attractive and at the same time imposing about it."[1] Yet in actual fact the inner man appears only to the inner eye, and that sees him more clearly in his writings than in portraits and copperprints, and especially in his passionate polemic against the weak spirit of the Enlightenment and for the spirit of celibacy. For in this institution (to borrow an expression used by Möhler himself of the celibacy of the priest in the following of Christ), living and learning, inner and outer, being and consciousness, divine and human meet together in such a way that the world must close its eyes while believers will see.

The writing, which appeared anonymously for the first time in 1828 as a review in *der Katholik*, and which will here be referred to as the *Examination*[2] (= *Beleuchtung*), grew progressively beyond the confines of a mere book review and developed into a confession of faith by Möhler, containing insights that he himself had only gained a short time earlier through the study of the Church Fathers and

---

1. Stephan Lösch, *Johann Adam Möhler*. Vol. 1: *Gesammelte Aktenstücke und Briefe*, 551 pp., Munich 1928; here 497ff. (No further volumes of this work appeared.)

2. Johann Adam Möhler, "Beleuchtung der *Denkschrift für die Aufhebung des den katholischen Geistlichen vorgeschriebenen Cölibates*," in *Der Katholik: eine religiöse Zeitschrift zur Belehrung und Warnung* 8 (1828) 1–32, 257–337.

through a personal conversion. It was soon known to be authored by Möhler in wider circles, and in the same year it appeared as an off-print.[3] Today it is very difficult to find a copy. The easiest way to access it is in a collection of Möhler's writings put together by Döllinger, the text of which is generally the foundation for the present one.[4] It is not only, as the term *Beleuchtung* suggests, an "examination," a reading of the well-meant, but forced Freiburg *Denkschrift* of the year 1828 whose purpose was to abolish the celibacy requirement for Catholic priests: but it is also the product of a personal revelation which had only recently been vouchsafed to Möhler.

A few years earlier he would have found the program of a few southwestern [German] professors much less offensive and unspiritual and much less cold and detached from experience; for he himself had once thought like the authors of the *Denkschrift*, who took their guidelines not from the Bible and the history of revelation, but from the "context of our age and our nation."[5] In the view of the learned Freiburgers [of 1928], the celibacy requirement for priests does not suit the age—so it must be eliminated. But tailoring measures to our age will always be liable to trigger a winter for the Church. This kind of thinking has ceased to regard time as flowing up to the coming Kingdom of God and it assumes that we learn what the Kingdom of God can and cannot be from the intellectual movements and trends of the age. It contains the threat that if wise professorial foresight is not listened to—which "in such cases counsels us to look not just at the immediate present but also to the experiences of the past and the possibilities of the future,"[6] and if celibacy is not abolished, then the future powers of the Church will be damaged; here I am expressing an anxiety of Möhler's time in the language of today.[7] This was the thinking of 1828, and we can see that anxiety about the future

3. Johann Adam Möhler, *Beleuchtung der an die Ständeversammlung in Carlsruhe eingereichten Denkschrift für die Aufhebung des den katholischen Geistlichen vorgeschriebenen Cölibates,* Mainz 1828.

4. Johann Adam Möhler, "Beleuchtung der *Denkschrift für die Aufhebung des den katholischen Geistlichen vorgeschriebenen Cölibates.* Mit drei Aktenstücken," in *Gesammelte Schriften und Aufsätze,* ed. J J I Döllinger, Regensburg, 1839, 177–267.

5. *Denkschrift für die Aufhebung des den katholischen Geistlichen vorgeschriebenen Zölibates. Mit drei Aktenstücken.* Druck und Verlag Friedrich Wagner, Freiburg, 1828; here, 65.

6. *Denkschrift,* p. 144.

7. Cf. Franz-Xaver Kaufmann/Johann Baptist Metz, *Zukunftsfähigkeit. Suchbewegungen im Christentum,* Freiburg, 1987.

troubled the Church greatly in the past too—or at least it troubled
a few learned gentlemen who classed themselves as belonging to the
Church. Before venting their anxieties, these gentlemen felt it necessary first of all to make the point that they were members of the
Church as a class.[8] Möhler happily acknowledges that theirs may be a
prophetic voice, perhaps the priests are lost in slumber and the Church
in Germany in danger of being killed in its sleep. These men may be
like the Old Testament prophets who were impelled by divine inspiration to stand up and shake the people awake, proclaiming the laws and
works of God to man.[9] But "the prophet who prophesies peace can
be recognized as one truly sent by Yahweh only when his word comes
true" (Jeremiah 28:9), and so a look at the prophetic quest of that time
to ensure the salvation of the faithful through the elimination of
celibacy will help us to be discriminating about the prophets of today.

It is easy to be pious among the pious and noble among the
noble, but such people were as rarely to be encountered in the Catholic
Church in Baden of those times as they are in the Catholic Church
of our reunified Germany of today, where many theologians want
to make the mass media the pulpit for their propaganda and to mould
the future of the faith through polemic. Möhler opposed uncatholic
and unbelieving expressions of opinion in his own day, and this
continues to come through in his writing down to today. We can test
our own courage by the courage of his little book, which sifts the
arguments against celibacy so effectively that little remains of their
substance. Today's objections to celibacy are the same as yesterday's:
in the first place, we are told that it doesn't suit the spirit of the
age—and in the second place we are told that there are not enough
priests. The first argument masquerades as respect for the spirit of
the bible ("Jesus himself did not leave any celibacy rule to his disciples") while the second hides behind an apparent concern for the
future of the Church.

There are no other arguments and there cannot really be any,
for these two cover the objections to religious virginity from its origins
and down to the present day. Möhler is a Church historian and he
pursues the refutation of the *Denkschrift* on the terrain of Church

---

8. Cf *Denkschrift*, p. 3, or Part V, note 32 above.
9. Cf. Chapter 1, this volume. p. 1.

history. He demonstrates how every age is at odds with celibacy right down to his own time. An uncatholic and unspiritual way of thinking does not understand celibacy at any time and never wanted to do so, and anti-celibacy thinking has always sought to explain [vows of] poverty, celibacy, and obedience to Jesus as being gratuitous additions to his message of the Kingdom of God. The only legitimate point in the *Denkschrift* is that the Christian must have courage. Quite right too! We can all heartily agree with its authors on this, it is something that has undoubtedly always been the case. It definitely requires more courage to make the promise of celibacy and chastity before a bishop than to climb a Himalayan peak twenty-five thousand feet high. There is no point in warning courageous people that climbing mountains is not for the cowardly! (Courage on its own is not enough for that, incidentally, it also requires a head for heights!) Möhler was like a new Stephen, whose wisdom and spirit the Libyans and Cyrenaicans could not withstand—as it says in the Acts of the Apostles! (Acts 6). It is worth recording that Möhler's premature death marked the beginning of a 100-year ceasefire in the celibacy battle, with the Catholic Church flourishing just as he had predicted. Möhler transcends the shallowness of his environment and gazes into the future, which he sees very differently from the futurologists of the day—predicting that the most distinguished young persons will follow the inner promptings of their nature as purified by God's Spirit, and calling it the highest freedom to have done so.[10] With Möhler's vision we are not so far from that of a Pierre Teilhard de Chardin (1881–1955), who foresaw the transformation of a yearning human nature—if the world survives: either adoration or decline![11] In his *The Eternal Feminine* he shows that chastity is the highest form not just of Christian but also of evolutionary life.[12]

In the "Examination of the *Denkschrift*" we are presented with the essence of Möhler's inner life as priest, theologian, and historian, and we are granted much more than a picture of his personal life,

---

10. Cf. Chapter 5, this volume, p. 66.

11. Ida Friederike Görres, "Die Evolution der Keuschheit" in Id., *Sohn der Erde: Der Mensch Teilhard de Chardin*, 184 pp., Frankfurt 1971, 144–165.

12. "Christ has given me salvation and freedom. When he said: *melius est non nubere*, men took it to mean that I was dead to eternal life. In truth, by those words he restored me to life, with Lazarus—with Magdalen—and set me between himself and men as a nimbus of glory." (Pierre Teilhard de Chardin, *Writings in Time of War*, London: Collins, 1968, p. 315, and "The Eternal Feminine," p. 197.)

much more than a saint's life, much more than a biography, and much more than a classic or a pioneer work of modern theology. Möhler neither makes a parade of his life nor does he put forward detached, analytical, historical, cool, objective, or scholarly arguments. His territory is rather the border area between the private and the public, where what is spiritual in man turns away from the outside world to the inner realm and enters into conversation with God. Only a spiritual director and father confessor can be involved in this inner conversation in a modest way. But Möhler lets himself be challenged from outside, even when distraction and misunderstandings are to be feared, because in this provisional world the inward and outward realms do not yet agree; spirit and nature, person and history still compete. The spiritual existence of a person in the world unfolds in this border area, and the Church History specialist, aroused to anger, perceives that the position from which the battle against the "fortresses" and "bastions" of celibacy is conducted is an unspiritual and uncatholic one. He enters into the arena to strengthen his own existence as priest and to strengthen the faithful in the Church. He does not want the Church to come into line with this world, he does not want to see it become an established church of the state or get sucked into the shallow life of society.

He says what can be said openly. He lets the knower of hearts sense what is in the depths and gives courage and arguments to the beginner who is vaguely seeking a spirit-filled life without really knowing where he is going. Möhler has long since realized that books cannot bring about the abolition of the celibacy rule, for its maintenance is not the work of books, it was not introduced by books, and it will not be driven out by arguments and counter-arguments in books or special issues of journals.[13] It is not human will that is at work in this institution, but the Spirit of Jesus Christ who himself lived poor, celibate, and obedient. Möhler would have preferred to impose an eternal silence on himself and all fellow-polemicists and to entrust no

---

13. The *Theologische Quartalschrift* in Tübingen devoted a special issue to the abolition of the celibacy rule under the title "*Viri probati.*" *ThQ* 172 (1992) 1–78. That ordination of married and "proven men" is only a pretext and that celibacy in the Church is to be completely eliminated is made clear in the introduction to this issue. There it is argued that the "*viri-probati*-ruling" will allow priests to "legitimize" their relationship to a woman (p. 1). How could that be? I thought the argument was only that proved married men are to be ordained? And now the illicit is to be legitimised? Oh for order, order in our minds!

further word on this subject to paper, were it not that the most disad-
vantageous consequences of the *Denkschrift* and similar polemical writings were there right in front of his eyes.[14] The person who is doubtful
of the value of a way of life cannot expect to see any commitment
to it, all he does is discourage it and leave men in their solitude, unable
to dispose of themselves freely. Möhler moves here on the borderline
between the inner and the public, between spiritual experience and
verifiable argument, between God and the world, and it is there that
the voice of the noble heart is heard.

The writing of the young Tübingen scholar is infused with
nobility and energy. He was not simply a learned man, but first and
foremost a spiritual man and a priest who knew something of the
life of the parish community, of the outwardly often bitter existence
of the priest at the coalface, of the generosity that can dwell under a
small roof and that is a sign of the indwelling divine Spirit even in the
remotest backwater. It is worth reading what he could say of the agony
and the ecstasy of the priestly life in an apparently so lackluster and
humiliated Church as that of 1828 [Germany], in which no member
of the aristocracy would think of educating his sons for a Church
career, since after the secularization of 1803 this Church had no positions of honor, rank, and repute on offer.[15] Möhler's fellow-students
were not for the most part endowed with much worldly wealth
and the stipend of the priest was one of the motivations for their calling. They were amazed at Möhler when they found out he came from
a wealthy family.[16] As if released from his pride, as if experiencing a
personal conversion, as if born along by an infinite power which he
had no need to comment on, he wrote on behalf of Spirit-filled
celibacy in cheerful tones. At the same time, his is a perfectly prudent
and clear vision that faces squarely up to the spiritless condition of the
Church for centuries and in his own century. Courageously addressing
the facts as they are, he can discern in them the gentle breath of
the Holy Spirit against the shrill storm of the world, and it is precisely
in the Church that he senses it, the Church to whom the Spirit is
promised, to nobody else but the Church and to nobody apart from

14. Cf. Chapter 1, this volume, p. 1.

15. Cf. Chapter 5, this volume, p. 66.

16. Cf. Balthasar Wörner, *Johann Adam Möhler. Ein Lebensbild. Mit Briefen und kleineren Schriften Möhlers*, ed. Pius Bonifacius Gams, osb, 408 pp., Regensburg, Manz 1866, p. 12.

her. Like a thorn bush that burns without being consumed! So Möhler does not give in to a mood of resignation like the professors of the *Denkschrift* then or a few theological professors today, for whom being different from the world is just too painful; they would rather give up on the discernment of spirits and pursue the eternal pattern of secularism "in the context of our time and our country."

There is no pride in the *Examination,* nor is there any arrogance, it is no sharp spotlight casting a harsh light over its object while leaving everything around in darkness. What shines out from this essay is the bright light of a spring sun in Baden or Württemberg, a warming ray of blue heaven; precious things are to be found everywhere in it as well as an unfettered sense of smiling humor which can occasionally provoke outright laughter—sometimes even to the point of being side-splitting. I confess that I have not laughed so much in recent years as when reading this text—and I don't only read theological literature that is full of solemn courage and wants to make the world a better place! This writing contains none of that pride that is always tinged with anxiety lest some modest sense of power felt momentarily should be lost. We have here someone who seems to have experienced what the Spirit is, what life is, and how grace is quick to go before us, accompanying and perfecting us. Möhler is not at all pleased when grace is mocked in true Enlightenment fashion and condemned as scholastic nonsense.[17] Nature is not capable of doing the works that make celibacy and the Church comprehensible and that indeed bring both to life. Again and again he speaks of noble inspiration, of noble joy, of the noble people and priests with an abundance of conviction and spirit. The spirit of generosity, which Thomas Aquinas calls *Magnanimitas* or great-heartedness of the soul that strives for the highest,[18] suffuses this whole writing on celibacy from the first page to the last. Surely every noble Catholic priest, he asks, can use his freedom to offer a sacrifice of generosity and so obtain his part in the gospel?[19]

It is with such a spirit as this that we have to do in this essay, a spirit of inspiration, a spirit of delight in the inspired word, a spirit

---

17. Cf. Chapter 1, p. 1.

18. "Magnanimitas est virtus, quia tendit ad maxima, secundum rectam rationem." *Summa Theologiae* II-II q. 129 a. 3.

19. Cf. Chapter 1, this volume, p. 1.

that knows how to accept the sharpness of the bible message of the end of days and the sobering facts of history or of the frequently rather mediocre appearance of the clergy. His mind is firmly on the situation of his own time, and he has in his sights a polemical text whose several authors he addresses very bluntly as opponents, but sometimes also as "My dear people!"; he even expresses respect for the author of the second part, though it is a greater respect than he wants to grant to the author of the first part.[20] However the piece is in no way purely a product of a particular historical situation, nor is it dependent on "progress" in exegesis or in the study of Church history, for external progress can only be alienation from the message of Christ in which the nearness of the Kingdom of God is announced.

Paradoxically, modern exegesis has rediscovered the thoroughly eschatological message of Jesus: unfortunately, this has not always led to a deepened faith, for it has often been a matter of mere intellectual curiosity without any real sense of purpose. Starting with the orientalist Reimarus in the eighteenth century, exegetes have been rediscovering the eschatological message that Jesus fully intended to communicate: the message that the time of this world was coming swiftly to an end and that the Kingdom of God stands directly before us. As a deist, Reimarus could only shake his head over this, and his discovery combined with a mix of personal motivations to arouse a burning hatred in him.[21] Others clung to nature and to a belief in the constancy of its laws in preference to accepting the end as proclaimed by Jesus. They transformed the perspective of the truth of Jesus, his life, and his teaching into a myth, a beautiful dream on which nobody can base his life. David Friedrich Strauss is emblematic of this kind of exegesis, an exegesis enslaved to the scientific spirit of the time, offering to the nineteenth century the spectacle of the theologian turned unbeliever.[22]

---

20. Cf. above Chapter 1, this volume, p. 1.

21. See Albert Schweitzer, *The Quest for the Historical Jesus. A Critical Study of its progress from Reimarus to Wrede*, 410 pp., London, A & C Black, 1945; "For hate as well as love can write a Life of Jesus, and the greatest of them are written with hate – that of Reimarus, the Wolfenbüttel Fragmentist, and that of David Friedrich Strauss" (p. 4); "Reimarus was the first, after eighteen centuries of misconception, to have an inkling of what eschatology really was" (p. 23).

22. Cf. also Johann Adam Möhler, "Gedanken nach der Lektüre des Lebens Jesu von Strauss" in: (see note 182), 245–256.

Möhler rises above historical distances, he rises above learned abstraction, he abandons the sceptical attitude of the mere observer, he points to what is the very best means available to the spiritual man for the proclamation of the end of time and the final fulfilment in which absolutely everything will become good again. That means is celibacy! Celibacy is the real freely-chosen symbol that the era of an ever-striving and desirous nature has come to an end because it has been fulfilled in Christ. Christ has saved me, cries Teilhard in a sober intoxication of spirit, and the otherwise futile sexual powers have transformed into a nimbus of glory.[23] Unbelieving scholars discovered the eschatological message of Jesus, felt very proud of their cleverness, but kept their distance from the new Kingdom of God and returned to the endless circle of nature. Since the time of Jesus the Church lives the end of times, and for this reason the spirit of the evangelical counsels and the spirit of celibacy are constantly developing. The world's obduracy is also constantly developing—as you would expect—it does not want to believe in the end of the times and puts all its energies into pushing it away. That is where the difference between teaching and life is!

It is this freedom from the prison of mere nature in which finite man is enclosed that moves and inspires me to make available again to the public Möhler's text of 1828, a text that made little impact when it was first published, a text that was quickly sidelined, a text lost to view almost the moment it appeared: I want to demonstrate its relevance to our situation today. It is little known or not at all. Even the specialists of the Johann-Adam-Möhler Institute in Paderborn don't know what to do with the *Examination,* they slip it in among his miscellaneous works[24] or even omit it entirely from their anthology of his writings.[25] His main works are of course *Einheit in der Kirche* (1825), *Athanasius* (1827) and the *Symbolik* (1832). But then there is also the *Examination* of 1828, whose force, depth, and general cheerfulness

23. Cf. above, note 12.

24. E.g. Harald Wagner, "Johann Adam Möhler" in, Heinrich Fries/Georg Kretschmar (eds.), *Klassiker der Theologie II. Von Richard Simon bis Dietrich Bonhoeffer,* 486 pp., Munich 1983, pp. 111–126; here p. 120.

25. Paul-Werner Scheele, *Johann Adam Möhler, Reihe "Wegbereiter heutiger Theologie."* 374 pp., Graz/Vienna/Cologne 1969. Nonetheless I owe much gratitude to the Johann-Adam-Möhler Institute for Ecumenics and also to the *Erzbischöflichen Akademischen Bibliothek* in Paderborn. Both were exceptionally helpful to me in my quest for books and pictures.

of tone help us to understand celibacy so much the better. How could it not be so, since the dual existences of Möhler as scholar and priest as a life-calling are at one in his personal commitment?

The present essay is also a policy statement, an ecclesiastical policy statement then and now in the battle for the shape of the Church and the priestly office. Möhler's aim is liberation from the historicist thinking that obeys the dictate of some kind of progress idea of the *Zeitgeist*. We cannot call the writing either modern or purely historical, although it is actually both at the same time. Its main aim is to release us from the pressure of the times. For that reason I read it with pleasure and publish it with the same pleasure. It is as though the ink from Möhler's pen has scarcely dried, it feels as though just a few weeks or months must have elapsed since he wrote this *Examination*, we find ourselves rubbing our eyes. Abstracting from the Romantic style of expression, all the arguments for and against have remained the same. But the year was in reality 1828, when things were so bad for celibacy and the priestly way of life that there was officially no monk and no nun to be found in the whole of Germany,[26] and when all the tendencies of the times as the Freiburg Professors had diagnosed them were hostile to the idea of celibacy being mandatory for the priestly office. The monasteries had been suppressed by the state, the spirit of the time looked to harness all energies to the service of society in the name of progress after the Protestant pattern, wanting to draw the Catholic Church and her clergy too into this. Instead of encouraging a spiritual readiness for the Kingdom of God, the Church was concerned as state church for the earthly service of Prince and people. Or rather, the Kingdom of God was to be utility, it was to be understood as economic, political, social, technical, scientific, and cultural progress. In Berlin the theologian of the day proclaimed that the Kingdom of God was simply identical with the advance of civilization.[27] What are monks and nuns to do in such a time, for if they are what they are, they are waiting for the Kingdom of God, while at the very same time—if the prevailing opinion is to be believed—they are actually hindering the coming of it? What is the role of a celibate in the service of the Kingdom of Heaven? It was a time when heads of

26. Cf. Chapter 4. p. 48.
27. See Karl Barth on Friedrich Schleiermacher, cf. Part I (note 9), p. 435.

seminaries, professors, deans, and even bishops were in despair, thinking that the noble experiment of spiritual virginity must be ended on account of its all too meager results. Taking up arms against the pressure of the negative Enlightenment perhaps required more courage from Möhler than did his later enterprise of giving a clear presentation of the doctrinal contrasts between Catholics and Protestants for the first time, though that is the enterprise on which his fame has been founded up to today.[28] For the truth is that his essay on celibacy brought upon him enemies in his own household and at the same time in a personally very sensitive area. Wörner, his first biographer and his associate from his student days, could remember the strength of the impact made by the *Examination*. "Those who found it rather close to home manifested their displeasure by airing various personal insinuations against the author."[29] Such machinations and rumour-mongering are a testimony to how powerful instinctive reactions can be in this area—the uncontrollability of the tongue is a proof of that, and it is amply backed up by the bible. How difficult it is for knowledge to penetrate the heart of the Christian! "Someone who does not trip up in speech has reached perfection and is able to keep the whole body on a tight rein" (James 3:2).

There is always a certain delusion about nature that sets itself against celibacy. Nowadays we only know nature, we do not know grace any more, as Möhler complains when lamenting the shallowness of Enlightenment thinking.[30] In the eighteenth century it was the Enlightenment's unlimited will to progress, in 1930s Germany a *völkisch*-racial fantasm, today it is an insidious psychologizing delusion which aims to bind man to his subconscious drives. This kind of mindset is eternally opposed to celibacy and quite instinctively knows it has to attack celibacy. The same in every age, naturalism makes the *Examination* as up-to-date today as it was then and as it was in between in the era of "Blood and Soil" ideology. Indeed a new abridged edition of extracts from Möhler's work on celibacy appeared (anonymously) with the title *The Undivided Service* in 1938. It printed from a

---

28. Cf. Johann Adam Möhler, *Symbolik oder Darstellung der dogmatischen Gegensätze der Katholiken und Protestanten nach ihren öffentlichen Bekenntnisschriften*, ed. Josef Rupert Geiselmann, Cologne/Olten 1960/1961; 1ˢᵗ ed. 1832.

29. Cf. Wörner (see note 182), 371ff.

30. Cf. Chapter 1, this volume, p. 1.

third to a half of the text along with an introduction and notes. At that time the writing was a useful antidote to *völkisch* "Blood and Soil" naturalism—which refused to recognize anything German in celibacy and thought it would result in the people's fertility being reduced. Its anonymous editor and commentator proudly announced that "along with his numerous other writings Möhler had produced the most sensitive modern study on the celibacy of the priesthood."[31]

What connects the non-theological Freiburg professors of 1828, the Blood and Soil ideologists of 1938, and the Tübingen professors of 1992 whom I have taken as typical of today's opponents of celibacy? I do not want to push the comparison too far and I just want to mention one point: it is the way their thinking is imprisoned within the categories of nature, science, and power. It is a mindset focused on success, failure, and pastoral plans. It is the thinking of this world! No doubt there is a great difference between the professors and the Nazi ideologues: the latter were obsessed with the idea of power while the former believe in the power of ideas, for they have gone through the school of the critique of ideologies. They like to warn us against the abuse of institutions, not dreaming that the most danger-ous institution of the day is not as yet encapsulated in any idea, it is the mass will of the democratized populations of the northern hemi-sphere; they want prosperity, they want it at any price, and they will have nothing to do with any idea of sacrifice.[32] That is the lack of faith of western civilization, which has no intention of giving anything up for the sake of the service of the Church: the result is that statistically there is a shortage of priests. In the long run this cannot be a good thing—and I am not for the moment thinking of spiritual life and celibacy, but rather of the global consumer culture and its plundering of the planet. The idea of modernity has consisted in wanting to use the finite to build the infinite through science, reason, enlightenment, politics, economics, education, Marxism, or consumerism. These are good things in themselves, but unfortunately they are not able to help us attain to the infinite: and yet the infinite is precisely what we cannot

---

31. Johann Adam Möhler, *Der ungeteilte Dienst. Von Grösse und Fährnis jungfräulichen Priestertums* (Annotated selections from Möhler's *Examination of the Denkschrift*), Salzburg-Leipzig , 1938, p. 7.

32. Cf. Carl Friedrich von Weizsäcker, "Gehen wir einer asketischen Weltkultur entgegen?" in Id., *Deutlichkeit*, Munich 1979, 73–113.

stop striving for. We find God only insofar as we let him come to us: Christ, the God who has come. This knowledge that the infinite cannot be reached through the finite must spell the end of modernity. Are we really under an obligation to show reverence to the transient spirit of the times just because a few unspiritual priests or communities are sulking?

As always it seems that the clergy themselves are the problem: in 1828 they were said to be "but a shadow of spiritual men," in 1938 they were apparently so numerous and so full of inner strength that German blood was impaired by their unwillingness to procreate . . . where is the flashpoint in 1992? Modern clergy are certainly well educated, and in view of the overpopulation of the earth they are clearly in tune with the times, but apparently it is the communities that are suffering, for there are too few priests, according to today's Catholic scholars. The differences between the three situations are certainly great, but they are really only on the level of tendencies, for all the convictions involved are totally this-worldly. The categories have remained the same: nature, influence, power, or (to use the modern slogan) fitness for the future: and the common assumption is that we must hold the reins in our own hands if we want the good for men, for the poor, for the oppressed, for neglected members of the community. But in truth the real Church has never thought in these terms: she has always looked to the Lord and asked how she could imitate him in proclamation and suffering.

Möhler's text reads for all the world as if it had been written for today. The same constellation of arguments is on offer in the theological world of today as it was then, and as it was in between. The battle is fought out against the background of the modern determination to assign to nature an autonomy apart from God and apart from grace. The issues that are paraded as crucial are "a deepened understanding of the Bible," "human rights in the Church," or "the need for adequate fundamental pastoral care"—this latter being another term that entered the vocabulary of modern pastoral theology from the time of the Enlightenment via utilitarian-style thinking. There are three kinds of benefit to be gained from a reading of this work: it is spiritually fortifying, it develops our theological knowledge, and—last but not least—it offers elevated literary pleasures that can awaken a sense of the meaning of words. And over it all there presides a benign

Easter smile, a heavenly cheerfulness, a humour that is often ironic but never cynical. Why should anyone despair when he is celebrating the presence of the Kingdom so close at hand in his own life!

Commentary on the Text

(I) Möhler begins by taking stock of the current situation:[33] how do things stand in the year 1828 with regard to the Catholic Church in Baden and Württemburg? What does she look like? What do things look like to the Freiburg lay professors who put together the *Denkschrift* and who claim for themselves a particular competence in questions of the spiritual life on the ground of their elevated "degree of education and knowledge"? They claim to belong to a particular class of Catholics that is equipped to reflect on matters regarding the Church and to have the right to pass judgement on those matters in the light of current ideas of morality and religion.[34] We too must ask what is the situation of the Church [today].

Of course it is in crisis—but then things were not going too well for her in those days either, when there was also a worrying shortage of clergy. On that point Möhler is quite at one with his opponents, and he praises them without the least hint of irony for having raised their voices publicly against shallow and worthless clerics who are a disappointment to him as well. Where have all the capable clergy gone? Have the priests gone flocking back to the fleshpots of Egypt? (Exodus 16:3) Clearly the clergy of his day must have been falling prey to a material and worldly lifestyle, they were obviously not a pretty sight.

Möhler does not make any attempt to gloss over the picture, and indeed he has personal knowledge of this situation, having witnessed it at first hand in parishes and seminaries. As a professor in Tübingen he criticized a parish priest in Ehingen for his "mincing about and his lack of zeal and industry."[35] The state of the clergy seems to have been lamentable and their general demeanor was gravely lacking in spiritual depth. Though they were not entirely ignorant, there was a lack of spirituality about them and they seemed to be remote from

---

33. Chapter 1, this volume: "Celibacy in the year 1828."
34. Cf. Chapter 5, note 30.
35. Cf. Lösch (see note 1), 352.

any higher realm. So Möhler was not at all unsympathetic to the claims made in the *Denkschrift* about the prevailing materialistic orientation among the clergy.

Nor is the Church in Germany and Europe in a good state 165 years later. That is how far back we need to look to see our own present situation in context. Spiritual, political, and economic developments are constantly opening up space for similar experiences. There is a Roman program for the New Evangelization[36] but the Church worries about her future. It is true that since the time of Möhler she has outlived all her opponents, though without doing a great deal of the fighting herself—like Gideon of old, who reduced his soldiers to a total of 300 and let the Lord fight for Israel (Judges 7:8). She has been repeatedly and severely oppressed and tyrannized—by Bismarck's nationalism, by Hitler's Nazism, and then by totalitarian Marxism, each of which all set out to crush Christianity in general and the Roman Church in particular. Even the secularization thesis, according to which religion will slowly die out, has turned out to be the opposite of the truth.[37] The Church's situation today is nonetheless not good, at least not as regards either the general mentality of her members or that of the holders of priestly office. Today's Tübingen professors tell us that there is "widespread discord among the clergy," and so they march to the razing of the bastions; as a means of remedying the prevalent low morale, they offer strategies for the conquest of the "mighty fortress," the "bastion of mandatory celibacy."[38]

On the subject of morale—then as now—there is nothing to discuss. When someone says he is in low spirits, then he is just that. This kind of state of mind is self-generated and feeds on itself, we all know that. The widespread discord of today echoes the worldly orientation of the clergy of Möhler's time, though there are certainly

36. Cf.: *Die europäischen Bischöfe und die Neu-Evangelisierung Europas. Rat der europäischen Bischofskonferenzen,* published by the Secretariat of the German Bishops" Conference, 423 pp., Bonn 1991 (*Stimmen der Weltkirche* no 32).

37. See the remark by [the then] Bishop of Rottenburg, formerly professor in Tübingen [now—2007—Cardinal Walter Kasper]: "The theory about the irreversible march of secularization has apparently proved not to be true. Sociologists of religion are meanwhile talking about religion's continued existence" (Walter Kasper, *Theology and Church,* 231 pp., New York: Crossroad, 1989, p. 14).

38. This is the angry mood of the issue of the *ThQ* mentioned above (see note 13); quotations: p. 44; p. 1.

differences. The accusation that the clergy have very materialistic tendencies and are therefore hypocrites, supposedly dedicated to the pursuit of spiritual values but actually living in the opposite way, seems of only secondary relevance today. Many Catholics today would be delighted to see their priests conforming more to the general lifestyle and living in a more worldly way, for then they too could go on happily following the predominantly hedonistic lifestyles of our day with undisturbed consciences. This may be their real motivation, but it is cloaked under a very different argument: the shortage of priests! So many communities desperate for a priest, so many needy people longing for pastoral care, so much work to be done in the vineyard of the Lord, so few laborers to do it! If the new evangelization of Europe is to be undertaken—so runs the argument—the people must be prepared for the task, but where are they? Talk of low morale is far from being dreamed up out of nothing, for it can be backed up with statistics. Our numbers are rapidly diminishing, we have been shrinking for 30 years, mass attendance and confessions are dwindling, the number of weddings is halved again and again, reduced to a third or a quarter! We have no people, the Eucharist is denied to communities, the nearest community is three kilometers away, etc. Surely it is entirely appropriate for bad figures to engender low morale?

There was however much the same need for a new evangelization 165 years ago in the Catholic Church after it had been laid waste and drained of life by Napoleon, in the spiritual desert of the Church made visible by Napoleon. The *Denkschrift* makes obeisance to the spirit of the age, which did not want public celibacy—or at least the educated elite didn't want it. But the truth is that it was the personal needs of the flesh which awakened the humane convictions of the learned men of Freiburg at that time. And Möhler? How then does the bright young Tübingen theology professor Johann Adam Möhler respond? Is celibacy to be abandoned? Are we first to fill up the fortresses—to use the technical military expression of the Tübingen professors of 1992—with "viri probati," married men ordained in maturity, and then have their numbers topped up with young men? Does he see the need? He certainly does, and he knows how to give powerful expression to it. He had had his own personal experience of the unspiritual atmosphere in the *Wilhelmsstift* in Tübingen and later in the Rottenburg seminary as well. When an initiative

for a petition to the Baden Chamber of Deputies for the abolition
of celibacy was set in motion in 1819, news of it was greeted at the
seminary by the deacons, of whom Möhler was one, with "loud
cheers."[39] His conversion to being a "fierce advocate of celibacy"—
as he was later called—came about through the study of the Church
Fathers; they it was who helped him to stop seeing celibacy as an
outward disciplinary rule and start seeing it as an inward spiritual
insight not dependent on pastoral plans or the events of the day.

Möhler knows how spiritual need can be met and he knows
what means are to be used to foster in the Church the joy of life
and a spirit of courage and effectiveness in the service of men. "Who
will give us wives!" If he utters this refrain so loudly, that is because
it reflects something out of his own past, from his own days as a
deacon in 1819; by 1828 however it has become a quotation from the
younger days that he himself has actually left behind while his contemporaries have still not evolved. He personally has made his peace
with this demand, it sounds so ironic and indeed humorous coming
from his lips, but at the same time it carries overtones of caustic
bitterness towards those who still seriously think they can help the
Church and the faithful to a deeper life by taking this road. Möhler
is no longer the agitator of old, and that is a real sign of maturity!
He explains to us very carefully why he himself stood for a while under
the spell of the liberal *Zeitgeist*, and his explanation is very simple.
The prevalent spirit among his teachers was one of contempt for everything spiritual and Catholic, for the popes, for bishops, for Councils,
and for monks, and nobody was more vehement in this respect
than the theologians among them. But ten years down the line the
scales have fallen from his eyes and he can see that those professors
are themselves among the prime causes of the unspirituality and
the weaknesses they are so busy lamenting. It was in this kind of shallow "enlightened" atmosphere that a newspaper like the *Freimütigen*
could flourish and publish its exceptionally violent attacks on celibacy.
The young Möhler was very vulnerable to all this, so much so that
in his Vicariate year of 1820 the noble Father Haas felt compelled
to challenge the charming young priest to develop "a more Catholic

39. Cf. Wörner (see note 16 above), 11.

mind."[40] Eight years later the desire expressed by Fr. Haas was to be fulfilled!

Möhler had experienced from the closest quarters in Tübingen just what that level of education amounted to which enabled middle-class Catholics to think they were entitled to reflect on spiritual things and then to categorize celibacy as a purely disciplinary measure, a measure with nothing—absolutely nothing at all—to do with the experience of the Spirit of Christ, something essentially disposable should the Church fail to move in the direction desired by the professors.

Möhler was converted to the spiritual view of practical problems much sooner than many of the others from his early days in Tübingen, such as Johann Baptist Hirscher. Möhler may have been granted a shorter lifespan yet he managed to become a brilliant and superior advocate of celibacy—not the kind of celibacy that is stipulated as a rule for Catholic priests by a diktat from Rome—but the kind that is written in their hearts by a calling from above. Are the hearts of men moved by pastoral/theological plans? Not in the least. If the Church does not live by the Holy Spirit, she becomes a humanist association that regulates spiritual needs psychologically as a task of the state, and if that doesn't work, through the agency of the police. If in Möhler's time there were 549 Catholics in Southwest Germany for every priest and now there are more than 3000, that does not tell us much about the right of the communities to the Eucharist, it merely tells us that attendance at the Eucharist has diminished faster than the number of priests.[41] Must the Holy Spirit be present fivefold or sixfold in the 3000 Catholics of today by comparison with the 549 of those days? Today there are at most half as many present at each mass with the one priest as there were 30 years ago. In comparison with 1965, we do not have a shortage of priests but a surplus of priests in Germany. Statistically there may be a shortage of priests, but not in reality.

Möhler saw all this with unusual clarity: the Freiburg professors of those days were dispirited, as are the Tübingen professors of today, as is the Church in Germany and Europe. But to cure only the symptoms and not the causes would just be quackery. So, to raise morale among the clergy and in the Church, he does not have recourse

---

40. Cf. Wörner (see note 16 above), 15.

41. Cf. *ThQ* 172 (1992) (see note 13 above), 11.

to natural aids and stimulants, but looks in the Acts of the Apostles at Barnabas, suggesting that the professors strike up a hymn or a sequence to the Holy Spirit. Instead of encouraging adaptation to insidious naturalism, he prays for a sign from above, for streams of divine grace. In other words, he urges the Freiburgers to raise their voices to God in prayer with full and devout hearts. I have no doubt whatever that more celibate priests would emerge from the Tübingen educational establishment today if the teaching body took to heart the recommendation of this famed alumnus of theirs to cultivate a more intensive spiritual life, including the practice of singing hymns together; otherwise it is all too likely that the Faculty will slide further towards an exclusively ratiocinatory science of religion. In that establishment as it is now, grace is a purely technical term, singing and spiritual life are private matters, and consequently it does not produce any priests.

It is a pity that all we have of the sound of Möhler's voice are written descriptions. It was a voice that was rather quiet than loud, but it must have sounded heavenly, especially when he struck up the Pentecost sequence: "Without Thy Godhead nothing can/have any price or worth in man." We have an account of how this voice sounded in 1836: "Never before have I been so impressed by someone's faithful celibacy on our first meeting. Big by nature, he was slight and delicate of build. His outward posture suggested nobility, dignity, and decency. His features were extremely fine and regular. His face had something magically winning about it. A gentle fire streamed out of his big dark eyes. A charm seemed to radiate from his countenance and suffuse his whole being. When he opened his mouth to speak, it was in a mellifluous voice and a pure accent. His manner of speaking was beautifully articulate and fluent. Using a deceptively simple vocabulary, he elaborated profound ideas with a clarity that was unusually lucid. There was something quietly seductive about his eloquence. The feminine but in no way emasculated aura that clung to his whole personality made Möhler seem much younger than he was. It was just a few weeks after his fortieth birthday, but to me he looked scarcely more than thirty."[42] It seems we have to attribute all this to pure grace, for according to official testimony from the Seminary from 1819 he was "lacking in any musical ear," and though he was acknowledged

---

42. Cf. above Lösch (see note 1 above), 507.

to be well-versed in liturgy, this was "apart from the actual singing."[43]
At this period the gaze of a bishop (Johann Michael Sailer) could cause
the shy Vicar great embarrassment.[44] But the pale expression must
have gradually transformed into a piercing radiance. Between 1820
and 1836 there was a huge revolution in the soul of Möhler, and the
effects of that revolution are most marked in this piece on celibacy
of 1828. His devotion to celibacy had turned him into a spiritual man.
Now for the first time he could be what he had always been and what
the shallowness of the age had prevented him from being. Where
earlier cool intellect had held sole sway, now the Spirit within him
could find a body through spiritual virginity. Surely a person's growing
realization of his true nature would have affected his voice as well?

The lesson to be learnt from Möhler is a timeless one, it rests
on a perception which can be termed "objective" only in a limited
sense, a perception which is not therefore given to "scientific" teachers
of the faith. Fortunately it is not these teachers who hold the teaching
office of the Church but the bishops, who—ideally—have proved
themselves in the spiritual life. For what is required if a person is to
understand how problems are self-generated is a spiritual way of life
which in the first instance follows the pattern of Christ and the saints,
looking only secondarily at statistics and refusing to be blinded by
them. The person whose life is devoid of spiritual ascesis does not
know what self-understanding and the self-generation of problems
means. Such people are for ever going round and round in circles
as they talk about "progress" and "times of crisis." The person whose
theology is uncatholic and one-sidedly rationalistic, the person
who treats Church history purely as a long series of scandals, the person
who sees the aims of the Church today solely in terms of the service
of spoiled prosperous citizens and not first of all in terms of teaching
the way to God, the person who talks only about the priesthood
of all believers on the grounds that distinctions are discrimination (as
they say in sociological jargon); such persons cannot be in the least
surprised—and indeed are rather secretly delighted (for all their croco-
dile tears) that vocations to the priesthood are so thin on the ground,
not thinking (as a result of their own lack of spiritual intuition) that a

---

43. Cf. Lösch (see note 1 above), 17ff.
44. Cf. Wörner (see note 16 above), 15.

young person will not give his life for anything that is nothing special. Even the world loses its interest in a Church whose orientation is primarily social or psychological. It is not a lack of priests we are suffering from in Germany and Europe but a lack of faith! Can inner life be created by imitating unspiritual thinking? Is the acceptance of a married priesthood and the extension of the bureaucratization of the servants of the Church really going to be the way to summon the Holy Spirit, through whom alone the Church lives?

What Möhler's approach highlights so starkly is the idea of the *self-generation* of problems. I do not know whether one priest was enough for the 549 statistical Catholics of those days—how are we to judge sufficiency? The truth is that given the modesty of the spiritual demands made by today's Catholics, one priest is quite enough for 3000 of them—indeed, one priest would be able to cater quite comfortably for double that number. Möhler had tackled this question in an essay of 1826, and he came to the conclusion then that a *plethora* of priests was an evil for the Church, and he believed he could ground this assertion historically. He considered that the catastrophe of 1803, in which the Church was robbed of her outward glory and of so many of her servants, was actually a blessing in disguise. He recognized the hand of God in it: "It is in the nature of things that there can only be a few priests. Only those who sense the breath of the divine Spirit, who receive the holy kiss, who have received the consecration of the Spirit, the anointing of the heart—they are the only ones who are truly priests of God."[45]

When so many Christians are Christians in name only with so little inward participation in the Church, to such an extent that they have little use beyond acting as data in the statistical argument against celibacy, a very serious problem is raised: how is the Christian—that very rare bird—to behave among so many apathetic and lukewarm fellow Christians? Is he to conform to their lifestyle? Is the Christian to make himself all things to all men in that kind of way? The real problem for Möhler is the un-spiritual atmosphere, the lack of faith and lack of spirit in the state, in society, in the Church, in the theological faculties, in the schools and seminaries! Let us listen to him: "Their complaint will also represent a powerful testimony against

---

45. Johann Adam Möhler, "Einige Gedanken über die zu unserer Zeit erfolgte Verminderung der Priester, und damit in Verbindung stehende Punkte," in *ThQ* 8 (1826) 414–451; here 436.

many principles hitherto prevailing in Baden, in the University of
Freiburg, in the Seminary at Meersburg, and in the Episcopal administration: it will confirm that nothing profitable has ever been done by
these principles nor ever can be done by them One of those principles
is the notion that celibacy should be abolished." Reform of head
and members—so desperately needed in the Church in Europe then
and now—can only ever come about through a spiritual deepening,
not by a lessening of the demands of faith. The lowering of the Church's
requirements for the priesthood would at worst be un-spiritual, at
best neutral as a means of healing our maladies; not only would it fail
to deal with their symptoms, but it would allow them to erupt and
consume the whole body. For conversion and turning to God is always
only His work: just as the walls of Jericho fell through the liturgical
trumpets and the Marxist East fell not least through the dogged
confidence and praying of a Pope from the East,[46] a new evangelization of Europe will not happen on the cheap as a result of the abolition of celibacy. I will explain further on the wider implications of this
and the way that clerical celibacy is oriented to the evangelical counsels in general.[47]

   Möhler, his eyes opened, can only utter an Olympian laugh
over the supposition that the spiritual condition of the clergy and the
Church can be bettered by means of the encouragement of married
sexual love. He does not in any way doubt the high value of this good
of creation which was renewed once more through Christ, but he asks
this question: how can a created finite good show the way to God,
since it must itself be shown the way first? And he goes on to say that
his hair stood on end at the thought that someone could have come up
with a remedy like this *first of all* and *alone* in an era of such spiritual
weakness in the church in Baden, Germany, and Europe. He confesses
that he has never heard anyone claim that the first requirement for the
renewal of paralyzed members in the love of Christ and the encouragement of enthusiastic vocations is the provision of *wives*. In a state
of Stygian darkness preventing any possibility of distinguishing between

---

46. As former Soviet President Gorbachev wrote on 3 March 1992 in the Turin Daily *La
Stampa*: "What has happened in Eastern Europe in recent years would not have been possible
without this Pope, without the great—even political—role that John Paul II has played in world
events." (Cf. *Frankfurter Allgemeine Zeitung* 4 March, 1992).

47. See the section below: "The Future of Celibacy."

friend and enemy or between good and evil, such an idea might just perhaps have come into someone's head. But nobody with the faintest inkling of true spiritual discernment would have dreamed of resorting to such a means. In any case, no natural means as such could stimulate faith; it was the Spirit, the uncreated One, who taught us in the right way what we should ask for. The Spirit had never recommended a married priesthood, though tolerating it with limitations in earlier times, and the Spirit was not at home in this way of seeing things.[48]

No natural means as such can stimulate our faith; no desire directed to a natural and finite end can bring us closer to God. After religions of nature and law came the religion of suffering, the folly of the cross, which knows that our identity cannot be bound up with the world, that there is no natural slide from earth to heaven, that grace only perfects nature when this nature—wounded by original sin—is first nailed to the cross. Anyone who promotes natural adjustment destroys grace, that is to say, blocks its flow. Since God himself is the ultimate uncreated grace, he thus destroys the way to God. Möhler studied the ups and downs of the history of the spiritual life too assiduously not to know that; he knew too much about the consistently austere, ascetic, Spirit-filled beginnings and the soft gourmet decline to have any faith in a theological orientation that seeks its salvation in greater "friendliness to the body." The Spirit brings discipline but also wealth, and wealth destroys discipline and thereby the Spirit. This is not just the law of the history of monks, but also that of recent history, for the spirit of capitalism developed out of a profoundly secularized monkish ethic, and it therefore represents a decline, because in the spirit of capitalism the means for attaining an infinite end are redirected to a finite one.[49] If not even an ecological crisis can be mastered by natural means, why on earth do theologians imagine that we can reach heaven, in which all earthly goals are included, by having more of nature?

It does not really matter what goal we have in the world, even if religion is entitled to be a part of it. When we are talking about finite ends such as cheaper energy, better medicine, more social justice, technical advance, outcomes are all too often the reverse of what was

---

48. Cf. Chapter 2, p. 13.

49. Max Weber, *The Protestant Ethic and the Spirit of Capitalism,* translated by Talcott Parsons, London: George Allen & Unwin, 1930, p. 292.

intended. There is a dialectic of reason, medicine, nuclear energy, national states, freedom, the concept—a dialectic of nature, in fact, which is simply a rerun of the dialectic of reason, since it has rehearsed its fluctuating identity in nature. But since there is no such thing as finite identity in time, every attempt to hold on to it veers round to its opposite, to contradiction and to destruction. What then is not sought in God, in a God who cannot be grasped by understanding, but who reveals himself of his own volition, and what is not expressed in greater ascesis of the body, that means in renunciation of the flattering delusion that our lives are in our own hands, converts into its opposite, is sin, because it opens the way to a greater catastrophe in the world. Our sins are failures of self-preservation, so God forgives them immediately if they are confessed to him.

This then is the spirit of revelation as opposed to the spirit of the Enlightenment. What Möhler observed was a failure of the biblical and concrete Catholic spirit both in the clergy at large and in the *Denkschrift*. These are not unrelated phenomena, for the one arises from the other. And as is so often the case in the area of guilt and sin, people accuse others of their own failings, a manifestation of the life of the soul into which the Apostle Paul had great insight: "So no matter who you are, if you pass judgement you have no excuse. It is yourself that you condemn when you judge others, since you behave in the same way as those you are condemning" (Romans 2:1). This knowledge is a ray of pellucid light, and Möhler focuses this light on the *Denkschrift*, showing that the authors are drinking at a well whose muddy waters are nauseating to the taste; yet all the while they are totally oblivious to what it is that is giving them this nausea. His prophetic calling sharpened by the study of Church history, Möhler feels the necessity to demonstrate that the *Denkschrift* emerges from the same climate of opinion that fundamentally conditions the outlook of the clergy of Baden, even while its authors are declaring themselves deeply unsatis-fied with that outlook and calling for an intensification of the lamen-tably paltry Enlightenment naturalism they are so deluded as to see as a remedy for it.

Möhler's main thesis then claims that the resistance to celi-bacy which has emerged in modern times uses the biblical way of thinking and its relevance to the community only as a pretext, arguing that in reality this resistance is "inwardly bound up with the whole modern spirit of hostility to the Church and the gospel" and has its origin in that. It is indeed fair to state that today's opponents of celibacy—often with the very best of intentions—want to treat the Church, Christ, and God as being there for finite ends, like social progress, world hunger, the rights of women, the protection of the environment, etc—and there is of course justification in the gospel for such a commitment. For the gospel is nothing less than the proclamation of the all-comprehensive salvation of man, and part of this involves enabling man on earth not to lose the hope that can all too easily be overwhelmed by poverty or indeed by consumerism. But it seems that we only reliably reach a finite end when we do not ignore the infinite end, for otherwise God is reduced to a mere function, a projection, a feeling, a myth. I am not entitled to make God into an empowerer or into opium for the people, even if I want to persuade myself that I myself belong to the people. The finest test of honorable intention is celibacy, which is supremely well-suited to distinguish whether people are seeking God or not, whether they want to be used by God or rather want to use God. For the more I surrender an original drive of nature and let it be transformed, the less I am able to confuse God with a particular appearance. Such an effect is produced even if I only acknowledge the call to celibacy or the evangelical counsels without actually living them myself.

I would not want to attribute this to all opponents of celibacy, but there is a very basic kind of attitude which is often to be met with in parishes; it involves functionalizing God and putting him into service and confusing the Church with a service institution. There are the great life events like birth and death along with a few lesser occasions like First Communion, Wedding, and Christmas. They awaken our spiritual taste a little and give us a desire to express ourselves more in word, song, and worship. But they do nothing to persuade a greater mass of nominal Christians to live their lives in accord with the standards of Christ. This expresses itself symbolically in the neglect of a culture of Sundays by so many Christians, indeed in its entire destruction. Servants of the Church—who they are is a matter of complete indifference—are expected to light a candle in connection with a few still always mysterious peripheral phenomena of life and mumble a few words, but otherwise the Church must avoid as much as possible disturbing the way of nature and society. It looks like total folly to such minds to state that everything is grace rather than nature, since for them grace is at best a peripheral phenomena in rare events. At a very basic level that is the confusion of ends and means. It is out of this consumer spirit that the opposition to celibacy comes in our European latitudes. Or is anyone seriously going to claim that it has emerged from a deepened Christianity? When the consumer culture dies, opposition to celibacy will die too. Let us hope that we do not have to wait too long for this.

Such a confusion of God with finite appearances is what I like to call *Naturalism*. It is really this that Möhler is campaigning against, because this "ism" is insatiable and demands a constant supply of sacrifices, but they are sacrifices that have no power to give spirit and life. There are myths and legends aplenty available to mirror our unrecognized and painful but self-generated problems. Just as I can use my hidden truth as a stick to beat others, I can also assent to a story, a legend, a myth buried in the back of my mind, whose conscious application would be too painful for me. The legends say of St. George, the knight that he freed a town from a great dragon, which the townsfolk had been appeasing with the daily sacrifice of two sheep and later—on account of the lack of livestock or else on account of its appetite having increased—two men. We can develop the application of the story to our own time. Once we begin to feed the young dragon out of fear at its power, what happens is that both our fear and the cause of our fear grow in like measure. The inhabitants of Silena in Libya—according to the *Legenda aurea* that was the name of the town in question—had been gradually nurturing their own problem. In the end they had lost all power to save themselves by themselves. Help had to come from outside if the vicious circle was to be broken. We all know how the courageous knight St. George helped the townsfolk in their desperate need and so found entry into legend and into the missal (April 23).

I think there is healing in this legend for the problem of naturalism. There has been a crisis of the priestly office since Vatican II, because many of the interpreters of the Council thought that the openness of the Church to the world should be understood in the sense of naturalism: Christians were called to the service of the world while priests were called to holiness not merely in the world but through the world. The difference between God and the world, between

symbols on the one side and realities on the other, was minimized—
though not completely abandoned. It is true that this difference
may have become too stark before the Council, when the lay Christian
was understood only as a non-cleric, so that the Church was equated
with the clergy. But the pendulum has swung too far. Over the last
thirty years the focus has consistently been on minimizing the distinction between the general and particular priesthood and ignoring the
difference between them. If the words *office* or *priest* have become so
unutterable in the Church, it is because for many Christians the idea
of a difference between nature and grace has become totally abhorrent.
Nature, science, planning is not everything in life—indeed it is not
even the most crucial thing! And the celibate priest walking through
the streets of the town or the city is a reminder of that, which is
why the world wants him out of its sight. The married priest offers
no such uncomfortable reminder to disturb our spiritual slumbers.

I will enumerate a few examples of how the difference
between nature and grace is (often unconsciously) blurred: the introduction of the permanent diaconate, numerous new pastoral roles
orientated to social work principles, the end of Latin as a liturgical
language, the weakening of the hours of prayer, the abandonment
of clerical clothing and monastic habits. The introduction of a married
priesthood would lead to the difference between general and particular
priesthood being consigned to isolated textbooks of dogmatics and
then soon to the history of dogmas. That is what I call naturalism, but
it can achieve nothing of value. A Church with a human face is not
really human, because the so-called human and natural flatter only for
a moment, but are not adequate for the seriousness of life, for life is
oriented to an infinite goal.

Naturalism is not only a reality within the Church, it is also
a reality in the relation of the Church—particularly the Catholic
Church—to the surrounding world. A look at Protestantism may
help us to a better understanding of the question of naturalism (even
though it may not be very opportune, and perhaps not even very noble,
because there is no real comparison). In Protestantism all the enlightened rational demands made so vehemently by the mass media have
been met, from the abolition of the celibate priesthood to the appoint-
ment of a woman as the Bishop of Hamburg. Has this enhanced
the life of the Lutheran Church? Is more of the spirit—I mean the

Holy Spirit—to be found there? I have to express my reservations and answer no: not the least bit more, and perhaps indeed the reverse. Have these things given the Lutheran Churches the power to withstand totalitarianisms in the world of the last 150 years? Hardly. Is there an increase in numbers that speaks for natural modernization? Not at all. Even modern man does not believe the modern version of Christianity.

Finally Möhler recommends—demands indeed—an end to initiatives for the abolition of celibacy, for they are pointless. The endless discussion of celibacy—and 165 years ago it was much more robust—wears down spiritual resolve and undermines it. In such a situation the priest is required not merely to possess the charism of celibacy, but also the charism of being against the spirit of the age. Only the noblest spirits like Möhler can withstand the battery of assault under which so many priests are reduced to leading a barren and unconvincing life. Anyone who is called to the priesthood today must have a twofold calling. He must hear a special personal call and at the same time have the calling to believe that there can in general be a calling. To put it another way, he must at one and the same time hold the ideal up high and jump over it himself. In the eyes of Möhler that is what robs many clerics of their initial cheerful naturalness, something so indispensable for a powerful life and spiritual effectiveness. One cannot live on probation, one cannot love on probation, one cannot abandon the world on probation. Then as now, constantly repeated attacks, doubt, and complaining provoke an inner conflict in the collective consciousness which exhausts all spiritual powers. The eternal emphasis on how difficult celibacy is, says Möhler, makes the priests—unless they have the dual calling to celibate priesthood and to the defense of this priesthood—appear weak, so that they hide away in some corner where their existence is tolerated. Meanwhile any priest who does not have this dual capacity, any priest who fails to find some niche where his celibacy is plausible, either breaks down or sees himself reduced to a shadow of his former self. The man who was so strong to begin with soon stands there like a "withered blossom," robbed of all the joy of life. And so the "widespread discord among the clergy" referred to above takes its rise.

(II) Although he was no great exegete, Möhler took considerable pains with his interpretation of the New Testament to try to dispel the shadows that had been thrown on virginity by the *Denkschrift*, in whose hands the Bible threatened to degenerate into an ideological weapon.[50] Ideology is the use of one idea for the concealment of another. The latter is for personal use, the former for public consumption. The difference between them is what produces the possibility of ideological deception. The professors of 1828 also made a distinction between that which was conditioned by the circumstances of the day and that which was authentic. What was held to be still valid in 1828 was the discourse of Jesus in the year 30 and of his apostle Paul a bit later, while the old time-conditioned vestment, the world-picture of that time, and the antiquated anthropology of the official Church, was held to be obsolete teaching. It just happened to turn out that the thinking of Jesus was exactly what could easily be understood by the people of Baden and the fatherland: amazingly, he got there even without the support and admiration of the learned gentlemen of Freiburg.

Möhler's reaction here is to be struck by the way that human nature, longing for comfort, prefers to see itself as flatteringly reinforced by Jesus, rather than opening itself with trembling humility to the way of salvation. He responds to the threadbare historicism of the *Denkschrift*[51] with a detailed and sensitive discussion of the teaching of Jesus and St. Paul on celibacy for the sake of the so-close Kingdom of God. He dismisses the historicizing distinction which alleges that everything incomprehensible and uncomfortable is time-conditioned, and shows—again with delightful humor—why Jesus is so radical, why he forbids divorce, why he himself lived celibate, poor, and homeless. Möhler explains this as the hundred-times better way, the needle's eye way into the Kingdom of God. For since in Jesus this Kingdom has come, in following him we can lay aside our natural anxieties and live according to our better intuitions, according to all the inspirations with which the Creator endowed us from the beginning, later to make us new in Christ. Therefore Jesus refers in teaching about the needlessness of divorce to this untarnished beginning (Matthew 19) which of course outwardly seems severe, but in essence it is a source of happiness. It is not nature that makes such a life

---

50. See Chapter 2 above. "The Biblical Counsel."

51. *Denkschrift* pp. 7–11.

possible from the start, but grace. Möhler stands firmly at this point, the lay professors at the standpoint of nature, and between them lies a gulf that allows for the odd disconnected call but not for any actual two-way communication.

It is very strange the way that any modernization and updating of the faith assumes it can quite legitimately appeal to the idea of a greater closeness to the Bible and to Jesus. Is the Jesus of history so much easier to accept than the Christ of faith? Are we going to succumb to the bogus alternative we used to hear so much about: "Jesus, yes—the Church, no"? Surely it is the Church that actually softens the radical demands of the incredible Jesus? Turning the other cheek, cutting your eye out, chopping off your hand and foot, leaving your family, readiness for suffering and death, and the totally unheard-of call to indissoluble marriage or celibacy to boot: let anyone who can do it, do it. Who could possibly live like that in reality or recommend such a way of life to a public in love with consumerism? And yet those are in point of fact the original actual words and deeds of Jesus. For more than a hundred years the depth psychologists have been fighting battles over the original call of Jesus for us to offer unlimited love to enemy and friend. Möhler instinctively develops the difference between nature and grace, which in questions of marriage and celibacy elicits all at once both anger from the Pharisees and astonishment from the disciples, whose response is the cry: "If marriage is like *that*, it is not advisable to marry."[52] Anyone who refuses to allow himself to be moved to a recognition of grace is reduced to remaining with the words of Jesus in nature, i.e. in the world. A greater closeness to the Bible then serves only as an ideological weapon for the spirit of the age, and references to the historical Jesus are a means to get even further away from him—further at all events than the Church does, with her awareness of the weakness and sin of the faithful. The ideological exploitation of the Bible homes in on the difference between Church teaching and the teaching of Jesus or between the life of Christ and the life of the Christian, but its real goal is to do away with both at the same time.

Romano Guardini was acutely aware of the ideological presuppositions of a purely historical picture of Jesus, seeing in it the

---

52. Cf. Chapter 2 above, p. 13.

naturalism of those who are constantly ready to doubt and rebel, preferring to believe in themselves rather than let themselves be healed through the knowledge of their weaknesses. "There is a connection between on the one hand the naturalistic dogma according to which history contains nothing else but man and the human, and on the other the Romantic yearning of modern man, with his highly-developed intellect, for the natural and original. So they strip everything out of the synoptic gospels" picture of Christ that is inconsistent with this yearning and we are presented with the "simple, pure, wholly religious Jesus." In truth anyone who wants to understand the synoptics must overcome precisely this way of looking at things with all its prejudices . . . The synoptics are not 'simple,' and the reason for that is that Jesus himself is not simple."[53] Indeed the truth is that the "historical" Jesus they present us with is actually less simple than the synoptic Jesus — i.e. less understandable, less acceptable, less believable for the moderns when they do not let themselves be converted and regenerated.

The synoptic Jesus is infinitely far from our modern approach to life, and we have little justification therefore for setting ourselves up as the measure of Jesus. Anyone who does not let the straightforward, pure, religious Jesus speak in his own voice, does not understand him. And what is the first thing he says? "The time is fulfilled, and the kingdom of God is close at hand. Repent, and believe the Gospel." (Mark 1:15) At the beginning of the twentieth century, Albert Schweitzer felt that the word "closeness" had of necessity to be understood in its chronological sense. But he knew that the simple modernistic criterion "in the context of our time and our country" leads only to historicism and does not bring the historical Jesus any nearer. He was convinced that through historical, history-of-religion, and psychological research, life had come back again to the figure of Jesus, as though he were stepping out of the dogmatic formulae and coming down through time to us. "But he did not stay, he passed by our time and went back to his own," and this drove Albert Schweitzer himself to retreat from theological activity.[54] He put more faith in the mistakenness of Jesus than in his own watch, went into the jungle and

---

53. Romano Guardini, *Das Christusbild der paulinischen und johanneischen Schriften*, 230 pp., Mainz-Paderborn, 3rd ed., 1987; here p. 38. (1st ed. 1940).

54. Cf. Schweitzer (see note 21, p. 620).

practiced the Kingdom of God that had arrived. He did not know how to put it into words, the Kingdom was near to him in a way he could not convey, and so he became a secular saint. He made himself useful to his contemporaries but without inflicting on them any irritating exhortations to conversion.

It is only in a secondary sense that the closeness of the Kingdom of God can be measured by the watch, and to explain what it means is seemingly quite impossible, since the world of objects and concepts has no word available for this unique kind of nearness to God. Guardini saw this problem all too clearly, and I will refer again to him. Revelation, he says, is its own testimony, so we have to renounce any attempt to measure it by what is given in philosophy and science, in logic and psychology, in the tools invented by human resourcefulness for the mastery of space and time. "Faith means willingness to accept the revealing *Gestalt* as it stands as the absolute beginning and even as the starting-point for thinking." [55] What Jesus says about marriage and celibacy can only be understood as a renewal from the roots up, as a restoration of the genuine creation, something that cannot be known and lived on the basis of experience with stumbling nature. Both the Freiburg *Denkschrift* and Möhler's *Examination* put before us that extraordinary phenomenon, the exception of eschatological celibacy, but they are at opposite poles from one another. The thinking of the *Denkschrift* is numerical, mechanical, and statistical, while Möhler's thinking is graced, organic, and in touch with reality. There can be no question but that the spiritual vision of Möhler is closer to the the intention of Jesus than the naturalism which in "cool" and "frigid" language (in using these expressions Möhler takes the temperature correctly) holds virginity to be "not impossible." There are two ways of looking at a rarity: either it may be something real, noble, and precious, a splendid goal only infrequently attained (the victory prize in a sporting event, which can only be won by a single person); or a freak, something that ought not to be, an abnormal exception, or something outdated and disconnected from the whole—in this case from the totality of revelation. In a seemingly unintentional way, the *Denkschrift* tries to push celibacy in the service of Jesus—an incontrovertible fact that it does not

---

55. Cf. Guardini (see note 53), p. 28.

deny—to the edge, to marginalize it. Jesus himself did not of course consider celibacy impossible, even though he did warn us against any over-confident adoption of that particular lifestyle, since of course virgin chastity encounters so many obstacles that it can only ever be a rarity.

Wisely, Möhler's response is not simply to praise virginity, but to offer evidence that both marriage and celibacy are rooted in grace. Actually both are incomprehensible to the world and to a church that is approved by the state—or as we would put it today, to a socially committed Church. Such a Church cannot see any point either in indissoluble marriage or in the relinquishment of sexual activity. This kind of abstinence has no natural advantage; in the eyes of a man inclined to sexual desire its only aim is a spiritual eternal one, and that he believes he can dispense with for the time being—until a finite judgement (the economic-ecological crisis) or eternal judgement catches up with him.

There is, however, something amiss with this argument of Möhler's in the *Examination*. For the parallel between Christian marriage and celibacy reaches deeper than is suggested by him. The connection between the two goes even further than the message in the doubly necessary verse so wonderful in its insight: "It is not everyone who can accept what I have said, but only those to whom it is granted." (Matthew 19, 11ff.) Möhler's argument is a *formal* one, and that may be right when dealing with the type of people by whom the *Denkschrift* was written. The formal explanation relating the first application of the verse to indissoluble marriage and the second to spiritual virginity runs like this: because Christ could hardly have wanted to say that only very few marriages will not end in divorce, he cannot here be prophesying that Christian celibacy will be a rarity, as the Freiburg professors want us to believe.

In this explanation Möhler counterposes grace directly to Mosaism, whose apparent gentleness is deceptive when it gives in to our natural drives and allows divorce for the sake of our hardness of heart. The Mosaic law knows little of grace and therefore it can barely raise itself above nature. In this one point of grace, marriage and celibacy are deeply tied together, but the Mosaic Law remains on the level of nature: it allows divorce and knows nothing of the value of virginity. For divorce is, in fact, hardness of heart, as Jesus says, not solely on account of its practical consequences, but on account of the way it perpetuates our addiction to life in this world, to a nature which rolls on and on endlessly without coming any closer to its fulfilment. Not one of those I have met who live under the sign of naturalism in this world understands the meaning of life. Naturalism is nihilism, it is hardness of heart. Marriage is a sign of the nearness of God, but—and here there is a difference—celibacy is an even more powerful sign of the same thing. Both are a gift from heaven. Marriage is a sacrament and celibacy is also a sacrament when in combination with the sacrament of priestly ordination, a sign of the presence of God in the finite world. We have to leave behind us the idea of celibacy as a rigid external disciplinary rule, a recommendation of Jesus which we are free to ignore, if we want to grasp its organic interconnection with the gospel of the Kingdom-of-God of Jesus. Then marriage and celibacy relate to each other as time relates to eternity. Both are granted to creation by grace and not by our own merit. Now we can make sense of the other message of Jesus in this connection: in heaven there will be no more marrying, because in heaven time finds its fulfilment in eternity. "Jesus answered them, 'You are wrong, because you understand neither the scriptures nor the power of God. For at the resurrection men and women do not marry; no, they are like the angels in heaven.'" (Matthew 22:29ff.)

The Freiburg *Denkschrift* doesn't just reject the Gospel, it also rejects the teaching of the Apostle Paul. He would like everyone to live without cares as he does, hence unmarried—for Christians should be concerned only for the things of the Lord. The Freiburg gentlemen try to marginalize this key statement, claiming that it is to a great extent conditioned by the context of the times, and they argue that the recommendation has no place at the heart of the freedom from the law proclaimed by Paul. They conclude that it has no normative power at all for later times like ours, which are very different from Paul's day.

Möhler makes short shrift of such casuistry and prevarication, pointing out that we have no evidence of any particular persecution of Christians in the days of the Apostles in Corinth. What the authors of the *Denkschrift* are trying to achieve is all too clear. In order to clarify the difference between command and counsel, Möhler applies himself to a broad presentation of the situation in Corinth at the time of Paul's visit as implied in 1 Corinthians 7. If we compare it with the passage in Matthew, Paul's way of expressing his desire that people may have a life free of cares is actually able to touch hearts more deeply even than Jesus himself. Jesus speaks about facts of the present and the future, while Paul goes on to make a value judgement and issue a challenge. Jesus speaks in the indicative, Paul in the optative or imperative, and a distinction or a postulate offers much more scope for objection. Paul tells us that it is better and a real mark of distinction when a person chooses not to marry. Jesus made no such comparison, he only stated what there are and what there will be, namely celibates for the sake of the Kingdom of God. Paul by contrast recommends, suggests, and advises us to regard virginity as better both on account of the greater freedom from care in the world it brings with it and for the sake of the greater care for the Lord it allows us to have; nonetheless at the same time he is also able to praise marriage. So it was that he triggered the debates about the better state of life that have continued to rage right down the Christian centuries.

What I have said here has been confirmed by the Church, most notably at the Council of Trent and the Second Vatican Council. Trent excludes everyone from the Church who says "that it is not better and happier to remain in virginity and celibacy than to be united in matrimony." [56] For all the joy in the world manifested in the Constitution on the Church *(Lumen gentium)*, Vatican II uses the comparative to concede to the evangelical counsels a modest precedence for the sake of "the richer fruit," [57] to be harvested from an unhindered glow of love and fullness of honor given to God. That is exactly the Pauline recommendation right down to the use of the comparative. But ultimately every comparative entails a comparison, and for all Paul's deliberately eirenic language, the comparison involves a discrimination, for it assumes a difference,[58] and this is a cause of particular displeasure to the authors of the *Denkschrift*.[59] Grace affirms the other, nature wants to see otherness removed, grace attains its goal

---

56. Cf. DH 1810.

57. ". . . uberiorem fructum percipere queat, . . . liberari intendit ab impedimentis . . ." (LG 44).

58. *discrimen* (Latin) = differentiation.

59. "Where is there here even only the faintest allusion on which to base the notion that marriage might be downgraded in the slightest? Several utterances of the Apostle Paul are connected first of all to this passage . . . ." (*Denkschrift* p. 8).

in being at oneness with the other, in nature oneness disintegrates into contradiction.

It is right that Paul makes a comparison, but the point of the comparison is not the higher or lower valuation of the one as against the other, but the choice of the good or the better by one and the same person. If Paul had to make his point today, he would probably say: "if anybody asks me what he should do to follow Jesus, then I reply to this concrete person standing in front of me—make up your mind! If you can, remain without a wife or husband, try to lead a simple life without luxury, and commit yourself to a service in the Church. For the Church is the body of the Lord. If you do not do this but decide instead to live as Christian in a career and in marriage, then that is good too. I venerate the sacrament of marriage, marriage is a way to God, it is a place where Christ is encountered, and if you want me to, I will come to your wedding. My respect for the spirit of celibacy does not prevent me from having close friendships with many married persons." That's the kind of way the Apostle Paul would express himself in the language of today!

Desirous of playing down Pauline celibacy, our Freiburg professors argued by contrast that when Paul gave these recommendations it was in response to an outbreak of persecution of the Corinthians, whereas in their day in the Baden territories there was no such persecution of Christians; therefore the Pauline counsel had ceased to be applicable. In times of persecution and hardship it is of course very wise to postpone marriage and devote oneself to coping with the crisis of the day. As far as the Freiburgers were concerned, since in Baden in 1828 the rights of citizens were not denied to Christians, nor were they threatened with poverty and death, the justification for priestly celibacy and chastity had vanished. We can well understand how Möhler must have been torn between anger and laughter at this argument, and how he could describe the *Denkschrift* as an apologia for the maintenance of an unspiritual state among men of an apostolic calling.[60]

Paul wants us to understand that the time is always short, that the earth is finite, that the form of this world is passing away (even if a further 2000 years have been put on the clock). Möhler calls this the

---

60. See Chapter 2, above p. 13.

moral or ethical viewpoint on celibacy for the sake of the kingdom of heaven. Today we would prefer to speak of the eschatological nature of the gospel of Jesus, which Paul reinforces in his own words. The time is short? The rediscovery of eschatology since the time of Möhler has sharpened the edge of the whole argument relating to priestly virginity. Möhler's fundamental intuition also emerges however in his moral-ethical point of view: the person who is not born again from God finds it incomprehensible that a man can raise himself above nature, for such a person sees no point in that. This spirit (or better non-spirit) which wants to see all religious life reduced to nature, state, society, psychology, and progress, is exactly what Möhler's *Examination* puts under the microscope, brings to the light, and drives out.

(III) The *Denkschrift* takes the program of marginalization much further, exploiting a type of argument much favored by critics of faith and the Church down to our own time. The essence of this critique lies in the idea of the vulnerability of the Church's faith to *external* pressures.[61] The Church is portrayed as lugging around with her all the baggage of history she has inherited from Jewish, Hellenistic, Germanic, Gnostic, Manichean, Platonist, and Aristotelian sources, so that she is for ever obliged to be modernizing in order to be comprehensible in the context of the day; otherwise she is liable to cease to be abreast of the times. Such critiques based on the idea of the Church's permeability to external influences shift their ground from *Zeitgest* to *Zeitgeist,* for the *Zeitgeist* always only understands the *Zeitgeist,* as Möhler so rightly sees.[62] The polarities current in the modern version of this thinking are progress/regress, modern/out-dated, human/legal, flexible/rigid.

The critique that focuses on external influences sees in the evolution of Church history great inherited historical burdens weighing down on the authentic Jesus, as if to crush him. The idea is that it is now time to undo two millennia of misrepresentations of Christianity. This exercise in rhetoric—I will not call it an exercise in thinking, since there is all too little thinking in it—is beloved in the circles of modern liberal theologians who feel obligated to human, national, or ecological ideas which carry weight with the public. The authentic

61. Chapter 3. "External influences."
62. See Chapter 2, above p. 13.

historical Jesus as presented by them turns out to have held precisely the opinions which please the public, and these opinions have been changing gradually from decade to decade. At the same time, awareness of external influences on the Church is found not just in unbelieving critics of the faith but also in spiritually well-grounded believers; but the latter do not think that between the time of Jesus and today the Holy Spirit has abandoned the Church and so permitted the proliferation of such a vast number of errors that now have to be painfully eliminated in order to make possible for the very first time in 2000 years the pristine revelation of the truth of Christianity as Jesus himself willed it. What do we mean precisely when we say that the Holy Spirit is here today? Has he been leading the Church in the wrong direction for 2000 years? Unbelieving critics pay no attention to this question because as unbelievers they want to ascribe everything that is difficult to understand to historical circumstance, so that they can claim that the early faith has only now happily been brought to light; then ultimately they can hold Jesus himself to be pretty much unworthy of trust and transform those same "historical inherited burdens" into the essence of a gospel that is no longer relevant. All this helps an unbeliever too to slumber on with a good conscience.

The real truth is however that on the question of celibacy a consideration of the wider religious context does not provide much ammunition for the supporters of a married priesthood. In fact comparative history-of-religion research points to conclusions that are rather unfavourable to their cause. The *Denkschrift* says that celibacy is only the continuation of heathen, Jewish, or other oriental customs[63] and that the Church's refusal to allow priests to marry is reprehensible *for that very reason;* but in reality on the basis of this argument a married priesthood would be even more objectionable since it is actually found much more often outside Christianity than celibacy is. Were the accusation really a fundamental one, it could easily be turned on its head and so refuted, yet a moment's reflection invalidates it. Nonetheless Möhler conscientiously takes on himself the responsibility of working through the various pieces of evidence that priestly celibacy was actually envisioned and desired outside of Christendom,

---

63. Cf. Chapter 3 above, p. 30.

even though it remained only an ideal. But equally he points out
that a married priesthood was natural, it was Jewish, it was normal,
with only small deviations towards virginity everywhere—and these
could have been the basis for something stronger and more substantial:
only not rightly so, because there was no basis in the existing still-
veiled knowledge of God for man to have been released from the bonds
of nature. But I will not say any more about this part of Möhler's essay,
for his crystal-clear text speaks for itself.

What all this really shows once again is that the natural
standpoint gives a rather shaky foundation for understanding issues
in the spiritual life. Anyone who has only one foot in heaven while
keeping the other firmly on the ground is in a very unstable position.
Religious history bears witness to a natural longing for what is uncon-
ditionally one and pure, but nature cannot give man such unity and
undividedness. On the other hand we cannot simply abandon nature,
as a few syncretistic sects have tried to do in their excess of zeal.
Möhler points to the Gnostics as an example of the opposite tendency
to naturalism; they sought salvation in a hatred and disapproval of
nature and this led them simply to prohibit marriage. Underlying both
the idolization and the denunciation of nature is the same lack of the
Holy Spirit, for he is given only to those who bow under the easy yoke
of Christ. Pantheism and Dualism, although at opposite poles and
at odds with each other, are in accord however on this one point: they
both spring out of a proud adherence to their opinion. Nature cannot
however be self-sufficient, for nature itself is not natural. Nor can our
human reason be self-sufficient, for it does not find its origin in itself.

There is food for thought for all critics in the fact that the
Church overall— Möhler speaks of the *whole Church*—has always at
the same time rejected the extremes both of the left and of the right.
She has always encouraged celibacy more strongly in monastic life and
the priesthood, while at the same time rejecting ancient and medieval
sects of contempt for nature and promoting marriage—which charac-
teristically collapses in a secular world. Whence this meticulous
pursuit of the middle road, this prudence and serenity that deserve
much more admiration than they receive? Möhler studies this question
in terms of the polarity of caricature on the one side and simple truth
on the other. Each sect or church division isolates certain phenomena
against the all-embracing Catholic truth and wants to appreciate it

alone, solely and exclusively. Möhler says nothing about how the way that holds the center ground so meticulously developed in questions of marriage and celibacy, but contents himself with giving historical examples, and they are indeed helpful. The process merits further reflection. Given the weakness and sinfulness of her individual members, how can the whole Church be sure as she passes through time that she remains in the intention of Christ and his mission and is not becoming a mere slave to the spirit of the age—a spirit to which she must on the other hand remain constantly sensitive?

Insofar as the Church uses her *freedom* to give God space, he himself does his works to and in man. All that is is good, for it ultimately stems from a good God. I do not mean that nature as such is good or that each particular idea is good and well-grounded, but that what God does is well done. Marriage is good because man and woman have a natural yearning for each other, but this desire must be purified at its origin, and that remains hidden from our natural vision. Celibacy too is good, it is indeed better, for it is a yearning for the fulfillment of time in eternity. This natural yearning must be purified too, but it may not reign alone in the world, for it is God himself who fulfils the time and not the ascetic. Hence world-renouncing sects are unchristian and they must be rejected. The Church needs to know that she is represented and led by Christ, in whom all time and finitude is fulfilled, and so it is that the personal office which represents this Christ and thereby leads his Church cannot really be different from the life of Christ. Therein lies the great security of the whole Church, because she praises all that is (except sin—which is actually nothing) and lets God act. Here is the most meticulously middle of middle roads!

(IV) The *Denkschrift* pursues its program for the marginalization or elimination of celibacy by seeking to date the point at which it was introduced into the Church as late as possible.[64] Not content to respond to this with a plain chronological counter-testimony and argue that priestly celibacy was praised or its neglect lamented here and there a few years earlier, Möhler asks about the conditions requisite if this spiritual form of life is to thrive. His conclusion is that celibacy was in fact never actually introduced but had always been there, and

---

64. Chapter 4 above, "Celibacy in the Early Church."

indeed as the expression of a high intellectual, moral, and spiritual level. In truth celibacy was lived in various forms in the Early Church— but then for many years it was completely submerged in the chaos of the tribal migrations and Germanic barbarousness. According to him, the lack of a feel for celibacy always equates to a lack of spirituality. This is because celibacy is the fulfilled prophecy of Jesus, the Savior himself, as Möhler says, it is the simple state of the soul opened up to God, it can be acknowledged in this way and no other by believing Christians. After all, Jesus pointed from the beginning to the amazing fact that there would be no lack of spiritual power in his succession, which would lead many to remain celibate for the sake of the Kingdom of God. Christ did not have to demand, to recommend, or to compare, he knew the simple directedness to God of a life that has ceased to focus its thoughts on this world alone. Spiritual virginity grows from the very beginning in the Church as a more intensive form of disciple- ship of Christ and reverence for God, but it grows organically as a gift of grace, not rigoristically as in the sects that go off the rails to left or to right. Even when it falls into abeyance for centuries it is continu- ing to grow. Its absence at such times is itself a sign that something is out of kilter with the discipleship of Christ in a Church whose life produces only a little spiritual virginity. Möhler shows how this constant growth finds its expression in later times in positive forms of intense spiritual life in monastic and clerical spirituality. It appears very early on with Christ and Paul themselves; it grows tentatively in early apostolic times and then blossoms in the Early Church. The Dark Ages represent a centuries-long intermission when a spirituality that was still immature was swept away by the chaos of the barbarian invasions and could not hold onto the standard it had once reached. It was only through Gregory VII [Hildebrand] and the program he pursued so vigorously of maintaining the freedom of the Church— *libertas Ecclesiae*—against the imperial state church order, that priestly celibacy began to blossom again, although not of course without being vulnerable to all the same failings we see in it today. Even in the Hildebrandine reform celibacy was not a matter of disciplinary rules, although it is true that there were repeated rulings of this kind with harsh punishments to suppress concubinage. A tighter discipline was also introduced to deal with the other bad practice of the day— simony (the buying and selling of clerical offices). The introduction of new rules and the strengthening of disciplines was prompted by the newly-awakened spirit of Gregory VII—so blessed by God—whose reforms were inspired by Cluny. The spirit of celibacy does not live in disciplinary rules, even though these can and must be introduced in difficult times as helpful supports to prevent the form of Christ from becoming extinct in the Church.

History teaches us that where a church is alive in a community, there are enough priestly vocations, and where that is not the case, the lack of faith produces a lack of a taste for celibacy. Decadence comes in various forms. It can exist on a highly civilized level of well-being, for luxury does not prove the elimination of barbarousness, but only that it is elegantly veiled. The outward appearance of spiritual culture can mask whether the spirit is really seeking God. As Möhler says, the uneducated man cannot understand celibacy, he inevitably experiences it as oppressive and rebels against it whenever he can. He has sunk too low morally to be able to imitate the ideal in his own life. It is madness to claim that in our own day it is particularly difficult to live celibacy—or at any rate more difficult than in earlier times. History teaches us something completely different. The seductive attractions of pleasure and comfort were always lively enough to affect people who were weak in their discipleship of Christ and devoid of real inspiration because of their carnal lives. The modes of carnal lust change but their spirit or their lack of the Holy Spirit remains the same down the ages, and it is sloppy thinking to suggest that historical developments have been making celibacy harder and harder, to such an extent that today it is no longer a feasible way of life. How did spiritual virginity ever manage to come into the Church? Was it because all the world already lived that way, or was it because instead Christians chose not to conform to the world and so succeeded in changing the world through a new kind of thinking? Far from lamenting the unfavorable nature of the times, we should reproach ourselves for having pinned our hopes more on nature than on grace. No time is unpropitious for its spirit to be opposed to the Holy Spirit—the more unfavorable the spirit of the times, the more powerful the opposition. Such observations dispel our melancholy, or at least point us to the causes of it; they show how the confused impression could arise that the spiritual life—and especially the one point of the evangelical counsels—is so extremely difficult to live.

The argument in Part IV provides useful material for an answer to a point that Karl Rahner once raised. He offered some profound reflections on the life of the priest, on the Holy Mass, and on the sacrificial idea,[65] but a growing divide opened up in his thought between theology and spirituality (as is well known). Falling into individualistic exaggeration, Rahner believed he could take every sacrifice on himself, while at the same time apparently expecting from others in the Church a great deal less—and even perhaps nothing at all. This may have been extremely noble on his part, but ultimately it was not very prudently conceived. For where there is no challenging form of life on offer, the natural man finds no grounds for letting the perceived intimations of grace—so strange to him of themselves— ripen into a form of life. It was because he overlooked this that the gulf opened up in Rahner's thinking. In the postconciliar era he said: "If the Church in a concrete situation cannot find a sufficient number of priestly congregational leaders who are bound to celibacy, it is obvious and requires no further theological discussion that the obliga- tion of celibacy must not be imposed."[66] Möhler's organic perspective demonstrates the precise opposite as a theological truth. The eras when there has been a paucity of priestly celibacy were also times of barrenness when very little of the Spirit of Christ could be seen. With Möhler we must say in opposition to Rahner: since the Church of Christ exists only where the Spirit of Christ reigns in the outward forms of office, an absence of priestly celibacy proves an absence of Christlikeness. Equally, in such times there are also few Christians for the priests to worry themselves about looking after.

My dear opponents of celibacy! How can anyone have dreamed up the idea of reducing the forms of grace still further and even of making away with them entirely, when they are in such short supply anyway? Of course the insight inspired by Möhler is extremely painful, but is it not necessary and honorable? Germany and Europe have little inclination for Christianity nowadays, as has been the case at many earlier periods, and perhaps even less than heretofore. A symptom of this is the lack of a feel for the spiritual life in general, something of

---

65. Cf. Karl Rahner, *Meditations on Priestly Life,* translated by E. Quinn, 288 pp., London: Sheed & Ward, 1973.

66. Karl Rahner, *The Shape of the Church to Come,* translated by E. Quinn, 142 pp., London: SPCK, 1974, p. 110.

which the distaste for celibacy is an illustration. Hence the difficulties in Church life! But would it bring more life into the Church—I mean the life of Christ and life in the Holy Spirit—if we got rid of the symptoms of the appearance of a lack by claiming that there is no lack, that there are enough office-bearers ready to serve, it just happens that none of them are celibates? Dear opponent, pause, take a deep breath, and then look once around you! Even better, look within yourself and open up to the fact that the Church is not going to be helped by structural reforms or by natural means. The removal of celibacy would actually be the simplest of all structural reforms in the Church but it would equally be the most perfectly spiritless of measures.

(V) Having rejected certain arguments against celibacy that appeal to the Bible, history, or pragmatism, Möhler comes to the actual theology of celibacy, in which this Christian form of life presents as nothing less than a seal of revelation.[67] Through celibacy the freedom of the Church becomes the freedom of Christ, the freedom he has over nature and the state and over everything finite. The real symbol of freedom is the connection of the spiritual office to virginity. No more and no less! One can only be a Christian when one acknowledges the Godhead of Christ and our freedom in regard to nature, state, and society. In priestly celibacy this acknowledgment happens either by a person's own ordination or by his acceptance of the celibacy of the Church's office-holders. Möhler thus refutes the small-minded who want to accommodate themselves comfortably to the finite identities and comforts of this world. All the arguments against celibacy aim at the subjection of revelation to nature, society, or the state, and in the era of mass individuality this also leads to subjection to psychological counselling. The thinking behind such arguments would wish to press the Church into service and harness it for the purposes of development and social programs.

"My kingdom is not of this world."[68] The Church thus arms herself with the word of Christ against subjection to earthly powers, she remains suffering and misunderstood predominantly in order to be rightly understood in the teeth of massive prejudice—just as Pilate too could not understand the Lord and yet understood him quite correctly.

---

67. Chapter 5, "On the Theology of Celibacy."
68. Cf. Chapter 5 above, p. 66.

Priestly celibacy and the evangelical counsels give to the Church as a whole and the faithful a part in the freedom of Christ. They need this *un*natural means to be able to live their freedom, for in the midst of the world they are not of the world. In his theology of celibacy Möhler proclaims this victory of Christ over the world, something that provokes so much mockery and slander from the world.

The last part of Möhler's text can be divided up accordingly into three sections. First of all Möhler illuminates the freedom of the individual in relation to the freedom of the Church. Then he investigates the spiritual victory over nature, and finally the victory of the Church over the secular pressures of the spirit of the age in state, society, and culture (where victories can still look like defeats in the eyes of the world).

If the only unitary subject was the Church as the free Christ stepping through the epochs, the first section could be dispensed with. But the freedom of Christ over against nature and state is at the same time the freedom of Christians in the world, and it is even more than that. For first of all the freedom of Christ develops slowly through history, and the Church in her individual members often experiences relapses into subjection to nature and society. Periodically epochs and continents fall prey to a slackness of spirit and the Christian no longer wants to know his Christ aright and falls victim to the anonymous intoxicating influences rising up from nature and society. There have been at least four types of such seductive influences sapping the responsibility of the person since the time of Möhler, three of which have now crawled back into the abyss from whence they came. I am referring to nineteenth-century nationalism, as exemplified by the events in Cologne in 1837 which elicited from Möhler his last piece of polemic,[69] and later by Bismarck's *Kulturkampf;* subsequently the monsters of National Socialism and Communism, destroyers of peoples; and presently the consumerism of the democratic societies; with every ploughboy wanting to play lord of the earth, it is setting the earth aflame and will eventually reduce it to dust and ashes.

The fundamental idea of the first section is easy to expound: the Church herself is free, and not just the individual believer within her ranks, so the accusation that she places a whole class in a straitjacket

---

69. Cf. Johann Adam Möhler, "Über die neueste Bekämpfung der katholischen Kirche," in: *Münchener Politische Zeitung,* 1838.

essentially misses the mark. Anyone who speaks of the Church as if
it were an institution and only an institution—namely a human thing
made for human ends—has no concept of the faith of the Church,
for he is incapable of recognizing the risen Christ and his Spirit in the
Church. If the Church were only an institution, she would have to
bow to the will of her members, since these would be her partners
and her participants. But Church membership in the people of God
involves participation in the body of Christ. To follow the will of the
majority is to sink to the level of nature, social coercion, and mass
comforts; it is infinitely far removed from the Spirit of Christ, who—
to repeat—lived poor, celibate, and obedient, and who had nowhere
to lay his head. Anyone who works along these lines is inspired by the
Spirit of Christ, anyone who works in the opposite direction is not.

Once he has passed through the narrow straits of this earth
and the needle's eye of natural worries, the spiritual man harvests an
abundance of fruits of the Spirit even in this life. Jesus promises such
fruits a hundredfold in the Scripture. One of the praiseworthy features
of Möhler's thought is the way that he explicitly draws out the hidden
connecting lines in life which the worried mind that builds only on
nature does not recognize. The commitment of one's life and joy in life
are one, they are two sides of the same coin. *Commitment is joy and
vice-versa.* Commitment is the ladder which connects heaven to earth.
A commitment can be made only with a view to one's last breath, with
a view to one's death bed. It is only when one has already died that
one can first begin to live. That is true for marriage and it is even more
true for celibacy.

In the second section, where Möhler represents the contradictions inherent in nature on its own, his humor sometimes deliberately
borders on satire. For a whole page and in spirited style he lauds
and praises . . . marriage! Seeing that the *Denkschrift* suffers from
a general paucity of ideas, acumen, and freedom, he comes to its aid
himself and launches his polemic with a paean of praise to marriage
as a way to salvation, simply so that his praise of celibacy will have all
the more striking force. Come now, he cries, we ourselves are going to
provide the best possible foundation for the viewpoint of finite thought!
At a stroke he thereby averts two potential objections. He proves
effectively that celibacy has not made him in the least insensitive, and
he also provides the proof that grace is able to pursue its restraining,

softening, and transforming work in him even where his sensitive nature wants to react strongly. The cheerful heaven that dominates Möhler's vision emerges from his sensitive nature, but not only or first of all from that. Putting a hymn to marriage next to a diatribe against marriage, he seems almost to be writing for the pages of a satirical magazine. Then, in a complete turnaround, nature is tamed and the tone becomes serious and free all at the same time. The sarcasm and the praise both arise from the same standpoint—the natural one—and their coexistence gives expression to the ambivalence of nature.

Natural arguments necessarily lead a person into contradiction, and Möhler puts forward completely contrary motivations that aspire to the same goals. The natural life is both egoistical and altruistical at the same time, but it cannot find its goal either in egoism or in altruism. Neither self-love nor selflessness have any sense in the natural world, but foster only despair. A great illustration of the contradictions in pure finite nature may be found in chapter seven of Paul's Letter to the Romans, which Möhler doesn't cite, but which describes outward dividedness as reflecting an inner one. Why is nature ambivalent? Nature is ambivalent because there is sin in the world. Möhler says so too, although he does not use the word "sin." No finite identity is durable, finite identities cannot have any development towards a goal, only a leap brings nature to firm ground.

Celibacy and marriage support one another. The abolition of priestly celibacy always means the abolition of marriage and other forms of faithfulness in life at the same time. Möhler gives very insightful expression to this connection. Where both are respected together, each individual form of life will also be respected. The great thing they share is commitment and the love of life, which is nourished from sources beyond nature. One cannot live as an experiment, one cannot love as an experiment. Everything earthly is hypothetical, only life, love, and God are not. Each individual event is like a rocket bursting through the walls of finite nature.

The third section brings us to a fervent finale of celibate cheerfulness, with historically accurate observations raising the tone up to its high point. Möhler has no victory *in* the world to celebrate here, it is at most a victory *over* the world. This kind of success arouses nothing but contempt or hatred in the eyes of the world, contempt arising out of a perception of some sort of weakness in celibacy, hatred arising out of a fear of some kind of frightening strength inherent in it. His explanation of the freedom peculiar to Catholics and the way he distinguishes that freedom from Protestant establishment speaks for itself. Celibacy is the very symbol of freedom, its sign and its instrument. The route which leads to this knowledge is quite clearly indicated. It is worth noting here the connection Möhler sees between the freedom of the Church, priestly celibacy, and the papacy, so that we can apply it to our own time. Möhler's intuition here seems to pierce through the thickest walls. For scarcely anyone—whether friend or foe—has really envisaged a *spiritual* connection between papacy and celibacy.

In the pope we are free! cries Möhler. There are so many ways this can be illustrated. In the past only the pope with his sovereignty recognized by the states could protect bishops and dioceses from the clutches of states; today a pope has played a significant role in liberating nations from the scourge of state terror in the East. That was yesterday of course, and spiritual laurels wither even faster than worldly ones, for in this case human praise is evidence of the confusion of spheres. The connection between papacy and celibacy goes much deeper. Both of them publicly represent the limitedness and finitude of a world which cannot find satisfaction in itself. When an era is determined to understand everything only finitely, "the heart of the Church must necessarily be attacked from the very same side that hates celibacy." I would like to propose to the opponents of celibacy as a topic for reflection the question whether thoughts of influence and power are entirely absent from the minds of those who call for the ordination of *viri probati* and the complete elimination of priestly celibacy! It is not that they have an eye for influence with the Pope and the Curia, their interest is in the proclaimed enemies of power in the Church. Why does the Roman Church and the teaching office really object to the liberalization in matters of marriage and celibacy that is so popular everywhere else? The reason why their attitude looks so peculiar and so unheard-of today is that the professors and the critics of celibacy are worried about power, whereas the pope and the bishops are not. From the standpoint of the natural, one can only describe the Roman-Magisterial conduct of the last decades as catastrophic for the Church. How much easier it would have been for parish priests and chaplains on the ground, how many opportunities the all-powerful media would have been deprived of for polemic, how much more spiritual growth could have been anticipated, if only this narrow-mindedness in regard to everything sexual was finally abandoned! How on earth is the new evangelization of Europe going to progress if there is nobody to do it? That's how it all looks from the standpoint of nature: surely it is a view that must be correct?

Yes of course, if our success is our goal, that's exactly how we have to think. But the truth is that our excellent spiritual leaders in Rome and elsewhere are in no way to be thought of as if they were the managers of a successful marketing business. The decisions they make are not in the least predicated on the assumption that one of the names of God is success. Many may not believe in the "outpouring of higher powers," as Möhler puts it, but perhaps the Pope and the Christians who agree with him do. Their power is the power of powerlessness, the charisma of office. The person who rules as celibate and obedient in his office has nothing more to lose on this earth.

The Future of Celibacy

In October 1990 the Episcopal Synod in Rome tackled the question of "the formation of priests in the present day." It had a great deal to say—among other things that the celibacy of the priesthood is a prophetic sign for our time. The Synod therefore wanted to remind priests "that perfect chastity represents a priceless gift for the Church and a prophetic value for today's world."[70] Jesus understood himself to be the one who fulfilled the prophets first in his words and then in his deeds. A few of his actions make sense only when they are understood as symbolizing the way the kingdom of God resists the spirit of the time—for example the entry into Jerusalem, the cleansing of the temple, the meals with sinners and so forth. However, it is not only the words and the deeds of Jesus but the whole existence of Jesus, who has no place to lay his head, that is prophetic. The prophetic office is the representation of a neglected but limitless reality. In discipleship of Jesus the whole man in all his physical reality—and not only his individual words and deeds—can become a symbol and in him the world translucent to God.

---

70. Cf. John Paul II, Post-Synodal Apostolic Exhortation, *Pastores Dabo Vobis*, 1992.

If today the prophetic sign consists in proclaiming the laws and works of God to slumbering Christians who have lost themselves in the drive to consume in a licentious society,[71] it is a proclamation that will be understood only by a few, for only a few can resist the brainwashing of the mass media. But celibacy and the other spiritual forms of life should nonetheless make sense to the few if they are to be capable of resisting social trends. Doing and understanding are of course not the same, but without doing there can be no understanding and without understanding there can be no doing. The priestly form of life therefore needs to be deepened in a twofold sense. It needs to be understood as an answer to the crisis of culture and the environment, and it needs to be connected much more closely with office in the Church: for celibacy is not merely something external added to office as a garment is added to the body. In the long term celibacy cannot then simply be the construction of a disciplinary law, something that even many priests are ignorant enough to believe could be eliminated at the stroke of a pen by Rome. If the virginity of the priestly office was introduced into the Church neither by paper nor by ink but by the Spirit of Christ, it will only look like an external matter of discipline and regulations as long as the reason why it is bound in with the mission of Christ remains unknown. The possibility of truly living a spiritual form of life is not something that can be fought for through changes of practice in pastoral planning or under the slogan of a right to the Eucharist. Everything has its time, including the knowledge of Christ, and two thousand years are not too great a distance to trace the workings of the Spirit of Christ, the Spirit "who will lead you to the complete truth" (John 16:13). The nearness of the Kingdom of God is not measured by a watch or by numbers. So how is it to be measured then?

The goals and functions of the priestly life differ from age to age. Today celibacy is a prophetic sign of the presence of God in an era that has become sexualized to excess and even to the point of insanity, an era when capitalist thinking turns even living and loving into a business. There is scarcely any legal restriction on business. But in the Nazi era celibacy pointed to something else, it was an antidote to collective racial madness, and in Möhler's day it served other purposes

---

71. Cf. Chapter 1 above, p. 1,

still. However, a spiritual form of life does not receive its power from its earthly goals, and though such a life is lived in the world, it is not of the world. Anyone who hears the call from God will in good time practice a different way of life which will reveal the contradictions of nature. But he should also *know* what he is practicing, and in this knowing lies the wisdom to be able to resist. In democratic times asceticism can only be more democratic, since the ideal of the democratic society is life without external authority, which means that I live without the benefit of the insight of another applied to me. The collapse of authority has shown itself in the pleasure with which taboos have been broken in "modern" societies. But the breaking of a taboo does not set us free, it merely leads to a painful recognition that there must have been something in the broken rule. Either insight develops or life loses its bearings. What in earlier times was authority now becomes painfully-acquired self-knowledge.

From this perspective the Church is always more democratic, since not only the clergy but each and every individual Christian bears responsibility for the mission of Christ. Commitment to a priestly calling has also become very democratic in our day, for it has become a lonely battle against numerous authorities. A person has to survive exposure to many secularized and unbelieving opinion-formers like schools, the mass media, and even the parental home, in order finally to obey God more than men. Vatican II could come out with an unprecedented strong statement about the Church as the people of God because the faithful of today are less reliant on authority and outside knowledge and more on their experience of God. Any Christian today who has no experience of God will amount to nothing. To live in a democratic Church of Christ means for the people of God to live like Christ, and he lived celibate, poor, and obedient. The orientation of this life is marked by celibacy and by the evangelical counsels, and these are not a mere discipline, for they involve a deep knowledge of the relationship between eternity and finitude, heaven and earth. One of them has to be chosen here.

At this point our own path must separate from Möhler's— or rather, it takes us beyond him. But there is one final inspiration we can get from him. Möhler recognizes that there is a necessity in the

Church for virginity, a kind of higher necessity, as he says, precisely because it is possible and is proclaimed by Christ.[72] But a short time later he turns round and describes celibacy as a disciplinary law. His organic understanding of the Church gives him a real flash of intuition, but it passes without Möhler seeming to register it. We must go beyond Möhler, but we must not be ensnared by the spirit of the age, for it firmly blocks out all spiritual life. Nor must we be discouraged by the Eastern Churches or Protestantism (on which as it happens Möhler throws a great deal of light in relation to priestly celibacy)[73] from hearing what the Spirit is saying to the communities. He is not saying to us "Fit in and get comfortable! Nature will get it right! Christ only says to you what you can already see by the light of your reason!" It just doesn't work like that.

It is not wholly implausible to speak of the end of modernity[74], even though so many of its newest and latest defenders continue to claim that our era is on the way to the summit of human existence.[75] The end of modernity is the impossibility of getting from finitude to infinity. The omni-presence of the ecological crisis is one reason why the "end of modernity" thesis is clearly plausible. It brings the limitedness of the earth a little bit more sharply into focus each day for the people of the first, second, and third world—indeed of the one world. Finitude is not the ultimate truth for humankind, for we crave deep, deep infinity. But it is *our* truth, beyond which we can go no further. We cannot set ourselves free by our own devices, for a thousand times finitude is always still finitude. Climb as we will up the ladder of progress, heaven remains for ever infinitely distant.

We can see that celibacy is recognizable as a prophetic sign at the point when it is integrated into the mission of Christ—who is the bridge betweeen infinity and finitude. Without its connection with the evangelical counsels, celibacy is neither understandable nor live-able. First of all priestly celibacy, a simple life, and obedience are a single package; first of all the outward rule of celibacy is organically bound

---

72. Cf. Chapter 5 above, pp. 66.

73. Cf. Chapter 4, p. 48 and Chapter 2 above, p. 13.

74. Romano Guardini, *The End of the Modern World*, translated by Joseph Theman and Robert Burke, 133 pp., London: Sheed & Ward, 1957.

75. Hans Blumenberg, *The Legitimacy of the Modern Age*, 728 pp., Cambridge, MA: MIT Press, 1985

up with the mission of Christ and the Church; first of all it is thus
recognizable that the creation is limited by a creator and finds the fulfilment of its yearning for infinity in him. I propose to set out the
deepened experience of the Christian mission in three theses: (a) The
ecological crisis is the modern day form of the finitude of the world.
(b) The Church recognizes in the evangelical counsels the finitude of
the world and thereby at the same time acknowledges the closeness
of the Kingdom of God in it. (c) The acknowledgment happens in the
real connection of the priestly office with the evangelical counsels.

    (a.) The ecological crisis is the present form of finitude.
I scarcely need to prove the fact of such a crisis or to dress it up in eloquent terms. Virtually unknown a mere thirty years ago, the concept
of ecology is becoming more and more widespread, for the rever-
berations emanating from an overburdened nature are increasingly felt
in all spheres. Nietzsche described the explorer Columbus as the symbol
of modernity, but 500 years later we are no longer on a journey into
the infinite, instead we find ourselves trapped in a one-way street!
According to Ernst Ulrich von Weizsäcker, ecology simply means the
politics of the earth.[76] There is no proof that not only the earth but
nature itself is finite. There cannot be a logical proof that we will not
find astounding new energies of the cleanest kind tomorrow, or that
the day after tomorrow we will not be able to live on the moon or on
Mars in settlements without any waste disposal problems. Any such
proof would itself be finite. Even if up to now all hopes for the discovery of the ultimate finite indivisible building block and a final law
of nature have been disappointed, it is logically not impossible that in
future times a finite object might be found that remains firm amid the
flux of time. So also with technology: logically a waste-free technology
is possible, even though such an expectation may not be realistic.
On the other hand we are entitled to ask: what will really happen to a
science that builds on finite identical quantities, what will be the end
result of a utopian technology that promises unlimited well-being,
even though there is no finite identity and no error-free technology?
The answer is that technology is only successful in particulars and
is forever producing unexpected effects and hence catastrophes.

---

76. Ernst Ulrich von Weizsäcker, *Earth Politics*, 234 pp., London: Zed Books, 1994, pp. 10 ff.

Why the success only in particulars? According to an explanation applied by many practitioners, the only abuse in the area
of technology lies in the imprudent or bad use of a technology that is
perfectly good in and of itself. On this theory, the ecological problem
is to be understood as a purely moral issue to be solved through
better education. Nuclear technology can either build bombs or it can
deliver cheap energy. Medicine can either lengthen lives or it can create
over-population. Gene technology can either reduce hunger or it
can create monsters. I have no desire to be sceptical of moral behavior
where it is in evidence, but such behavior is not capable of mastering
the deeper powers not subject to the will. Theory tells us that the
moral will is not in a position to avert the tragicness of the phenomena
I have enumerated. It is not a *bad* will that leads to tragedy but the
good will of a finite awareness that is concerned only for itself and wants
to preserve its own life. The natural sense of life consists in the preservation of life, but that is quite sufficient to produce the tragicness
of nature.

(b.) The finitude and tragicness of nature are far from being
a new experience for man. In the evangelical counsels the Church
recognizes—not for the first time in our century—the finitude of the
world and the nearness of the Kingdom of God. In reality, finitude
belongs to the most ancient forms of the self-perception of man, and
he can respond in two ways: "I believe," or: "I despair." It is the denial
of finitude that produces the roll call of historical disasters that are
presented to us so vividly in the first book of the Bible (Genesis 1–11).
Chapter one states that everything is good, but then come a series
of catastrophes. Man wants to preserve himself, that is his first concern
in the world, but then he sadly finds himself increasingly losing his
grip on his first goal of existence. The evangelical counsels are actually
deducible as a form of life from the natural drive to resist the transience of life. They are the recognition of the finitude of man but
without despair, while pure cognition plunges into the absurdity of a
desire that fails to reach its goal.

When man is bound up in his natural existence as an end
in itself and his desire to keep on extending his life span, then he has
to resist things that threaten to obstruct him on the race track of life.
The changeableness of life shows itself in the three dimensions of past,
present, and future. Three threats grow from them for the natural I,

threats which it resists. By self-determination—which I prefer to call I-determination, for thus the place is left open for the true self of man—it is kept free of connections to past history, it emancipates itself from the forms of the past in the interests of aims and goals that do not set any limits to his future. We arm ourselves against the uncertainty of the future with wealth, with the gathering of means to preserve our freedom to pursue our aims. The first frees the I from the past, the second from the future, creating the possibility for him to accomplish his will after and before—which means to preserve himself. The I of man wants to make itself independent of time. In sexuality the spatial difference is abolished between I and not-I, which offers him for a moment a liberation from the worried-I, a liberation that seeks its goal not in preservation, but in the momentary abolition of the I in pleasure, whereby however—paradoxically— finitude is actually further intensified. The case is in nature that when an animal has reproduced itself, it becomes superfluous, indeed a nuisance. Death is nature's trick to have more life. This threat of nature lurks behind every satisfaction of the senses.

There is no ultimate satisfaction in self-preservation, for life is constantly beset by dangers, sometimes nearer, sometimes more remote. The underlying danger is constantly present, it is sensed unconsciously and indirectly. Every need can be met, only worry cannot, for it creeps in through the keyhole and will always have its rights in the end. Nothing is any use, death taps the mightiest and the richest on the shoulder and summons them to come too. Thus nature utters a decisive "no" to the deepest desires of the ego and grants only a brief postponement. At most there are 70 or 80 years, says the Psalmist, and the best of them is only toil and burden (Psalm 90). What shall we use the time for? The majority of men use time to rebel against the end or to forget about it by plunging into work or pleasure. But there is a third possibility not provided for by nature, and that is the evangelical counsels. They too say no to natural striving and they are thus perfectly in accord with the final goal of nature, but they do it in complete awareness and without temporal postponement.

We now need to consider this no and its transformation into yes—which is the experience of new life from the Spirit. The no is the experience of the finitude of the world, which in the evangelical

counsels becomes the experience of the nearness of God. In anticipating the results of nature temporally, the evangelical counsels
confirm it and thus avoid the natural outcome of nature, its tragicness.
I am saying nothing new if I say that power in itself, wealth in itself,
sexuality in itself are all tragic, for they do not achieve the natural
end they have invested in. If we were to eliminate from Shakespeare's
works the tragedy of these three human motivations, there would not
be much left.

How does the recognition of finitude happen? First of all it
has to provide proof that it is not an evasion but a deeper view of
reality. It relativizes the realism of nature and entities derived from it
like culture, state, society, etc. to the last realities but one, which can no
longer occupy the first place. But they stand in a defined relationship
to the evangelical counsels. "The renunciation of needs symbolized in
the monastic vows of poverty, chastity, and obedience are a means for
growth in awareness, for a distancing from oneself. The deep transformation of human nature which becomes possible in this way shines
brightly in the culture involved. . . . This self-discipline thus serves . . .
not only the preservation of existing society, but the transformation of
man; what religion calls his salvation."[77] "Symbolic" means that again
the counsels cannot be understood, and a new cycle of finitude and
tragicness would begin here. And yet their effect is very real and present
in all cultures, while the number of those who freely deny it as against
those who are driven by nature or society into denial is quite small.
For the monk, the transformation of human nature or the world is not
the first motive of his calling. It is no accident that the preservation of
society does not come up there, since the original knowledge of God
gives rise to a general perception, not conceptually, but contemplatively,
penetrated by temporal and eternal being. A functionalization in
terms of political, social, or ecological goals would make such a life
impossible. Nobody can risk his life for finite goals.

The realism of the counsels prevents us from historicizing them
and pushing them back into the past. Though their actual emergence
is bound up with historical circumstances, they are not circumstances that become technically, economically, or politically obsolete.
In Buddhism they are the means of religion, they are the only way

---

77. Carl Friedrich von Weizsäcker, "Gehen wir einer asketischen Weltkultur entgegen?" in
idem., Deutlichkeit, Munich, 1979, 73-113; here p. 89.

of redemption as the end of all striving. In the Gospels and in the letters of the Apostles there is a pressing recommendation to the way of life of Jesus, who himself lived poor, celibate and obedient.[78] I will leave the differences aside for the time being. What gives the counsels their power, what makes them plausible, the fact that they are the counsels of Jesus or the ecological crisis? The answer is that we should not set the one against the other. The counsels of Jesus express the experience of the man who has recognized and acknowledged the finitude of life and who lives wholly from God. In the ecological crisis the situation of finite man is at the center again, it opens up the possibility of the recognition and acknowledgement of the limits of the natural ego. So the experience of the life of the counsels is at one and the same time strictly religious and (via negation) organically linked with our experience of the finite world. There is a scholastic principle that states that grace fulfils nature. With today's changed concept of nature, whereby it is defined by the struggle for existence, this principle can be restated in the light of the negation of the finite: nature destroys nature, grace hallows and perfects it.[79]

A look at history shows how realistic the insight embodied in the evangelical counsels is in its foundational monastic form. The life of the counsels is not a renunciation of earthly hopes of salvation in favour of something beyond, but a recognition of the indivisibility of salvation. Even earthly, finite, natural life (salvation!) is oriented to grace. The beginnings of Christian monasticism in Egypt and its golden age in the Middle Ages did not spring from some kind of *ressentiment* or fear of reality, but from a contemplative perception of reality which does not involve itself in the competition for power, because power is simply the repetition of the tragicness of nature. This experience, which does not think in terms of using things, is operative from the start of the monastic movement, even though later on a finite usefulness did develop as a by-product of it. It was no accident that the monastic life of the early church blossomed at the time when the Constantinian turn had brought the Church into the embarrassing situation of being an official religion. The same phenomenon was at work with the emergence and revitalization of medieval monastic

---

78. Cf. Chapter 2, above "The Biblical Counsel."

79. *Natura destruit naturam, et gratia sanat et perficit eam.*

life. The poverty movements did not arise out of a reaction by the
have nots against the haves: "The growth of prosperity, the appearance
of a monetary economy, the increase of an urban population, and
the beginnings of industrial enterprises . . . did not unleash a 'social
movement' of aspiring classes in opposition to the ruling strata . . .
a religious movement did take hold of persons of all strata who desired
to take seriously the demands of the gospels and the apostles, in the
midst of an economic upswing."[80] The founders of the Christian orders,
Benedict, Bernard, Francis, Clare, Dominic, Ignatius, Mary Ward,
in our day Charles de Foucauld and far away in Asia Buddha too, were
the children of nobles or princes or very rich men and they personally
experienced the limitations of finitude. Their experience of history and
God could thus become paradigmatic.

Here we see the emergence of a paradox. Between the knowledge of the finitude of nature and the acceptance of it there is a deep
abyss, an abyss which can be crossed neither by the will, nor by
morality, nor by laws, nor by education. The paradox of grace lies in
the difference between understanding and doing. The despair of the
moderns and the dialectic of the Enlightenment have their origins
here. Even when simplicity is so desirable for culture and the environment ("Small is beautiful!"), even when an ascetic world culture is
pressingly on the agenda, whether personally or socially it simply does
not *happen!* I can only give up my own interest when I see that this
agenda has already been completed. For the ecological program a
paradoxical demand is made which recalls the necessity of grace.
The paradox arises in the ecological question where what is at issue is
a finite salvation in the world, and this demands decisions on the part
of the general reason of humanity which the particular reason of
the individual is not in a position to accomplish. Hence natural life
is pointed in the direction of grace for its own preservation and
today's nature—which preserves itself—even more so, since it needs
grace not merely for supernatural fulfilment, but just for its own
temporal preservation.

---

80. Herbert Grundmann, *Religious Movements in the Middle Ages*, translated by Steven
Rowan, 443 pp., Notre Dame, IN: Notre Dame Press, 1995, 235-6. [Translator's note: I have
been unable to find the exact equivalent of Fr. Hattrup's quotation from the German original of
Grundmann's *Religious Movements*, but the one I have supplied has much the same sense.]

(c) The third thesis therefore states that the recognition of finitude consists in the *real* connection of office with the evangelical counsels. It seems to me that Vatican II already saw a prophetic sign in the evangelical counsels, though without being very conscious of the fact. There was an optimistic mood in the air at that time, and the first sacrifice offered to that optimism was the word "sacrifice" itself. The expression "ecological crisis" was as yet unknown. And yet in the Constitution on the Church (*Lumen Gentium*) the Council made a place for the evangelical counsels in the whole Church which they had not had up to then. In one sense they are initially devalued insofar as they are not to be the only way to holiness as against the way of a secular career and family. But while up to now God's dealings had related almost completely to the individual (as had been appropriate to earlier more stable periods of history), the Council recognized the paradox of grace for this historical hour by applying the counsels to the whole Church.

Aware of the paradox of grace, the Church has always associated her office with a certain form of the evangelical counsels, but now the connection emerges as real. The Decree on the priesthood sets out the interconnections between the whole Church, the life according to the counsels, and office.[81] In order to preserve the differences of the orders, the counsels *(consilia)* are referred only to virtues *(virtutes)*, but these turn out to be obedience (*oboedientia* 15), continence (*continentia* 16), and poverty (*paupertas* 17), and though these counsels are limited and suited to the pastor's life, they are in fact precisely the original elements of monastic life. It is the office of the priest that founds the interconnection of the virtues, he is sent into the Church and he has given himself to the one who has sent him of his own volition. And this makes sense, because Christ himself lived obedient, poor, and celibate.

There are however distinctions to be made. Obedience, which is founded by listening to the will of God, belongs to the essence of the office, there can be no question of exceptions. On account of its spiritual advantages, celibacy is certainly in many ways associated appropriately with office, but it does not belong to the essence of the priesthood, as a look into history and at the Eastern Church shows.

---

81. *Presbyterorum Ordinis* 15–17.

It is poverty that seems to have the loosest connection with office: priests may use earthly goods—though only with spiritual discretion and without heaping up property, the criterion being that they should not cause offence. Freely willed poverty is however recommended as the greater sign of the Christian.

Vatican II actually stresses the unity of the counsels, their interconnection with the priesthood, and their meaning in the whole Church more strongly than heretofore, and yet the theology of the counsels is not perfect. Here I want to mention three points.

According to the Constitution on the Church, the counsels are to stand *in relation to the whole Church,* but in what way they are to take their special place in the life of the Church is not clear. In chapter five this form of life is discussed several times along with other forms, and then in chapter six it is referred to separately once again, without the need for this special separate reference being made clear. Lacking a well-defined position in the Church as a whole, their connection with office remains vague and undefined as well, since ecclesiologically it is not the personal holiness of the priest but the sign dimension that must be connected with office. The vagueness of the relation of the counsels to the whole Church is mirrored in the structure of *Lumen Gentium,* where this vagueness is quite overt: "Thus, although the religious state constituted by the profession of the evangelical counsels does not belong to the hierarchical structure of the Church, nevertheless it belongs inseparably to her life and holiness." [82] Here two ideas are placed next to each other without there being any connection between them. The first idea is that the counsels are not to be a part of the hierarchical structure of the Church, and yet nonetheless they are so in fact, since ordination was always bound up with a certain form of the counsels. And since in addition they belong to the holiness of the Church, the life of the counsels should also theologically be reflected in this structure. For anything that belongs essentially to the Church must be present in the office by which the Church is represented and led.

This then is why I say that the *unity of the counsels* is referred to, but not comprehensibly. Initially it is taken for granted, but then the individual counsels are dealt with separately. This betrays an

---

82. Cf. *Lumen Gentium* 44.

embarrassing inability to grasp why the counsels have for several centuries always been presented as an inseparable threesome. Rahner, von Balthasar, and others sought to make the unity of the counsels theologically plausible.[83] But they presuppose the redeemed believing man in order to make out that the counsels somehow represent the simple acceptance involved in hearing and perceiving the self-communicating mystery which they praise—as Rahner does. Their unity is defined theologically, but without any indication as to how the counsels are an answer to the riddle of the finite world. And yet the counsels sometimes do make sense to a wider public, though only as the reflection of the experience of a defined society—quite apart from any evidence of their unity.

The third point at which the theology of the counsels remains imperfect is the *phenomenon of the variation in the degree of credibility* of poverty, obedience, chastity. A look at South America shows this. "While poverty is in practice a central theme in all the representatives of the 'Liberation Theology' school, for the most part the other evangelical counsels of obedience and chastity are consigned to the background in their thinking."[84] Where does the fluctuating evaluation of the counsels come from? For a long time the biblical guidelines could be connected directly with daily experience. People were poor, only a few could start families, obedience was self-evident in times when a few ruled and almost all obeyed. In other words, in many ways the life of the counsels in a world of ruling and serving was only a continuation and intensification of, and even inspiration for, a way of life practiced everywhere.

But when the modern era started gearing up for emancipation—from absolutism, in citizenship, in the socialist and capitalist revolutions, and down to the telecommunications society the life of the counsels turned into something remote and incredible. Progress dissolved the monasteries. Man seemed perfectly able to attain his natural ends. There did not seem to be anything for grace to contribute to the perfection of nature as seen like this, and the traces of it in contingent events were pushed back to the edges of conscious life. The

---

83. Cf. Manfred Scheuer, *Die Evangelischen Räte, Strukturprinzip systematischer Theologie bei H. U. von Balthasar, K. Rahner, J B Metz und in der Theologie der Befreiung*, 449 pp., Würzburg, 1990.

84. Scheuer (see note 83 above), p. 370.

counsels could preserve themselves therefore only by retreating defensively into a kind of ghetto. The walls of a ghetto are built on the boundaries of what is acceptable to the public. In the present day, however, there has been a dramatic revolution which is helping to give the counsels in general—and not just the counsel of poverty in a particular continent—a new credibility and a new place in the life of the Church. For the counsels are the comprehensive form of the limit experience of man, a limit which is pressuring humanity more and more each day.

What then is the place for the evangelical counsels in the light of the signs of the times and the Council? According to the Constitution on the Church *Lumen Gentium*, the counsels can have three places in the Church: the first insofar as they are an eschatological sign within the Church, the second insofar as they are an answer from faith to ecological limit experiences, and the third insofar as they are in certain forms *de facto* associated with office. How do these three relate to each other? Is there an inner connection between them? The sign dimension of the counsels was emphasized by Vatican II, our present experience of the ecological crisis arises from a destiny willed by nobody in particular, the connection with office has been a *de facto* development in the Latin Church. This factuality, which the Council considered perfectly appropriate, is neither of the essence of the counsels nor is it merely accidental, but it stands between the two, it is the most central of middle ways, as Möhler says.[85]

Though as a form of freedom and grace the counsels can be described as appropriate, the actual existence in the Church of a group or a class which obligates itself to the evangelical counsels—the religious orders—is a matter of necessity. According to the Council, the existence of the Church as a whole as a sacrament of salvation for the world is also necessary. It is not down to her to choose to be called together into a visible group with the goal of holiness. The choosing is done first by the individual, who has to accept his calling and then choose Christ who gave himself to God the Father in freedom and without whose choice the Church could not be a sacrament for the salvation of the world. But there is only *one* choice for her, in which she accepts the offer of grace and makes it a public sign.

---

85. Cf. Chapter 3 above, p. 30.

That is where the counsels are appropriate to office. In this choice is
expressed the paradox of grace in a finite world that cannot do without
it, a finite world that is not able to make grace present by itself. All
activities oriented to finite goals are subject to the ambivalence inherent in limited goals: to want the good does not make it present, and
only wanting the good ends up producing evil. The elementary task of
the spiritual choice is not to create good, but to affirm the good that
has appeared. This experience is in itself always present in the Church—
in the element of choice in the Exercises of St. Ignatius, for example.
But in the present-day experience of the world it acquires a public
quality, so that I would like to speak of a new place for the evangelical
counsels in the Church.

How can the personal experience of grace take a public form?
I cannot force myself to put the general interest before the particular
interest. If I do nonetheless manage to do so, I experience the capacity
not as my own activity, but as an incomprehensible gift accompanied
by a limitless peace. Experience has no directly public form, but it
can take the form of the performance of an action on which a claim is
to be based. If the claim is raised, it is spoiled. In this way of negation
we can see a parallelism with ecology. I can no more force others
than I can myself to renounce their interests in favor of a general
interest, namely in favor of the ecological balance. Since we are unable
to bring about this general renunciation, the temptation arises to
impose it by force, to eco-dictatorship, which many now no longer see
any possibility of avoiding.

The public choice of the Church to connect office in herself
with a particular form of the counsels corresponds wholly to the
paradox of finitude. The Church chooses the end form of her way as
the public form of the good, something which is not to be done by
men but received. She would like the days to be fulfilled. She calls out:
"Marána tha—Come, Lord." (1 Corinthians 16:22; Revelation 22:20)
Or as in the *Didache* "Let grace come, and let this world pass away"
(*Didache*, 10). If time nonetheless continues to run on, she accepts
that all the same and blesses marriage as a sacrament. To act coercively
here would be to summon up every force of distortion both within
and outside the Church. Socialism, which sought to enclose men
in a secular cloister for the sake of a sure salvation, went to its end
with moans and groans and many sacrifices. But the Church is

empowered by the divine grace she receives to appoint to her leading and representative office those persons who are also called to the life of the counsels. This is no gratuitous choice, it is a deeply appropriate one and it accords with the mission of the Church. Since the Church half shook off the Constantinian yoke with Gregory VII and wholly so after 1789, she no longer needs to be a state church, but is free as a whole subject to express her assent to grace publicly: office is fused with the evangelical counsels.

The connection of the counsels with office is *formally-logically* not necessary to its essence, as a glance at the disciples of Jesus and at the history of the Church shows. But the same glance also shows— and Möhler's instinct is sure here—that there is a tendency toward a celibate priesthood in the New Testament, in the history of the Church, and indeed both in Judaism and in heathendom despite the fact that Jesus never formally prescribed it to his disciples. How could he have done so, since he had to proclaim the limitlessness of the Kingdom of God to a still very limited Israel in which to be unmarried and childless was a source of shame! At best a person always starts with himself, and this is what Jesus did in his own path through life. So if there was no formal necessity for celibacy, the time would come of a *historical necessity* to connect the counsels with office in the Church. The more the Church became *de facto* a world church and hence the subject of history, the more the connection progressed from appropriateness to necessity. Then she became free in relation to historical development, free not only to proclaim the word but also to choose the good—which she does not bring out of herself but receives as produced by God.

Choice is the jumping-off point for the understanding of the counsels. Choice in this context does not mean that freedom to choose by which I myself decide once and for all what pleases me most; in relation to God, choice means that though the highest value is clear, I see no possibility of realizing it. This requires very careful explanation! First of all, choice assumes knowledge. The knowledge of the Christian is: this world time is passing away and it will come to fulfilment in the return of Christ, but it does not lie in the power of man to determine the time and the hour. Therefore the Church thankfully receives both, the time of waiting and the time of fulfilment, for time itself is an anticipatory form of eternity, it simply craves fulfilment. The time of waiting holds salvation present but concealed, we can see it in nature as in a misted mirror. Time is ambivalent, like clothing made from natural fabrics, for it can enhance the truth of the appearance or it can be used to deceive. The sacramentality of marriage has as its goal to elude this ambivalence of nature by a life of faith.

It is the desire of the Church to see time and ambivalence ended. In the office of service, the Church shows us Christ representing and leading. Can she want not to choose the end form of grace? But it is part of the finality of the world that milk and wine are bought in vain, that none must teach others any more, and that there will be no more marrying. That is the end form of life, and in it nobody is afraid any more to be poor, celibate, and obedient, because all desiring is already fulfilled. The counsels do not need to be lived by all, but without the recognition of this form of life there is no recognition of the life of Christ, in which the finite is limited in order to prepare the place for the arrival of the infinite. The recognition of the concrete life of Christ is possible when the Church ties her leading and representing office to the counsels.

It is much harder to pass up the better possibility than not to choose the necessary one. The person who passes up what is necessary might perhaps be heroic even though he is not really very bright: he denies the gravity of the earth, he thinks he can fly, he crashes to the ground. But the person who does not choose the better possibility falls below his own level. For precisely because the better possibility is placed within his choice, he denies his identity in rejecting it. The Church would fall below her own level if she eliminated celibacy and the counsels from the form of office. What was in the days of the Early Church but a dimly-perceived possibility that could go unrealized has in our time of greater knowledge become no longer merely possible but historically necessary. The married priest belongs with the eschatological message of Christ to a past era. Practical problems have nothing to do with this. Better a shrinking Church than the hypocrisy of a married priesthood which would be for ever having to make excuses for its ambiguity. Where the spiritual experience of the counsels is not present, there is no Church of Christ. Are we dependent on greatness and power in this world? Can shrinkage not be a greater truth than growth? Where do natural trees grow from? Where celibacy and the evangelical counsels are not lived by sufficient numbers of persons, there are no priests and therefore there is no Church of Christ.

There is a further issue that is related to the real connection of office and the evangelical counsels. Could not the question of the priesthood of woman be resolved, if the Church and her office were *really* connected together with the simple life, with celibacy and with obedience? When someone demands to be given an office of service in the Church, that person completely contradicts its character. The feminist movement may win emancipation in the world in this way, but not before God. Even in the world, the women's and men's emancipations of modern times are pregnant with catastrophe. In his *Exercises,* St. Ignatius of Loyola says that suitable men should be encouraged in the direction of the priestly calling as long as they are hesitant. But once they get keen on the idea, one must not speak of it more, so as to be quite certain that the voice of God has the last word.[86] Other masters of the spiritual life have taken the same attitude: if a person is desperate for an office, it should not be given him, whereas a person who is afraid of it out of humility and therefore is fitted to it, should be argued out of his reluctance and pressed to obedience for the sake of usefulness to others.[87] It is all too easy for the desire for esteem or profit to creep quite unconsciously into the priestly office. The counsels are in fact a unique means to distinguish those spirits that are from God and seek God. Of course this gives no guarantee of the good use of office, but we can deal with any misuse of office in the Church of Christ only by reform, not by a tired resignation which settles for imitating secular relationships in society. Anyone who is reduced to a mere "me too" or "we are all the same" mentality does not live by the Spirit of Christ.

---

86. "For though, outside the Exercises, we can lawfully and with merit influence every one who is probably fit to choose continence, virginity, the religious life and all manner of evangelical perfection, still in the Spiritual Exercises, when seeking the Divine Will, it is more fitting and much better, that the Creator and Lord Himself should communicate Himself to His devout soul." Ignatius of Loyola, *Spiritual Exercises; translated from the autograph by Father Elder Mullan, sj,* fifteenth annotation; http:www.ewtn.com/library/SPIRIT/EXERCISE.TXT – page 7.

87. ". . . as a place of rule should be denied to those who covet it, so it should be offered to those who fly from it," Gregory the Great, *Epistle to Cyriacum,* Book 7, Epistle 4, in *A Select Library of the Nicene and Post-Nicene Fathers of the Christian Church,* 2nd series, Ed Philip Schaff and Henry Wace, Edinburgh: T &T Clark/Grand Rapids, MI: Wm B Eerdmans, 1989, vol. xii, p. 210

There are perhaps other hindrances to the ordination of women which cannot be discussed here—theological or psychological limits—maybe a woman cannot personally represent the man Christ in that being a man or a woman is not a kind of outward clothing but an essential difference in human beings. But nothing done in this direction should be done in detachment from the evangelical counsels, which are so strongly tied in with the priesthood.

To conclude, how do we cope with our anxiety about the capacity of the Church to face the future? It is worth reflecting in this connection on a point made by a man who himself struggled with the commission of Christ, a man who at the same time as Albert Schweitzer—and just like him—could not see how one can proclaim the kingdom of God as having arrived, a man who was a theologian and who yet could not be a theologian, a man who was perhaps no more a theologian than his colleagues with their belief in progress. I am thinking of Franz Overbeck. He had a far-seeing gaze but he said little about what he saw, publishing practically nothing. Perhaps the deeper structures of history cannot be disclosed in words, maybe they just have to be waited for. Nonetheless in his lectures he made it clear that after the Constantinian turn of the Church it had been saved by the monks, who preserved it from the embrace of the state.[88] This was not just the experience of the Early Church however—it was also that of the time of Gregory VII, the time of Möhler 165 years ago and our own time. "Celibacy does of course provide unmistakable evidence of the non-unity of Church and State. As no clear-thinking person could fail to recognize, celibacy is an ordinance which could never have sprung from roots which the state removed."[89] Nothing that state, nature, and society can do has the capacity to lead the Church of Christ. What leads her is the grace of the Holy Spirit which finds its most beautiful expression in celibacy and in the evangelical counsels— because there it is supremely independent of nature.

---

88. Cf. J. B. Metz/T. R. Peters, *Gottespassion. Zur Ordensexistenz heute*, 103 pp., Freiburg-Basle-Vienna, 1991; here p. 78.

89. See Chapter 5 above p. 66.

Index of Persons

About the Liturgical Institute

The Liturgical Institute, founded in 2000 by His Eminence Francis Cardinal George of Chicago, offers a variety of options for education in Liturgical Studies. A unified, rites-based core curriculum constitutes the foundation of the program, providing integrated and balanced studies toward the advancement of the renewal promoted by the Second Vatican Council. The musical, artistic, and architectural dimensions of worship are given particular emphasis in the curriculum. Institute students are encouraged to participate in its "liturgical heart" of daily Mass and Morning and Evening Prayer. The academic program of the Institute serves a diverse, international student population — laity, religious, and clergy — who are preparing for service in parishes, dioceses, and religious communities. Personalized mentoring is provided in view of each student's ministerial and professional goals. The Institute is housed on the campus of the University of St. Mary of the Lake/Mundelein Seminary, which offers the largest priestly formation program in the United States and is the center of the permanent diaconate and lay ministry training programs of the Archdiocese of Chicago. In addition, the University has the distinction of being the first chartered institution of higher learning in Chicago (1844), and one of only seven pontifical faculties in North America.

For more information about the Liturgical Institute and its programs, contact: usml.edu/liturgicalinstitute. Phone: 847-837-4542. E-mail: litinst@usml.edu.

Msgr. Reynold Hillenbrand
1904-1979

Monsignor Reynold Hillenbrand, ordained a priest by Cardinal George Mundelein in 1929, was Rector of St. Mary of the Lake Seminary from 1936 to 1944.

He was a leading figure in the liturgical and social action movement in the United States during the 1930s and worked to promote active, intelligent, and informed participation in the Church's liturgy.

He believed that a reconstruction of society would occur as a result of the renewal of the Christian spirit, whose source and center is the liturgy.

Hillenbrand taught that, since the ultimate purpose of Catholic action is to Christianize society, the renewal of the liturgy must undoubtedly play the key role in achieving this goal.

Hillenbrand Books strives to reflect the spirit of Monsignor Reynold Hillenbrand's pioneering work by making available innovative and scholarly resources that advance the liturgical and sacramental life of the Church.